S0-BXC-028

18.15.

THE ROMAN CATHOLIC CHURCH AND THE NORTH-WEST SCHOOL QUESTION

MANOLY R. LUPUL

The Roman Catholic Church and the North-West School Question: a study in church-state relations in western Canada, 1875-1905

UNIVERSITY OF TORONTO PRESS

©University of Toronto Press 1974
Toronto and Buffalo
Printed in Canada

ISBN 0–8020–5301–7
LC 73–89844

LZ
114.2
N67 / 17,582
L86

CAMROSE LUTHERAN COLLEGE
LIBRARY

Contents

Preface

The separate school question is one of Canada's most enduring controversies, sharing that distinction with such other perennials as the British connection, 'Yankee' influence, and federal-provincial relations. A highly emotional issue, it touches basic assumptions about the nature of Canada's political destiny, for in Canada, in addition to the usual religious differences, there are the differing views of the French- and English-speaking communities about the nature of Canada's national identity: whether it is a bilingual, bicultural, or multicultural state or a single-language polity with one dominant way of life. The fact that most French Canadians are also Roman Catholics ensures that religious and ethnic differences are readily joined on the school question.

This book details the history of the question prior to 1905 in what is today Alberta and Saskatchewan. It describes the relations between the government of the North-West Territories and the Roman Catholic church during the period of church ascendancy in education before 1888, the establishment of state control in 1892, and the subsequent negotiations for a school settlement more satisfactory to the Catholic church. The advent of provincial autonomy in 1905 presented the minority with a major opportunity to improve its educational situation, and its efforts helped to precipitate a serious political crisis for Sir Wilfrid Laurier and the Liberal party. The school question as an electoral issue is also discussed as are the political debates at Regina and Ottawa. Although several earlier works, notably by C.B. Sissons, *Church and State in Canadian Education* (1959), and G. M. Weir, *The Separate School Question in Canada* (1934), treat the same question, this book is the first to use the very important episcopal correspondence in the Catholic archives in western Canada.

While the eastern Canada, British, American, and European roots of the question are not much developed, they are important, for it is from eastern Canada (Ontario mainly) and, to a lesser extent, Great Britain, northwestern Europe, and the American midwest that the first settlers to the North-West Territories came, bringing with them the dominant ideas of the time. The last quarter of the nineteenth century was an era of intense nationalism, with much emphasis on the primacy of the state and the need for a uniform system of common schools attended by all children in the state. To develop patriotism and to ensure the greatest possible financial support for its schools, the state as educator could tolerate no competitors – not even the church, the centuries-old custodian of learning. In western Europe, particularly, the anti-clerical policies of King Emmanuel in Italy, Bismarck in Germany, and Jules Ferry in France not only rendered public schooling more secular, but linked it with the aspirations of popular democracy which vigorously opposed all interference by the 'authoritarian' church. Accordingly, the teaching of religion was prohibited, clerical inspectors were removed, and religious orders were discouraged from teaching in public schools and were frequently harassed.

One of the religious orders to experience the wrath of the French authorities after 1879 was the Oblates of Mary Immaculate, engaged in missionary work in western Canada since the mid-1840s. The Oblates naturally followed European developments closely and were much concerned to check manifestations of *étatisme* in the sparsely populated west. To this end, they encouraged the Indians, Eskimos, and half-breeds to give the church a central place in their way of life. As a result, the church, having preceded state authority by almost forty years, had a firm grip on social development by the mid-1870s. Had the opposite been true, or had a missionary order with shallower roots in France taken up work in the west, or had Archbishops Taché and Langevin of St Boniface (both Oblates) been less influenced by the ultramontane (ultra-conservative) wing of the Catholic church in Canada (with that wing's strong dislike of politics divorced from religious influence), an accommodation with the territorial state in educational matters might have been less difficult to effect. As it was, church-state relations deteriorated steadily, particularly after 1888 when the popularly elected Legislative Assembly at Regina set about to secure its own supremacy against all comers, the federal government included.

If the federal government (mainly the Conservatives, in power for all but five years between 1867 and 1896) had been in a position to stabilize the situation, it is possible that many denominational aspects of territorial education might have survived the encroachments of the local assembly. However, the Conservative party was in the throes of disintegration after Sir John A. Macdonald's death in 1891, and not until 1896 (when it was too late) was it able to muster sufficient internal discipline to act as the kind of protector of minority rights that the British North America Act intended the federal government to be.

Nor could the Liberal party be more effective when its turn came during the school crisis in 1905. Although at the peak of its power, it had a long tradition of defending provincial rights and was in no position to increase the church's influence in the provincial school systems of Alberta and Saskatchewan. Thus the combination of federal weakness and impotence, on the one hand, and Catholic intransigence, on the other, ensured that the North-West school question would be a lively issue – and one worthy of study for the manner in which yet another region dealt with the classical issue in educational history: the establishment of a popularly controlled system of public schools in the face of differing conceptions of man and society, and (in Canada) of the country's destiny as a nation.

This book ultimately has a didactic purpose. It was written to bare the tensions and ill-feelings that arise when leaders in church and state, and the people generally, fail to recognize that public schools in an open society cannot easily further the metaphysical assumptions of any one group. Public schools, rather, are at their best when exploring the assumptions of all groups at the appropriate level. However, no single solution to the problem of church-state relations in education will satisfy both Catholics and non-Catholics. The most that legislators can hope to achieve is minimal dissatisfaction when establishing a system of public education financed and controlled by the state. It is to trace the origins and extent, and mainly to judge the validity, of Catholic dissatisfaction during the formative period of Alberta's and Saskatchewan's social development that this book was written. Perhaps it will help to calm the current unrest about the normative (and ultimately the metaphysical) direction(s) of public schooling in Canada.

This book has been published with the help of a grant from the Social Science Research Council of Canada, using funds provided by the Canada Council, and a grant to the University of Toronto Press from the Andrew W. Mellon Foundation. The writer is also indebted to the late Father Paul E. Breton, OMI, for the use of the Grandin Papers and for his help in obtaining access to additional church correspondence in Edmonton and St Boniface. Just as courteous and unstinting of their time were numerous archivists and librarians in Ottawa and several centres in western Canada. The patience, understanding, and counsel of Dr Israel Scheffler, Harvard University, and of the following members of the Faculty of Education at the University of Alberta are gratefully acknowledged: Dr H.T. Coutts, former dean, Dr H.S. Baker, Dr B.E. Walker, and Dr R.S. Patterson. Invaluable also were the guidance and encouragement of Miss M. Jean Houston and Miss Francess Halpenny of the University of Toronto Press, and the editorial assistance of Mrs A.M. Magee and Mrs Gertrude Stevenson. The sole responsibility for the final product is, of course, my own. Finally Dr Madeleine Monod and Mr Michael Kalinowsky of the University of Alberta are gratefully remembered for their help with the French translations and Mrs Mildred Folton, Mrs Darlene Haverstock, and Mrs Doris Dobbin for their careful typing of the manuscript and index.

M.R.L.
University of Alberta

To Natalie

Abbreviations

AAE	Archives of the Archbishop (Roman Catholic), Edmonton
AAStB	Archives of the Archbishop (Roman Catholic), St Boniface
ABM	Archives of the Basilian Fathers, Mundare, Alberta
AOO	Archives of the Oblates of Mary Immaculate, Ottawa
AUA	Archives of the University of Alberta, Edmonton
CSP	Canada Sessional Papers
Morice (E)	A.G. Morice, *History of the Catholic Church in Western Canada from Lake Superior to the Pacific (1659–1896)*, 2 vols. (Toronto, 1910)
Morice (F)	A.G. Morice, *Histoire de l'Eglise catholique dans l'Ouest Canadien du Lac Supérieur au Pacifique (1659–1905)*, 3 vols. (Montreal, 1912)
PAA	Provincial Archives of Alberta, Edmonton
PAC	Public Archives of Canada, Ottawa
RBE	Report of the Board of Education for the North-West Territories
RCPI	Report of the Council of Public Instruction for the North-West Territories
RDE	Report of the Department of Education for the North-West Territories
SAR	Saskatchewan Public Archives, Regina
SAS	Saskatchewan Public Archives, Saskatoon
TSP	Unpublished Territorial Sessional Papers, Saskatchewan Public Archives, Regina

THE ROMAN CATHOLIC CHURCH AND
THE NORTH-WEST SCHOOL QUESTION

1

State, church, and education
before the first school ordinance, 1884

On 15 July 1870 Hudson's Bay Company rule in western Canada came to an end, when the federal government acquired the North-West Territories and the Canadian west passed out of the romantic fur-trading era into the more prosaic period of colonization and settlement. During the next ten years the buffalo quickly disappeared, the North-West Mounted Police was established, Indian treaties were negotiated, and political institutions were introduced. In April 1875 the North-West Territories Act provided for a resident lieutenant-governor and council for the Territories, replacing the primitive form of territorial administration under the lieutenant-governor of Manitoba which prevailed from 1870 to 1876. To aid the five (six after 1877) appointed council members (including three stipendiary magistrates or judges), the act allowed for an elected representative from any area (not exceeding one thousand square miles) that contained one thousand adults, excluding aliens and Indians but not half-breeds. The act also contained an educational clause, with its all-important provision for separate schools, but language, whether in government or schools, was not mentioned.[1] In May 1882 the Territories were divided into four provisional districts – Alberta, Saskatchewan, Assiniboia, and Athabaska (Fig. 1), and in June the second governor, Edgar Dewdney, moved the capital from Battleford to Regina to be near the railway, then moving across the prairies at breakneck speed. With the coming of the railway the white population increased from approximately 1,500 in 1881[2] to 50,000 in 1891.[3] Most of the settlers came from Ontario; British immigrants, Americans from the midwest, and French Canadians from Quebec or New England were relatively few. Major centres of white

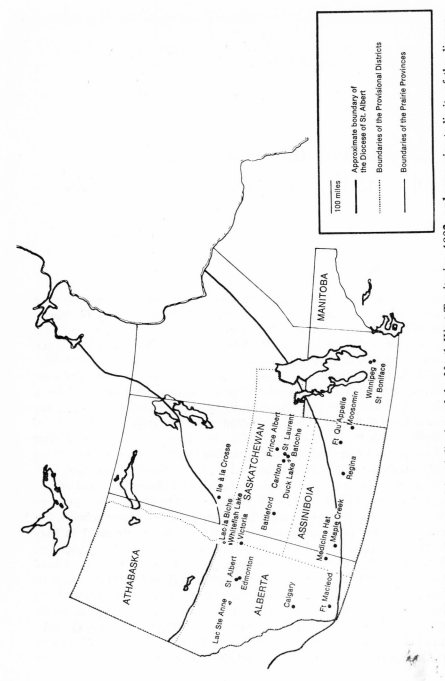

Figure 1 Manitoba and the provisional districts of the North-West Territories, 1882, and approximate limits of the diocese of St Albert before 1891 (Source: D.G.G. Kerr, *An Historical Atlas of Canada*, Toronto, 1959; P.E. Breton, *Vital Grandin*, Paris and Montreal, 1960)

settlement, outside Regina and Battleford, were Edmonton, St Albert, Fort Macleod, Calgary, Medicine Hat, Maple Creek, Moose Jaw, Moosomin, Fort Qu'Appelle, and Prince Albert. The whites were outnumbered by the half-breeds or mixed-bloods (about 5,500 in 1881[4]), with the English and Scottish half-breeds concentrated mainly at Prince Albert, Whitefish Lake, and Victoria and the more numerous French half-breeds (the Métis) at St Laurent, Carlton, Duck Lake, Batoche, Fort Qu'Appelle, Lebret, St Albert, Lac La Biche, and Lac Ste Anne.

The beginnings of the Roman Catholic church in the North-West[5] ante-dated the first resident government by nearly forty years. As early as 1838 two secular priests crossed the Territories on their way to mission fields in British Columbia, and four years later the first permanent Catholic missionary, the Reverend J.B. Thibault, spent the summer in and around Fort Edmonton. In 1843 he established a mission at Lac Ste Anne, about fifty miles northwest of Edmonton, 'out of the reach of the dangerous encounters of Crees and Blackfeet warriors.'[6] The next year the Reverend J. Bourassa, another secular priest, joined him and for the next eight years they evangelized the territorial north.

A systematic expansion of Catholic missions awaited the coming of the Oblates of Mary Immaculate, a missionary order founded in southern France in 1816 and brought to Canada in 1844 by Montreal's ultramontane Bishop Bourget. The first Oblates to come west were Brother (later Archbishop) Alexander A. Taché and Father Pierre Aubert, who reached St Boniface on the Red River in 1845. Six years later, Taché, a newly consecrated bishop returning from France, persuaded Father Albert Lacombe to join the mission at Lac Ste Anne. Together, early in 1861, they established the St Albert mission, which ten years later became the episcopal see of the Diocese of St Albert (Fig. 1). Taché and Lacombe were both born in Quebec. Two other prominent Oblates – Vital Grandin, the first bishop of St Albert, and Father Hippolyte Leduc – were born in France. Grandin, at Rome's request, took up residence in the projected Diocese of St Albert in 1868, three years before the ecclesiastical province of St Boniface, which encompassed the whole of western Canada, was created.[7] A missionary to the Indians and Eskimos in the far north since 1854, Grandin, in 1857, became bishop of Satala and coadjutor to Bishop Taché of St Boniface, with his episcopal residence at Ile à la Crosse, a permanent mission station since 1846. Father Leduc arrived in northern Alberta in 1867 to aid Lacombe and Father René Remas.

Relations among the four main church leaders were always good. The short and stocky, round-faced Taché was highly regarded for his diplomacy and political astuteness.[8] He was a strong supporter of the Conservative party and the third member of the ultramontane triumvirate of Bishop Bourget and Bishop Laflèche of Three Rivers, Taché's close friend and former colleague in the North-West (1845–56). Although Taché did not press his political views on his subordinates, he did set the political tone for the Catholic church in the west. As a result, Grandin too favoured the Conservatives, though politics interested him very little except when church interests were involved, and even then he seldom expected much at the hands of non-Catholic politicians. A patient, retiring man, barely familiar with English, Grandin leaned heavily on his metropolitan for guidance in secular affairs, as his lengthy and frequent letters testify.[9] Taché, however, had a vast archdiocese to administer and, as the church's school difficulties multiplied, the lack of close co-ordination was occasionally annoying. Nevertheless, the two remained close friends to the end (Taché died in 1894; Grandin in 1902) and a break comparable to that in 1905 between their successors, Archbishop Langevin and Bishop Legal, over school question policy would have been inconceivable.

To aid them, both prelates relied heavily upon Fathers Lacombe and Leduc. The former has become an heroic, almost legendary, figure in the west, as much for his numerous activities under primitive and frequently dangerous circumstances as for his longevity (he died in 1916).[10] To his knowledge of the west, and in particular his influence over the much-feared Blackfoot Indians, he brought a ready wit and an open pragmatic manner which increased his value as an ambassador-at-large in the service of church, state, or the Canadian Pacific Railway. Lacombe shared Taché's interest in politics but lacked his political acumen. Under stress, he could be outspoken, even impulsive, as shown by his private letter in 1896 to Wilfrid Laurier, leader of the Liberal opposition in Parliament, threatening him with church opposition at the polls if Liberal policy on the school question were not changed. Unpredictable, opinionated, and on occasion critical in private of his religious superiors and colleagues, Lacombe, though popular, was too independent to be trusted with high office. Even so, he served his church well, for he was comfortable with politicians, adept at lobbying, a gifted raconteur, and undoubtedly the best known and most colourful religious personality in the west.

Lacombe got along well with Leduc, the master administrator whose efficiency may have helped Lacombe appreciate his own limitations in that respect. Next to Grandin, Leduc was always the most important figure at St Albert.[11] Devoted to his bishop and anxious that diocesan affairs prosper, the high-strung Leduc suffered much as the church's influence in education steadily declined. As school inspector in 1887 and a member of the Catholic section of the Board of Education from 1888 to 1892, he was the church's chief educational spokesman. His numerous diocesan offices, however, left him little time to anticipate the adroitness of political leaders on the school question. Finally, in the mid-1890s, with the church's educational fortunes at their lowest ebb, he lashed out at its lay tormentors in *Hostility Unmasked*, a polemical pamphlet suggested by Archbishop Adélard Langevin,[12] whom Leduc, like Grandin and Lacombe, willingly followed, but for whom neither could be expected to have the warm attachment so frequently displayed towards their pioneer-colleague, Taché.

By 1883, then, the year the first school ordinance was proposed, the Catholic church was well established in the Territories. Although most of the early missionary work was among the Indians and Métis, white communicants increased steadily. By 1891 Catholics made up 19 per cent of the total territorial population,[13] a figure that changed little thereafter. The influx of white settlers raised the question of how well a predominantly French-speaking clergy could meet the needs of a mixed population. The number of English-speaking Catholics cannot be estimated for the early period, but by 1880–1 they were likely still a minority if all the 2,896 settlers and their families of French origin in the census are assumed to be Catholics (4,443).[14] No comparable figures exist for 1890–1, but by 1901 the French Catholics had become a distinct minority, with only 7,000 settlers of French origin out of a total Catholic population of 30,070.[15] Yet so deep were the Oblate foundations that clergy of French descent continued to dominate the church well beyond 1905, the end of the territorial period. In 1903, for example, in the ecclesiastical province of St Boniface almost 75 per cent of the clergy were French and over 50 per cent were Oblates, excluding the predominantly Indian vicariate of Athabaska-Mackenzie, where the twenty-seven clergy were all French Oblates.[16] In fact, so firm was the hold of the French clergy in the west that in 1912, when the episcopal see of St Albert was transferred to Edmonton, there were still practically no English-speaking priests to serve Edmonton's Catholics, of whom the greatest majority 'by far' were English-speaking.[17]

The Oblates, like the Jesuits (and other Bourget protégés), were 'a strong conservative influence' in Canada[18] and Oblate correspondence is strewn with strictures against liberalism, freemasonry, communism, socialism, and all forms of anti-clericalism with its correlate, *étatisme*, the elevation of state over private interests, including the church. As a result, state schools, the invention of Protestantism (the root also of liberalism and accompanying evils), were highly suspect and compromise on the subject was not easily achieved. The Oblates, recruited mainly in France and Quebec, brought with them 'the dream of a Roman Catholic French-speaking populace throughout the vast regions of the northwest'[19] and held on grimly as the influence of that populace steadily declined.

Although the North-West Council held regular sessions after 1877, it did not pass its first school law until 1884. The few white settlers and the absence of municipal institutions caused the delay. The people either maintained schools on the subscription principle or patronized the nearest Protestant or Catholic mission school. By 1883 the most important Catholic mission schools were at St Albert, Lac Ste Anne, Lac La Biche, Ile à la Crosse, St Laurent, and Duck Lake. They enrolled mainly Indian and Métis children, but a few white children were undoubtedly also present as Indian, Métis, and white inhabitants mingled freely in a region where whites constituted less than 3 per cent of the total population in 1881. Only in Catholic mission schools at Edmonton, St Albert, Macleod, Prince Albert, and Battleford did white children predominate.

The schools were supported in the main by charity. The problem of obtaining adequate support, although serious, was not insurmountable until the white population increased rapidly in the late 1870s. The increase was accompanied by an intensification of conflict between the French-speaking Catholics and the English-speaking Protestants, with the unfortunate English-speaking Catholics (as always) in between. The conflict had existed during the fur-trading era, but as long as the population was small the vast and mighty wilderness minimized ethnic and religious differences. Bishop Grandin, however, had been apprehensive about the future ever since Confederation. The union, he thought, would undoubtedly increase Anglo Protestant immigration and undermine Catholic church influence through Protestant schools. Catholic schools were needed but he admitted he lacked the means to establish them.[20]

Increasingly after 1880 the main concern of the territorial Catholics was to avoid becoming a hopelessly small minority. To meet the challenge more colonists and more schools and churches were needed, all of which required more money. The problem was circular, for with the right kind of settler funds would be available, but the lack of funds made it more difficult to attract the right kind of settler. Grandin and Taché appealed to the Quebec episcopate, who, though usually sympathetic, disliked the prospect of recruiting French, Swiss, and Belgian urban immigrants, exposed to the vulgarities of revolution in Europe, to replace the faithful and reliable French-Canadian habitants departing for the North-West.[21] And French Canadians in the United States not only were reluctant to leave New England for the Canadian prairies, but attracted more French Canadians from Quebec, the very ones whom the clergy were unwilling to send west.[22] The political instability of France and Italy, hitherto important sources of financial aid,[23] meant that western missionaries had increasingly to look to Quebec for charity, a charity which only spurred Ontario Protestants to greater missionary efforts in the west.

There were, in addition to Quebec, three other possible sources of financial aid: the Catholic laity, the federal government, and the newly established territorial government. None was dependable. The piety of many settlers and their enthusiasm for education, especially church schools, did not impress Bishop Grandin. Most Catholics were either indifferent towards education or preferred state schools where, they were convinced, their children would be better prepared for employment by learning English.[24] This attitude, as we shall see, changed little, even during the most crucial years of the struggle for Catholic schools. The quality of French-Canadian settlers, especially from the United States, also distressed him. He confided to Taché that he preferred good Protestants to French Catholics ashamed of their nationality and religion.[25] Yet nominal Catholics were better than no Catholics at all. Missionaries might well view European anti-clericalism and the American public school as minor challenges after battling well-entrenched medicine men for the souls of suspicious Indians. But to obtain churches and schools for evangelizing, funds were needed, and so Bishop Grandin issued his first mandamus (bishop's letter) in October 1883, assessing the faithful in grain or money according to occupation and marital status. The clergy were counselled to use tact with passages that might offend.[26]

As between the federal and territorial governments Bishop Grandin had good reason to expect favourable consideration from the former. The territorial government lacked powers of direct taxation and derived its income from fines, the sale of licences and permits, and the annual federal grant. Of necessity it had to be parsimonious. The federal government, on the other hand, was not only better situated, but it had frequently relied upon the Catholic clergy to help negotiate Indian treaties, explain government policies, and pacify Indians who threatened to impede the construction of railway lines. There was also Archbishop Taché's dramatic and hurried return (at Ottawa's request) from the Vatican Council in 1870 to deal with the political crisis in the Red River settlement. The church therefore might well expect generous treatment in the appointment and advancement of French Canadians in the public service, in the disallowance, repeal, or amendment of obnoxious ordinances passed by the North-West Council, and in the support of mission education.

Bishop Grandin made his first request for federal aid to mission education in 1873.[27] An order-in-council allotted three hundred dollars per annum
to each of five specified schools in Manitoba and the Territories on condition
that each have an average attendance of sixty pupils (later reduced to twenty-
five[28]). When aid was slow to arrive Grandin complained in 1875 and
Ottawa sent three hundred dollars for the school at St Albert.[29] A request for
similar amounts for Lac Ste Anne and Ile à la Crosse followed, and in 1877
the government sent another three hundred dollars for St Albert and a like
sum to be shared by Ile à la Crosse and Lac La Biche.[30] A five-year campaign
to obtain three hundred dollars for each school failed, probably because
negotiations with the new territorial government were already under way
to place school aid on a more stable basis.

The negotiations originated with an 1877 petition to the North-West
Council by the Métis of St Laurent requesting a grant in aid of education.
The council considered the objective laudable and sent the petition to
Ottawa.[31] In 1880, after considerable correspondence, a federal order-in-
council approved the governor's suggestion[32] that Ottawa pay one-half the
teacher's salary in all mission and voluntary schools enrolling an average of
fifteen pupils and aid in the construction and furnishing of the school house.[33]
There is no evidence that either Grandin or Taché helped to draw up the
petition, or even knew that it existed, although Father André, the parish
priest at St Laurent, who had earlier assisted the Métis to write a constitution
for their winter camp,[34] may have helped to phrase it. Bishop Grandin was
not impressed by Ottawa's subsidy. The great difficulty, he wrote Taché,
was not to find funds for teachers' salaries but to provide teacherages once
schools were established.[35] Moreover, schools in charge of teaching sisters
were superior to anything the Protestants could establish anyway.[36] But with
the Protestants quick to take advantage of the federal aid plan, it was not long
before Grandin was writing Father J.L. Antoine, superior-general of the
Oblates in Canada, for English-speaking or bilingual priests and teachers
who could staff the schools.[37]

Even though little financial aid could be expected from the territorial
government, the church authorities could hardly ignore the governor. David
Laird, the Liberal journalist-politician from Prince Edward Island who
became governor in 1876, was practically an autocrat in the Territories.[38]
He had been Alexander Mackenzie's minister of the interior and had considerable influence at Ottawa, so that many of his recommendations became
law. Accordingly, very soon after Laird's appointment Bishop Grandin
acknowledged his authority as a loyal and devoted subject and allowed that
the spirit of the people, especially the Métis, required close co-operation

between church and state. Religion alone, he believed, could make good citizens of the different peoples in the Territories.[39] Laird, replying in French, was pleased that the Métis were good subjects of the queen and complimented Grandin for his zeal in protecting their interests. However, the Presbyterian governor foresaw a looser relationship between church and state. While religion was important, in Canada the state could favour no religious denomination, though individual missionaries might be encouraged in the pursuit of their arduous tasks.[40]

Early in 1882 Grandin greeted the second governor, Edgar Dewdney, with a still more explicit statement of the ideal church-state relationship:

Autant que possible, Monsieur le Gouverneur, nous ne nous occupons pas de politique, mais nous professons le plus grand respect et la plus grande soumission à l'autorité légitime et au lois du pays, surtout si cette autorité et ces lois ne sont point contraires aux lois divines et ecclésiastiques et respectent les libertés religieuses aux quelles nous tenons plus qu'à la vie. Dans de telles conditions, Monsieur le Gouverneur, vous n'aurez point à vous plaindre de nous; nous serons vos plus fidèles administrés et par notre exemple et au besoin par notre influence, nous faciliterons votre tâche dans le pays.[41]

Dewdney's position, however, was as neutral as Laird's: 'Whatever action is taken upon your several prayers,' he wrote Grandin in another context, 'permit me to assure you, that such action will be based upon their [sic] merits solely, without regard to the religion professed by your lordship.'[42] Dewdney, an Anglican and a staunch Conservative ('A man who lives in a teepee,' he once wrote Sir John A. Macdonald, 'should not be considered a householder *unless he is a Conservative*'[43]) and a great admirer of 'Sir John,' was careful that territorial problems should disturb the federal government as little as possible and representations that threatened to become major political issues in the North-West were decidedly unpopular.

Bishop Grandin presented the church's position to successive governors with the Indians and Métis primarily in mind. The latter, though more numerous than the whites, were not represented on council until the second session (1878), when in response to petitions from St Laurent and St Albert,[44] Pascal Breland, a 'Merchant of Cypress Hills,'[45] joined Laird and the three stipendiary magistrates, Colonels Hugh Richardson and J.F. Macleod (commissioner of the Mounted Police), and Matthew Ryan as an appointed member. In the only other change in the council's membership between 1878 and 1883, the Métis in the electoral district of Lorne (Carlton, Duck Lake, and Prince Albert[46]) helped to elect Lawrence Clarke, Hudson's

Bay Company factor at Prince Albert, in 1881. Easily befriended, the Métis were an unstable political force in the Territories and the despair of French Catholic leaders when French and/or Catholic interests had to be defended at the polls.

Grandin's expressed concern that social stability was impossible where religion was either proscribed, frequently embarrassed, or merely tolerated was undoubtedly strengthened by the effects of European anti-clericalism after 1870. As a result, he was always apprehensive about the development of political institutions in the west. In the embryonic social setting political authority could hardly be neutral; it was bound to place the stamp of the Protestant English or the Catholic French upon the institutions that developed. In 1877 he said he was rather uneasy about the future of the French Catholic population under an English Protestant government.[47] If the Protestants were allowed to become the majority, he observed in 1880, they would fill the government places and dominate in a few years.[48] It was not long before he saw Protestant intrigue and English diplomacy behind each government delay and each evasive answer. In 1882, after a particularly unsatisfactory talk with Hayter Reed, then Indian agent at Battleford, Grandin complained to Leduc that all who governed them were Anglo Protestants and that French Catholics would soon be treated as a conquered people.[49] The future would indeed be difficult, especially once the North-West Council raised the question of providing non-Indian children with state education on terms satisfactory to the church.

II

Catholic educational interests in the Territories were safeguarded by two important statutes, the British North America Act (s. 93) and the 1875 North-West Territories Act (s. 11). Both defined government responsibility in education and still serve as yardsticks to test the constitutionality of legislation affecting Catholic educational interests in Alberta and Saskatchewan. The confederation of Canada, it is generally agreed, was a compromise and section 93, the school clause, was one of its most important achievements. Since 1841 Protestant Canada West (Ontario) and Catholic Canada East (Quebec) had been governed by a single legislative body. In 1866 the Protestants of Canada East, anxious to improve the legal status of their dissentient schools, had failed to obtain additional guarantees from the legislature. With the Catholics of Canada West also concerned that the act of confederation secure the legal status of their separate schools (as defined in 1863), the large Protestant majority in Canada West reluctantly agreed to a permanent guarantee for the Catholic separate schools on the double understanding that the Separate School Act of 1863 was a final settlement of the question in Ontario and that the Protestants in Quebec would be given a similar guarantee in law to the dissentient schools in existence since 1846.[50] The resulting clause read as follows:

93 / In and for each Province the Legislature may exclusively make Laws in relation to Education, subject and according to the following Provisions:

1 Nothing in any such Law shall prejudicially affect any Right or Privilege with respect to Denominational Schools which any Class of Persons have by Law in the Province at the Union:

2 All the Powers, Privileges, and Duties at the Union by Law conferred and imposed in Upper Canada [Canada West] on the Separate Schools and School Trustees of the Queen's Roman Catholic Subjects shall be and the same are hereby extended to the Dissentient Schools of the Queen's Protestant and Roman Catholic Subjects in Quebec:

3 Where in any Province a System of Separate or Dissentient Schools exists by Law at the Union or is thereafter established by the Legislature of the Province an Appeal shall lie to the Governor General in Council from any Act or Decision of any Provincial Authority affecting any Right or Privilege of the Protestant or Roman Catholic Minority of the Queen's Subjects in relation to Education:

4 In case any such Provincial Law as from Time to Time seems to the Governor General in Council requisite for the due Execution of the Provisions of this Section is not made, or in case any Decision of the Governor General in Council on any Appeal under this Section is not duly executed by the proper Provincial Authority in that Behalf, then and in every such Case, and as far only as the Circumstances of each Case require, the Parliament of Canada may make remedial Laws for the due Execution of the Provisions of this Section and of any Decision of the Governor General in Council under this Section.[51]

Education was thus made a provincial responsibility, subject to certain restrictions where 'Denominational' or 'Separate' or 'Dissentient' schools existed at the time of Confederation or were subsequently established. To tamper with the rights or privileges of such schools was to invite federal intervention and risk the indignity of remedial legislation. The clause, however, was not without its ambiguities: What or who constituted a 'Class of Persons?' What was 'a System of Separate or Dissentient Schools?' Who would decide when a right or privilege was 'prejudicially' affected, and on what basis? What would happen if the provincial authority ignored the remedial legislation?

Section 93 was, then, as Father Breton has observed, 'loosely-worded and imprecise.'[52] In 1875, however, its 'Denominational' or 'Dissentient' school principle became the separate school principle of section 11 of the North-West Territories Act:

11 / When and so soon as any system of taxation shall be adopted in any district or portion of the North-West Territories, the Lieutenant-Governor, by and with the consent of the Council or Assembly, as the case may be, shall pass all necessary ordinances in respect of education; but it shall therein be always provided, that a majority of the ratepayers of any district or portion of the North-West Territories, or any lesser portion or subdivision thereof, by whatever name the same may be known, may establish such schools therein as they may think fit, and make the necessary assessment and collection of rates therefor; and further, that the minority of the ratepayers therein, whether Protestant or Roman Catholic, may establish separate schools therein, and that, in such latter case, the ratepayers establishing such Protestant or Roman Catholic separate schools shall be liable only to assessments of such rates as they may impose upon themselves in respect thereof.[53]

The North-West Council (and later the Assembly) could thus pass school laws, but the minority, whether Protestant or Catholic, could always separate from the majority without incurring the penalty of double taxation. Section 11, too, was not without its difficulties: Could the majority, even the Catholic majority at St Albert or St Laurent, really establish such schools as it 'might think fit?' What would happen if the schools did not suit the lieutenant-governor, who could pass school ordinances with the consent of the council or assembly? When a Catholic separate school was established, did all Catholics have to support it? Would the taxes from rate paying corporations support the separate or public school? If both, how would the funds be divided? These were some of the questions that later exacerbated the contentious North-West separate school question in western Canada.

The 1875 Act was passed by the Liberal administration of Alexander Mackenzie, the thrifty, austere-looking Baptist from western Ontario, who opposed separate schools as much as did his political idol, George Brown.[54] The act was not much discussed by either Mackenzie, Laird (then in the federal cabinet), or Alexander Morris, lieutenant-governor of Manitoba and the North-West.[55] Laird alone raised the subject of education in a letter to Morris after Mackenzie had introduced the bill in the House:

You ask for details of the North-West scheme. I enclose the Bill as introduced. I understand there is a clause to be inserted in Committee providing that a similar right is to be given to the minority with respect to Education as exists in Ontario. Probably other amendments will be made as the Bill has been too hastily prepared for such an important question ... Mr. McKenzie [*sic*] took the matter in hand himself and gave the heads of his scheme to Col. [Hewitt] Bernard, who prepared the Bill.[56]

In his short introductory remarks Mackenzie said nothing about a school clause. When Macdonald, in opposition, also ignored the subject, Edward Blake, a prominent government supporter, became disturbed. If Parliament hoped to promote immigration into the new region, the people had to know their rights beforehand. 'A general principle' governing education was needed to prevent 'the heart burnings and difficulties' with which other portions of the Dominion and other countries had been afflicted on the subject. Mackenzie explained frankly that education had escaped his attention until he came to discuss local taxation; a school clause, however, would be inserted in committee.[57] Subsequent discussions of the bill were brief and it passed without division.

In the Senate, however, the school clause provoked a spirited debate and played havoc with party loyalties. Even before the bill's second reading in the Commons, J.C. Aikens, a Conservative associated with the Ottawa Auxiliary Bible Society (Methodist) who became the governor of Manitoba in 1882, expressed disappointment that separate schools were being introduced before the North-West had its own government. Senate government leader, Richard W. Scott, a Catholic who had introduced the Separate School Act of 1863 in Canada West, defended the administration for taking 'precious good care' to eliminate complaints on the subject in the future.[58] This was only a skirmish. On Scott's motion for third reading Aikens moved to eliminate the separate school provision in section 11.[59] George Brown and Billa Flint, both Liberals and Presbyterians (the latter close to the Presbyterian Sabbath School Association of Canada), followed with the usual arguments against separate schools: they were contrary to the BNA Act which gave each province 'absolute' control over education; territorial Protestants, unlike Quebec Protestants, did not require protection from Catholics; education and the people would benefit where youth were trained together; religious instruction could be provided by the clergy of each denomination or in Sunday School; and the issue was not separate schools but freedom to settle the question locally in order to eliminate it in national councils.

The defence of separate school supporters, led by the Liberal Scott and the Conservative William Miller, was also typical: the provision for separate schools would remove a source of future discord in the North-West ('They could do now safely and easily what they might not hereafter be able to accomplish when powerful conflicting interests had grown up in the territory,' Miller admitted); the BNA Act did not refer to territories, where parliamentary wisdom, not provincial rights, ruled; parents had a right to educate their children as they pleased; Catholics, almost half the Canadian population, were strong enough to resist injustice in the Territories and if necessary elsewhere; children should acquire secular and religious knowledge simultaneously; and the separate school clause did not necessarily mean separate schools – it only gave the minority the same right as the majority to choose its own schools.[60] On division Aikens's motion was defeated on a close vote (24–22), and separate schools thus became a permanent feature of the school system in the North-West.

Brief references to section 11 were made in Parliament in 1876 and 1880,[61] as separate school supporters carefully screened related legislation for possible dangers. In 1876 Senator Miller questioned Liberal sincerity on the separate school question, illustrating thereby the kind of political manoeuvring that was a regular feature of discussions involving the school question:

The Bill of last year had been carried through the House of Commons to gratify a number of Roman Catholics, but the moment it came to this House, the head of the party, Hon. George Brown, opposed and did his best to defeat the measure. It was an understood thing that it should pass in the Commons to please the Roman Catholics, and afterwards be killed in the Senate, and then it would be accepted as a matter of course. If it were not for the generous support of the leaders of the Opposition and their friends, the Bill would never have been passed through this House.

Four years later he maintained that, even if the separate school clause were repealed, separate schools would still prevail because 'the British North America Act provided that, wherever the system of separate schools was established in the Dominion, it should continue in force for all time.' No one challenged the statement and the matter was dropped, not to come before Parliament again until 1890.

There is no evidence that Bishop Grandin or Archbishop Taché noticed the NWT Act or the debates it engendered. Neither Taché's protégé, Senator Marc A. Girard, nor Louis F. Masson, the ultramontane member of Parliament for Terrebonne, Quebec, both of whom wrote the archbishop regularly during the 1875 session, mentioned it. Nor did Grandin and Taché raise the matter in their correspondence.[62] Taché was deeply involved in the Riel amnesty question in 1875, and Grandin's silence may be attributed to the small territorial population and the meagre provisions for schooling, which made separate schools of little immediate consequence. Still the silence of the two leaders who could best appreciate the potential value of section 11 is significant. Silent also was Manitoba's *Le Métis*, the French newspaper founded in 1871 by another episcopal protégé from Quebec, Joseph Royal, who would succeed Dewdney as governor in 1888. Its lengthy editorial of 10 April discussed the act without mentioning the school clause.

III

With section 11 merely permissive, the North-West Council made no attempt to establish a school system until Frank Oliver, the independent-minded editor of the *Edmonton Bulletin* and Edmonton's first member of council whose political career extended to 1911 (after 1896 as a federal Liberal), introduced his school bill on 13 September 1883.[63] The bill probably surprised few residents in his district, for during the electoral campaign in May Oliver and his opponent, S.D. Mulkins, had stressed the need for municipal organization and a system of taxation to facilitate public schools.[64] Oliver represented a large constituency which included the French Catholics around St Albert, and in his campaign he had tried to avoid racial and religious issues, deemed detrimental to the united front which most territorial politicians believed important in a frontier community. Opposition to separate schools was a natural corollary, but neither in this nor in his opposition to special privileges for the French was Oliver's attitude typical of the doctrinaire Anglo Protestant.[65] To him, public education was not only the basis of a united populace, but the logical outcome of another principle: the separation of church and state, *irrespective of denomination* (he himself was a Methodist). He was no more anti-French than he was anti-Catholic. While he took the primacy of English for granted once the trend of settlement had been established, he showed little of the enthusiasm in opposing French which he later displayed in attacking the languages of immigrants from continental Europe. In 1883 Oliver was also opposed by Francis Lamoureux of Fort Saskatchewan, generally recognized as representing French Catholic interests. Thus race and religion did become factors in the campaign,[66] even though Lamoureux himself referred to neither, emphasizing only a preference for schools to roads and strongly advocating lowering the average attendance from fifteen to ten under the federal plan of 1880.[67]

Governor Dewdney, in 1883, made no reference to school legislation in his address to council.[68] There had been no general movement for a school bill. Apart from the *Saskatchewan Herald* (Battleford), which thought schools were of 'paramount importance' in a new country,[69] territorial newspapers had paid little attention to the subject. Although the *Macleod Gazette* made a strong plea for a local school in September 1882 and recommended, a year later, that it be 'absolutely non-sectarian ... somewhat on the plan of Eastern Canadian common schools,'[70] it said nothing about a school system, even though the second editorial was obviously prompted by Oliver's bill.

The proposed school bill did not pass. After examination by a special committee it was printed for consideration by the people.[71] Catholic educational interests were affected mainly by sections 118–25, labelled 'Separate Schools.' Section 118, with its provision for separate schools, was the most important:

In accordance with the provisions of Section Ten of 'The North-West Territories Act, 1880' providing for the establishment of Separate Schools it shall be lawful for any number of property holders resident within the limits of any Public School District or within two or more adjoining Public School Districts or some of whom are within the limits of an organized School District and others on adjacent land not included within such limits to be erected into a Separate School District by proclamation of the Lieutenant-Governor with the same rights, powers, privileges, liabilities and method of government throughout as hereinbefore provided in the case of Public School Districts.

The first separate school districts, then, would be very flexible in the sparsely populated North-West. Although there was no provision for a central educational agency, it would appear also that the regimen of all schools would be the same. The remaining sections described the manner of erecting a separate school district, the most important condition being a petition to the governor signed by all the electors in the proposed district. The property of separate school supporters, however, would continue to pay off debenture indebtedness incurred prior to separation. Public school trustees would collect all the school taxes, separate school trustees receiving funds in proportion to the amount paid by separate school property. The trustees or the lieutenant-governor-in-council would authorize books (s. 86(2)) and teachers would submit to the trustees' secretary a signed statement of particulars to be read at the annual general meeting, including 'the religious faith professed by the children, or their parents on behalf of the children' (s.

108(a4)). Religious instruction and religious holidays, apart from Christmas and Easter (s. 140), were not mentioned.

Bishop Grandin first discussed the proposed school ordinance with Archbishop Taché early in 1884 and found it rather liberal. However, public schools ('en réalité des écoles protestantes') would predominate as long as school districts originated with petitions from the people. Manitoba, he thought, had an excellent school law[72] and he wished the same for the North-West. Anxious about his own ability to meet the new challenge, he offered to resign: the times required someone who could defend Catholic rights before their enemies.[73] When urged by his advisers to visit Regina, he refused because the Oblates had no foothold there and because of his own difficulties with English.[74]

Taché warned Grandin against the dangers of legislation which appeared liberal but was susceptible to hostile interpretation,[75] and advised him to consult Judge Charles B. Rouleau, the Ottawa lawyer who had replaced Ryan as stipendiary magistrate in the North-West to fulfil a promise made by the federal government during Grandin's trip to Ottawa early in 1883. Grandin saw Oliver first and was informed that the vastness of the country made it difficult to bring together a board of education as in Mantioba. Oliver agreed, however, to work for a division of the North-West into such school districts as would give Catholics and Protestants their own schools, each under clerical supervision.[76]

Gradually Catholic pressure and persuasion at Regina mounted. Before the end of March Grandin had seen Rouleau and written to Dewdney,[77] Colonels Macleod and Richardson, and Bishop Henri Faraud of Athabaska-Mackenzie, who had not heard of the bill.[78] Judge Rouleau became the key figure – the intermediary between the clergy and the government at Regina. A native of Quebec, he had been appointed to secure 'justice aux intéressés,' as Hector Langevin, minister of public works, informed Grandin in October 1883.[79] As a stipendiary magistrate, he joined Colonels Macleod and Richardson on the North-West Council, where he remained until the 'legal experts' disappeared in 1891. A resident of Calgary until his death in 1901, Rouleau became one of the five members of the territorial Supreme Court in 1887.[80] Devout and deeply conscious of his ethnic origins, he was the most able, and at times the sole, spokesman for French Catholic interests in the council and, after 1888, in the North-West Assembly. In 1884, with Oliver's school bill before the people, Rouleau visited St Albert in March, and the bill was amended by tacking in clauses from the Manitoba school law relating to the formation of a board of education.[81]

From Amédée E. Forget, clerk of the North-West Council who for many years also worked effectively behind the scenes to advance French Catholic interests at Regina, Taché learned, on 1 July, that Dewdney and Richardson had seen Rouleau's amendments and appeared to favour them. Forget encouraged Taché to come to Regina when the bill was in committee to give Catholic supporters in council moral support.[82] In the meantime, Father Lacombe had already discussed the proposed school legislation with officials at Ottawa.[83] By mid-year, then, the ground had been carefully prepared to ensure that Catholic educational interests would not suffer when the first school legislation passed at Regina.

2
Church ascendancy in education, 1885-7

Frank Oliver's school bill was re-introduced in the council on 7 July 1884, and sent to the school committee, which included Oliver and Judge Rouleau.[1] The next day Rouleau introduced the St Albert amendments. Oliver's bill, he said, was 'a very good one in many points,' but it did not give the religious aspects sufficient attention. Oliver admitted that his bill was not perfect and offered to help frame one that would satisfy all classes in the Territories.[2] From Rouleau, Taché learned that the council was quite willing to adopt the amendments.[3] Dewdney, in a dispatch to Macdonald, was less optimistic: 'The School Bill is the only one which I think will create much feeling or discussion ... The feeling is with Oliver. I have not gone into it much myself but suppose it is the old fight. I am trying to get them to agree among themselves and submit a Bill acceptable to both.'[4] The governor was successful and a compromise bill passed without division on 6 August.[5] 'We have had no trouble,' Dewdney informed Macdonald, 'a little bold talk from *Oliver* who's [sic] last session I hope we have seen. Roleau [sic] was great help to me. [He] has plenty of pluck & sense.'[6] There is no evidence that Taché, in Regina to consecrate the first Catholic church when the school bill passed, influenced its passage. As Dewdney's guest at Government House,[7] however, he may have discussed it informally.

Not surprisingly, the first eight sections of the first school ordinance were practically a carbon copy of the Manitoba School Act.[8] A twelve-man board of education to be appointed by the lieutenant-governor-in-council was divided into Protestant and Catholic sections, each controlling its own schools, licensing its teachers, selecting its books and apparatus (books having reference to religion and morals for the Catholic section being 'subject to the approval of the competent religious authority'[9]), and appointing its school inspectors. In short, the dual school system of Quebec, first established in Manitoba in 1871, was now carried into the North-West.[10] In this respect, at least, the triumph of Catholic principle was complete. Otherwise, the ordinance differed little in principle from the original school bill, and the separate school sections, complete with the obnoxious public petitions, were identical.[11] Oliver apparently accepted Rouleau's provisions for the board of education and Rouleau accepted Oliver's for separate schools. The latter, however, were mandatory under the 1875 Act, and Oliver was obliged to include them.

The ordinance also had its unique features. Under the heading, 'Conduct of School,' it detailed the provisions for religious instruction. A form of prayer adopted by the trustees could be used at the opening of each school day (s. 83), but there was to be no religious instruction in any public *or* separate school until three in the afternoon, when 'such instruction as may be allowed under this Ordinance and permitted or desired by the trustees' could be given (s. 84). Any child whose parents or guardians differed in faith from that expressed in the name of the school district could leave at three or remain without participating in the religious instruction (s. 85), and any trustee, inspector, or teacher who attempted to deprive such exempted child of 'any advantage that it might derive from the ordinary education' would be disqualified (s. 86). Christian holidays, apart from Christmas and Easter (s. 81), were not mentioned. Thus the partial triumph of Protestant principle was also secured, for the opening of school with prayer, the postponement of daily religious instruction until after the completion of secular studies, the local option or voluntary principle, the conscience clause, and recesses confined to Christmas and Easter were all-important to the Reverend Egerton Ryerson and the Protestants of Ontario,[12] where such practices originated in Canada and from where they now made their way into the North-West.

The dual school system was to be established simply by each school district declaring whether it was Protestant or Catholic, public or separate (s. 10). The owner of land, whether outside or within the limits of a district, could petition the governor to have his land included in an adjacent district when the latter was of his faith (s. 37); every district would receive aid from the General Revenue Fund of the Territories (s. 91); the taxes on property owned by a Protestant and occupied by a Catholic tenant or vice versa would be paid to the trustees of the district to which the owner of the property belonged (s. 98); Protestants and Catholics who held property jointly would pay taxes to their respective districts in proportion to their interests in the property (s. 97). In no case could a Catholic be compelled to pay taxes to a Protestant school or vice versa (s. 131(1)).

The ordinance was not without its difficulties: How stable would district boundaries be where land could be transferred at will from one district to another? Could a company owned by Catholics and Protestants be accountable to two sets of trustees? How effective would the conscience clause be in a one-room Protestant school, where a few Catholic children rode together with Protestant children and had to remain in school until the end of religious instruction, which only the Protestant parents wanted? With two sections of the board, could the same standards be maintained in licensing teachers, appointing inspectors, and selecting textbooks? Future legislators had, of course, to cope with the difficulties. The first and last were dealt with almost immediately;[13] the second was only settled after Saskatchewan and Alberta became provinces;[14] the third was ignored.

The ordinance, it should be noted, said nothing about the teaching of French; in fact it was altogether silent on the language question. It may be that the prevalence of French in the Territories and its natural use in mission schools in homogeneous districts like Batoche and St Laurent made the question momentarily unimportant. Still, Archbishop Taché had shown some interest in Ottawa's 1877 amendment of the North-West Territories Act,[15] which recognized French as a language of debate in council and in proceedings before the courts, and provided for the publication of the council's journals and ordinances in French;[16] and it is perhaps worth noting that neither he nor Grandin pressed for a legislative guarantee to French schools, at a time when evidence that English settlement was outstripping French settlement was mounting and the possibility that French schools might soon be in jeopardy was becoming more real.

With both Catholic and Protestant principles only partially reflected in the ordinance, it is possible that neither group was entirely satisfied with the council's first efforts to create a school system. Amendments during the next few years indicate as much, at least where the non-Catholics were concerned. Catholics, on the other hand, were little disturbed. In the episcopal correspondence for 1885 and 1886 there were no letters of complaint to Regina, The only incident was a brief flurry during Oliver's campaign for re-election early in 1885 when, at a political meeting in St Albret, Father Leduc referred to the new ordinance to support his view that Catholics should support the Catholic candidate, who would certainly be in the field before too long. While he believed Oliver had tried to be fair to both parties, only someone like Judge Rouleau could know which sections of a law were likely to interfere with the Catholic faith. In a follow-up letter which appeared in the *Edmonton Bulletin* of 10 January, prompted, he said, by a misinterpretation being given to his words, Leduc protested against all insinuations that he intended to raise 'a cause of dissatisfaction' between Catholics and Protestants. Rather, he had spoken to strengthen the union of Catholics at St Albert and Fort Saskatchewan and 'to exhort them to be always united and on friendly terms with the people of Edmonton and neighborhood.'

At a public meeting in Edmonton, a week later, Oliver discussed the passage of the ordinance and criticized 'the somewhat uncalled for conduct' of Rouleau in revising the bill. Leduc followed with another address at St Albert and, in Oliver's presence, gave him full credit for the ordinance, but found him 'rather too much in opposition.' When the Irish Catholic Daniel Maloney, an enthusiastic supporter of Matthew McCauley, one of Oliver's political rivals, asserted that Rouleau was the real author of the ordinance, Oliver explained that it had passed through the legislative stages in his own handwriting, 'with the exception of the clauses relating to the formation of a board of education, which were simply clipped from the Manitoba act by Judge Roleau [sic] and tacked in. Inasmuch as the provisions of those clauses directly contradicted the provisions of the rest of the ordinance, it could easily be seen that both parts were not the work of the one man.'[17]

Father Leduc did not pursue the matter. Neither Oliver nor his eventual opponent, Dr H.C. Wilson, made any mention of it in their electoral advertisements and it was also ignored at the nominating convention in Edmonton.[18] Although Oliver sustained the only defeat of his long political career, the school question was not a factor, because the northeastern part of the electoral district of Edmonton, where the Catholic vote was concentrated, was separated early in August to become the new electoral district of St Albert.[19] At the St Albert nominating convention in September Maloney promised to guard the educational rights of his constituents with special care, but the delegates paid little heed, choosing Samuel Cunningham, an Irish Catholic half-breed popular with the Métis, who was elected by acclamation.[20]

II

Changes in the 1884 Ordinance began immediately. A few touched fundamental principles and reflected the hostility of several elected council members towards the dualism of the system. In 1885 the focus of discontent was the composition of the board of education; in 1886 it was the organization of separate school districts. And from the beginning the state pressed the church for more control of the developing school system.

With the 1884 Ordinance largely inoperative for lack of a General Revenue Fund from which the council could vote school grants,[21] a board of education had not been appointed. In 1885 Colonel Macleod, chairman of the school committee, raised the matter of appointments in council and brought immediate opposition from Rouleau. The Territories, the latter contended, were unable to support 'two sets of officials,' one Catholic, the other, Protestant. As to membership, Rouleau did not doubt the ability of his colleagues, but a board should consist of the 'best and most fitting' men, such as the bishops, who were 'well educated and had the best interests of the youthful population at heart.' Thomas W. Jackson and William D. Perley (later Senator Perley), although both representing the Qu'Appelle district, where the Catholic Métis vote was decisive, countered that education should be non-sectarian and pointed to Ontario as an example of how education prospered with the people's representatives in control. Rouleau wondered which members of council were qualified to examine teachers and grant certificates. But he was not apparently wholly opposed to the immediate appointment of a board, for at one point he thought a five-man board, two Catholics and two Protestants, with the governor as chairman, 'might work.' Yet when Jackson moved a five-man board Rouleau insisted upon seven members.[22] Jackson, however, prevailed and on 15 December John Secord, a Regina lawyer, and Charles Marshallsay, a Whitewood merchant (both elected members of council), and Judge Rouleau and Father Lacombe were appointed to the Protestant and Catholic sections respectively. Governor Dewdney became the chairman and his secretary, James Brown, served as the board's secretary.[23] The two sections could meet separately or sit together as one body, in which case the governor presided.

What interpretation can be placed on Rouleau's attitude to the actual creation of the board, the body he himself had worked to include in the ordinance? '... Bishops,' Jackson had said, 'had no more right than other men to sit at a Board of Education.'[24] With bishops excluded and other well-educated men scarce on the frontier, the great need, from the Catholic point of view, Rouleau may have concluded, was delay until territorial Catholics could become numerous enough to ensure more Catholic representation on the council, the most likely source of future board members. As unrealistic as that hope might appear to be, there were few alternatives. Did not Jackson and Perley already say that the best school systems were controlled by the people's representatives? But the minority had also to be judicious. Once it was apparent that a board (with its two council members) would in fact be appointed, it was best to ignore the board and concentrate on weakening the local movement for responsible government. The board was, after all, a body *appointed* by the governor, with no direct responsibility to territorial public opinion. The religious minority, unable to count on popular support at the polls, could at least count on the board to protect its educational interests – but only if the cry for local political autonomy did not become too strong among the elected members of council. Accordingly, Rouleau flatly rejected assertions that 'local self-government or local assemblies' were widely desired in the Territories. Council members were restricted in handling federal funds because the governor alone was responsible for spending the money. Rather than 'ventilating' their views on all sorts of subjects, they should aid the governor, whose position, after all, was different from that of the governor-general, who was bound to follow the advice of his ministers.

Needless to say, Rouleau's stand did not endear him to his elected colleagues on council. Edmonton's Dr Wilson insisted that his constituents 'strongly desired' responsible government; if Rouleau thought otherwise, he did not understand the sentiments of the people.[25] Even more important, however, Rouleau's remarks indicate how early he had come to realize that the minority's first line of defence was Ottawa, not the territorial government, and that the minority's best strategy was to pressure the federal government to control its remote subordinate. Rouleau's position may have been prematurely defeatist; worse still, however, it flew in the face of responsible government, which the majority equated with territorial progress. Because the council (and later the assembly) always contained an overwhelming number of Protestants,[26] the chances for amiable relations between the church and the state were probably never too good. But it did not help to have a Catholic stipendiary magistrate throw cold water on the pet projects of elected representatives. The latter had long memories and in due time took their revenge.

Sharp differences also arose in 1885 over the selection of school textbooks and the certification of teachers. Perley objected to spending public money on books that might not 'materially advance' children in 'civil pursuits,'[27] but with Rouleau's help the selection of textbooks remained with the board's sections.[28] On teacher certification the outcome was different. Rouleau objected to teachers in religious orders going before a single board of examiners to secure certificates, but Macleod insisted that 'the whole thing' would be in the hands of the Board of Education (which appointed the examiners)'[29] and the change was made.[30] A similar amendment, carried without debate or immediate Catholic reaction to the gradual undermining of the minority's position, transferred the appointment of inspectors from the sections to the whole board.[31]

The importance of the last two changes should not be exaggerated. The examiners set few common examinations and the inspectors visited only schools of their own religious persuasion, as long as appointments were strictly along religious lines. Still the changes were notable departures from the strict principle of dualism. They were the first steps in 'a movement toward secularization' – 'les premières agressions'[32] – and indicated legislative dissatisfaction with religious dualism in education. Much later, in 1894, Forget, one of the Catholic representatives on the Board of Education from 1886 to 1892, explained that 'owing to the particular composition of the board of education, these changes offered no immediate danger, although they indicated a new and hostile tendency.'[33] The council had adopted the board as its administrative agency in education, but from the beginning it was uneasy about the separation encouraged.

Another important change in 1885 restricted the earlier legislation for religious instruction to the public schools, leaving separate schools free to teach religion as they saw fit (s. 78). At the same time the provision for permissive prayer at the opening of each school day was repealed.

In 1886 amendments to the ordinance continued, apparently unopposed by Rouleau, even though one of them, according to Forget, later proved 'fatal' to the organization of Catholic separate school districts.[34] This change, made by a school committee that included Rouleau, affected the formation of separate school districts. Hitherto it had only been necessary to be near some organized school district(s) to erect a separate school; the change required ratepayers organizing a separate school to reside 'within the limits of an organized public school district.'[35] No separate school could now be organized in advance of a public school; and if a Protestant majority refused to establish a school district, Catholics, too, could be without a school. (The reverse, of course, was also true.) The size of the separate school district, broadly and vaguely defined in section 11, was now made more explicit, but the new definition was less permissive and put a check on the spread of separate schools. Because a Catholic in a Protestant public school district or vice versa might now be required to pay taxes to a Protestant school district, the provision barring such an eventuality was repealed.

A second major amendment in 1886, again with negative consequences for Catholic interests, involved the religious designation of public school districts. A district was not prevented from using a religious prefix, Catholic or Protestant, but it was no longer necessary (s. 4). As a result, a third group of public schools emerged: those without religious designation. With the whole Board of Education empowered to appoint inspectors and examiners and to select textbooks for the undesignated schools,[36] the threat to the dual school system was serious. Moreover, it soon became very real. In March

1888 the whole board directed the trustees of undesignated schools to select textbooks authorized by one of the board's sections. If the trustees chose Protestant texts, Protestant inspectors and examiners followed.[37] This meant that Protestant schools could drop their religious designation (the only ones to do so) and represent themselves as public schools externally, but continue internally to all intents and purposes as Protestant schools. Catholics who refused to attend such schools could be accused of divisiveness, and the battle was on between supporters of the 'public' schools (usually Protestants), who cast doubt on Catholic patriotism, and supporters of the separate schools (usually Catholics), who questioned Protestant sincerity.

The last important change in 1886 returned school inspections and teachers' examinations to the respective sections of the board (see Table I).[38] For the Catholic section the change was a gain in principle only, for practice, as we shall see, did not necessarily follow changes in the school law.

As in 1884, the Catholic clergy took little notice of the school legislation of 1885 and 1886. Shortly after the 1885 session Fathers J. Hugonard and L. Lebret spoke briefly at a public banquet in Qu'Appelle for T.W. Jackson, but neither mentioned the school question.[39] Archbishop Taché greatly disliked the board's power over teachers' examinations[40] and after a visit to Regina during the 1886 session,[41] the appointment of examiners for designated schools returned to the sections, with the whole board appointing 'a Board or Boards of Examiners' for only the undesignated schools (s. 1). But neither Taché nor Grandin noticed the limitation placed on the organization of separate school districts. In fact, late in 1887 Taché, disturbed by the new school bill before him, termed the 1886 law 'favorable' and asked Sir John A. Macdonald to wire Dewdney 'to leave the Catholics in possession of their rights, as secured by the School Ordinance of 1886.'[42] This was the clergy's only comment on the 1886 law and explains why no formal protest was lodged at Regina or Ottawa against a limitation which Sir John Thompson, the federal minister of justice, would term 'objectionable' in 1890.[43]

The silence of both prelates is very difficult to explain, but was probably the result of prolonged diocesan absences in 1887. For most of the year Grandin was in Europe or in eastern Canada and Taché visited the east from 14 February to 5 July.[44] On at least two occasions, however, they met for several days[45] and, had they noticed the change, could have reminded the political authorities that limitations on the organization of separate school districts were contrary to the spirit, if not the letter, of the law. But careful as they were to scrutinize legislation passed at Regina, the two prelates either overlooked or did not fully appreciate the 'fatal' change made in school boundaries in 1886.

III

The attitude of the clergy, unperceptive, perhaps even negligent in 1885–6, changed abruptly in 1887 after Dewdney announced a new school bill 'consolidating and amending previous legislation.'[46] Taché, suspicious of Protestant intentions, wrote Dewdney (who had sent him a copy of his address) immediately and confessed to 'a feeling of uneasiness': 'The subject is so delicate and the views of some of your subordinates are so diametrically opposed to our's [sic] on that subject [see Table I for earlier administrative changes] that I always dread a law framed altogether outside of the participation of some one who thinks as we do on the matter.' (The Protestant section, Dewdney informed Macdonald, had proposed the bill and Dewdney himself had helped to draft it without consulting the Catholic section, one member being 'away on leave and the other unable to be present.'[47]) Taché hoped the bill would not compel Catholics to take a stand 'contrary to the harmony which has prevailed so far.'[48] Dewdney assured him that the stipendiary magistrates would secure the minority's interests: 'Should there be any difference of opinion between them as to this, I shall refer the matter to Ottawa, but I am unable to bring any pressure to bear upon my Councillors (who have their conscientious scruples) beyond impressing upon them the necessity of doing ample justice to all parties interested in the cause of Education.'[49] With Ottawa thus proclaimed the final arbiter, Taché asked Macdonald to wire Dewdney not to disturb the educational status quo. Macdonald, unaware of the bill, promised to review the legislation to ensure that Catholic rights were 'fully maintained.'[50]

Father Lacombe in the meantime had already become a one-man lobby at Regina, soon to be joined by Grandin and Leduc. After interviewing Dewdney he consulted Forget and Judge Richardson, attended council when the bill was introduced, and on Colonel Macleod's invitation presented a memorandum of the minority's objections to the school committee.[51] Lacombe reported to Grandin, who concluded that a real conspiracy had been conceived to impose laws which were restrictive and most anti-Christian.[52] Together they met Macleod, Cunningham, and O.E. Hughes (Prince Albert), who appeared to share their views, but Grandin was disheartened. Even sympathetic members, he informed Taché, did not seem to understand the unfavourable aspects of the new bill.[53]

During the next few days Lacombe made three appearances before the school committee[54] and Grandin and Leduc saw Dewdney and Hayter Reed, now assistant commissioner of Indian affairs and a member of council. The discussion in the governor's office was neither calm nor pleasant, with both the governor and Leduc losing their tempers.[55] The future, Lacombe wrote

TABLE 1

Powers exercised by the Board of Education and by its sections, 1884–92

School ordinance (date and year)	Control and management of schools	Cancel teachers' certificates	Arrange examination, grading, licensing of teachers	Appoint examiners of teachers	Select school textbooks	Appoint inspectors	Determine appeals from decisions of inspectors
1884 (6 Aug.)	Sections	Sections	Sections		Sections	Sections	
1885 (18 Dec.)	Sections	Sections	Board	Board[1]	Sections	Board	Board
1886 (16 Nov.)	Sections[2]	Sections[2]	Sections[2]	Sections[2,3]	Sections[2]	Sections[2]	Board
1887 (18 Nov.)	Sections	Sections	Board	Sections[4]	Sections	Sections	Board
1888 (11 Dec.)			No changes				
1889 (22 Nov.)			No changes				
1890 (29 Nov.)			No changes				
1891–2 (25 Jan.)	Sections	Sections	Board	L-G-C.[5]	Sections	L-G-C.	Board
1892 (31 Dec.)	C.P.I.[6]	Superintendent[7]	C.P.I.	C.P.I.[8]	C.P.I.	L-G-C.	C.P.I.

SOURCE: *School Ordinances of the North-West Territories, 1884–92*

1 'A Board or Boards of Examiners,' appointed by the Board of Education, was to select the textbooks on which the teachers would be examined
2 The whole Board of Education was in charge of undesignated schools
3 Technically, the number of boards that could examine teachers was increased to three: one for the undesignated schools and two for the Catholic and Protestant schools. In practice, however, all non-Catholic teachers wrote the examinations set by the Protestant members on the single Board of Examiners
4 'A General Board of Examiners,' of four members (one-half nominated by each section) was to examine all teachers in common. Each section, however, retained the right to select teachers' textbooks in 'history and science' and 'any additional subjects'
5 Lieutenant-Governor-in-Council. Each section retained the right to select textbooks for teachers' examinations in 'history and science' and in 'additional' subjects
6 Council of Public Instruction
7 Appointed by the Lieutenant-Governor-in-Council
8 Two or more examiners to constitute 'a Board of Examiners'; 'history and science' clause disappeared

Taché, looked dark; a big storm was brewing on the horizon. The English, he said, with their fanaticism and usual brutality would attack in the legislature and in the press when the school committee brought its report to council.[56] On 28 October Rouleau, who had been holding court in Edmonton,[57] finally arrived, and after a long talk[58] Grandin left for eastern Canada and Leduc returned to Calgary. Lacombe, on orders from Taché, remained in Regina.[59]

What substantive issues had caused this concentration of Catholic power at Regina? On 28 October, with the new school legislation public, Lacombe gave Taché the gist of a revealing conversation he had had with a reporter from the *Manitoba Free Press* (Winnipeg) about French-language instruction in the Catholic schools, then under legislative attack for the first time. Told the new legislation would abolish the French schools by making English the sole language, Lacombe replied, ' "I hope the ordinance will not pass. Even suppose it will pass at Regina, the last word will not be said, because there is another question to be settled, the one that the French language is as well official as the English." '[60]

The status of French in territorial schools was still not clarified by 1887. The number of schools in which French had been the exclusive language of instruction cannot be estimated, but by 1887 there were apparently only three extant.[61] More typical were bilingual French-English schools, though their number too is not known. What is clear is that the place of language in the schools was a question which greatly troubled the French-speaking clergy. Before 1885 it was the preference for English among New England expatriates which gave the most difficulty. As a result, both French and English were taught at St Albert as early as 1875[62] and the school contemplated for Edmonton by Grandin and Leduc in 1877 was to be bilingual.[63] One was actually established at Cunningham, near St Albert, by the Reverend J.T. Quévillon in 1885.[64] But lay Catholics who preferred English schools were also active, and in 1884 an exasperated Grandin wrote Lacombe of French-Canadian farmers between St Albert and Edmonton who had constructed a school house and hired an English schoolmaster without consulting anyone.[65] After 1885 the problem was compounded by the split among the Métis in their attitude towards the clergy subsequent to Louis Riel's unsuccessful rebellion. Thus in December 1888 the Métis of Carlton petitioned the territorial assembly to make the teaching of English compulsory in all schools.[66] Two months later the Métis at Prince Albert petitioned Ottawa against the same compulsory language clause.[67] The attitude of the less numerous English-speaking half-breeds is not apparent. Despite their common Indian ancestry and strong territorial and maternal linguistic bonds with the Métis, the religion and language of their fathers divided them and, though they worked together in the Prince Albert–Duck Lake area to secure their lands before 1885, there is no evidence that they made common cause on religious or language questions.

The French-speaking clergy themselves were, of course, of one mind on the question. Although the 1877 federal bilingual amendment and the territorial school ordinances ignored French-language instruction, it followed that a bilingual North-West would require a bilingual school system, and any challenge to the French language would be strongly resisted. Acting on the thesis, first enunciated in 1866 by Bishop Laflèche of Three Rivers, that to lose one's language was to lose one's faith,[68] the clergy established a necessary connection between French speech and Catholic worship and ensured that bilingual education in Catholic schools would be as explosive an issue as the schools themselves. For the moment, however, calm prevailed. When the question of 'exclusively teaching English' came up in council, 'it was shown that only three schools in the Territories taught French alone,' and the matter was left optional.[69]

Another issue was the size of the Board of Education and its Protestant-Catholic ratio. Dewdney, in debate, suggested the board be increased to ten members, seven Protestants and three Catholics. Secord preferred a six-four ratio. Rouleau proposed a four-three ratio, but oddly enough declared, without elaborating, that the Protestant number did not matter as long as the Catholics were given three members. The matter was settled on a slightly hostile note when John G. Turriff (Moose Mountain) moved a five-three ratio, limiting the term of each member to two years. (Dr Wilson had insisted that the board had 'too much power' and suggested a two-year limit to strengthen the council.[70]) On 2 December the following were appointed to the reorganized Board: *Protestant* – the Reverend W.C. Pinkham, bishop of Saskatchewan and Calgary (Church of England), Judge E.L. Wetmore, the Reverend A.B. Baird (Presbyterian), the Reverend J. McLean (Methodist), and J. Secord; *Roman Catholic* – Judge Rouleau, Father Leduc, and A.E. Forget.[71] At the board's first meeting Bishop Pinkham was the unanimous choice as chairman.[72]

A third issue was the control of the certification of teachers. Was the whole board or its sections to control certification? The existing legislation favoured the sections but the council favoured the board. From the *Morning Call* (Winnipeg) Lacombe learned that David F. Jelly (Regina) and Hayter Reed feared the possibility of dual certification standards emerging. The suggestion that Catholic teachers might be considered inferior to Protestant teachers angered Lacombe, who urged Grandin (then in Ottawa) to warn the federal authorities of impending strife. In particular, his friend Thomas White, minister of the interior, should realize that his officials in Regina were creating many difficulties for him. Lacombe had defended Dewdney, Reed, and others, even at the risk of offending his superiors, but, he added, if official hypocrisy and bigotry forced him to turn against the government, he would become an adversary perhaps as formidable as the Blackfoot.[73] In a letter to Reed he came to the point directly:

If, by your declaration, you mean that our certificates of first class are not worth third class of the protestant, which is untrue and what you must know, by your own experience, you prove to me that you are a man of a party, opposed to us, their tool and moved by the bigotry of your co-religionists, what you have denied always before me. If so doing, you think to make your advancement, in favoring them, and underground to crush us down, I tell you, you are mistaken. This conduct will bring you to fail in your honor and one day will come, when you will understand that you made a great mistake. I am sorry to break with you, but your conduct forces me to do so. I cannot longer join with a man, whom I thought to be *the right one in the right place*, who now is not true to his promises and good words towards me. Of course, that's your own business and of your advisers. All right, have the new ordinance to pass as it is, but I can promise you that 'sowing wind, you shall reap whirlwind,['] and perhaps soon. This mistake, you will understand but it will be too late.[74]

Dewdney, in reply to a telegram from Macdonald,[75] gave the following account of the incident:

... Reid [sic] suggested that all teachers [sic] certificates should be graded alike that is on the same standard of examinations – for if thus was not done a teacher in one section might have a first class certificate on an examination which another section might only give a third class to – and stated most particularly that this might occur in either the R.C. or Protestant sections – however one newspaper made it appear that he referred particularly to the R.C. section and this meeting the eye of Père La Combe brought about the enclosed letter to Reid. He consulted me as to what course he should take. At first I thought he should read the letter in open Council but on second thought advised that he draw attention to the remarks in the paper and ask the Council what was their understanding of the remarks. They all supported Reed's contention.

Reed then asked Macleod, Richardson and Roleau [sic] to meet him in my room. They came and he read the letter. Roleau said he was much surprised at the tone of the letter and would write to Père La Combe asking and advising that he should withdraw the letter.

He did write a very strong letter and gave it to Reed to post – and the matter rests. I only wish La Combe had written that letter to me instead of to Reed. I know he intends it as much for me as for Reed.

This French business or domination won't work in the Territories – it is taking root already.[76]

Rouleau said nothing to Taché of his role in the Reed affair. He termed the school bill iniquitous and blamed it on Dewdney, Secord, and Marshallsay, with Reed, Jelly, and Frederick W.G. Haultain (Macleod)[77] indirectly responsible. The upshot of the Reed incident, he added, was that all teachers' examinations would come under a single general board of examiners appointed by the sections, with each section in control of examinations in subjects that contained religious and historical materials. That was, he believed, tantamount to victory in principle.[78] Macdonald, too, was satisfied with the new ordinance. Neither he nor Sir Hector Langevin, minister of public works and Macdonald's lieutenant in Quebec, could see that it injured Catholic interests 'in any way.'[79]

It would appear, then, that the Catholic lobby at Regina had been highly successful in retaining an acceptable school system. By comparing the ordinance with Taché's objectives, as outlined in a letter to Lacombe in October,[80] it is possible to gauge more precisely the results of the campaign conducted at Regina. Taché wished to make the two sections of the board completely independent, with the board responsible only for general questions which did not affect any religious principle either directly or indirectly. Only once (in the abortive 1884 Ordinance) was such an absolute separation on the statute books; the tendency after 1884 was to de-emphasize the role of the sections. Even so the 1887 Ordinance, in re-establishing a single board of examiners (s. 9), gave each section power to select teachers' textbooks in 'history and science' as well as 'exclusive jurisdiction' over 'any additional subjects' prescribed (s. 10), thus ensuring independent Catholic action where it counted most. On the subject of a single school curriculum Taché was very explicit that the sections alone were to control the course of studies. Although the ordinance authorized eight compulsory subjects, it allowed trustees to authorize additional ones (s. 83), again ensuring freedom of action and continued freedom for French teaching. To Taché, this provision was probably a compromise at best, as initiative in the matter rested with lay Catholics, who, as we have seen, were not always friendly towards French-language instruction.

The religious holidays listed by Taché were not granted, but trustees were empowered to declare additional holidays, 'not exceeding one day at a time' (s. 82). And, after a two-year absence, public schools could again open with prayer (s. 86(1)). Archbishop Taché, it would appear, had little reason to find fault with the new ordinance. It is true that section 8, which defined the powers of the board's sections, did not contain, as he had hoped, all that the ordinance of the previous year had contained, but the new law did not repeal the dual principle, which he admitted, was the fundamental principle of the old law. Moreover, the new ordinance did contain several benefits: the opening of school with prayer, an additional Catholic representative on the board and definite powers (however discretionary) regarding religious holidays and the teaching of French. There were, of course, some anxious moments before the bill passed in council. However, only one issue, teacher certification, gave rise to any marked bitterness. It would appear that Catholic leaders could have been less suspicious of the council's intentions in 1887. Certainly the council was never as hostile as the assembly which succeeded it. On the other hand, the religious lobby did help to maintain the status quo for at least another year, with the discretionary and optional clauses quite likely the direct result of Catholic pressure at Regina.

IV

During the period of church ascendancy, the school system that actually evolved was a mixture of dualism and uniformity. The Protestant and Catholic elementary school curricula, although drawn up separately, were similar from the outset and, except for religious instruction in Catholic schools, were practically identical by March 1888.[81] School textbooks were entirely different, however, with the Protestant, the English Catholic, and in time the French Catholic schools each having their own.

To staff the schools teachers were first issued provisional and non-professional certificates. The provisional certificate, requiring no minimum academic preparation or examination, ranked as a third-class non-professional certificate.[82] A two-man board of examiners (increased to four in 1888), staffed by Protestant and Catholic clergy appointed by the Board of Education, introduced first-, second-, and third-class non-professional examinations in March 1886 to test the academic background of teaching candidates.[83] In April the Board of Education and the board of examiners chose the textbooks on which these examinations were based. Unlike school text-books, they were practically identical for the English-speaking candidates of both sections, the lone exceptions being in history and catechism. French Catholic candidates for the French and bilingual schools wrote on the same subjects as English Catholic and Protestant candidates, but their textbooks were entirely different.[84] The first non-professional teachers' examinations were held in January 1887 at ten centres in the Territories.[85] Thereafter examinations were held semi-annually.

In June 1887 the Protestant section introduced the professional certificate for teachers and required holders of provisional and non-professional cer-tificates to acquire it within a year. A provisional certificate would lapse even sooner if the holder failed to pass the semi-annual examination for a third-class non-professional certificate. Holders of non-professional certificates with at least one year's teaching experience could obtain professional cer-tificates by presenting their certificates, properly endorsed by the school inspector, to the Protestant section.[86] In March 1888 both sections adopted the same conditions for granting non-professional and professional certifi-cates, based on the Protestant regulations of the previous year. The textbooks for the non-professional examinations, however, were now different for the Protestant and English Catholic candidates and similar for the French and English Catholic candidates.[87] Separation for English Catholics was to be on religious not ethnic grounds. Finally, in March 1889 the Board produced a secondary school curriculum[88] and in 1890 the Protestant section desig-nated Standards V and VI (introduced in 1889) as the first and second high school standards. The subjects of Standards V and VI became the subjects of examination for third- and second-class non-professional certificates. For Catholic candidates the equivalent subjects were the Intermediate and Superior courses.[89] Initially, then, the work of the secondary schools was very closely tied to providing elementary school teachers with suitable aca-demic preparation.

In March 1886 the board had appointed eleven inspectors (six Protestants and five Catholics) to look after the six inspectoral districts into which the Territories were divided. Sixty and 50 per cent of the Catholic and Protestant inspectors respectively were clergymen.[90] When the inspectoral staff was increased to fourteen in 1888 (seven for each section), the percentage of Catholic clergy increased to 71, while the Protestant percentage dropped to 43.[91] The first school inspections, made in 1886, were conducted along denominational lines, even though all inspectors were appointed by the whole Board of Education under the 1885 Ordinance[92] and could be expected to inspect any school in their district. The development of dualism in practice, even when the law encouraged the opposite, may have prompted the 1886 amendment that set limitations on the organization of separate school districts. Members of council who wished to discourage sectarian or separatist education may have concluded that increasing the powers of the Board of Education *at the top* of the educational structure was far less effective than curtailing the flexibility of school district organization *at the bottom*.

If the feeling did exist (and it is difficult to account for the 1886 amendment without it), it certainly would have been strengthened once the regulations governing non-professional teacher certification, adopted by the board in April 1886, became public. Here again, according to the 1885 Ordinance,[93] the whole board was to arrange for the certification of teachers (see Table I). The board established a uniform curriculum, as we have seen, but it preserved the sectarian or separatist principle in three ways: Catholic candidates could offer catechism as an additional subject, Protestant and English Catholic candidates could use different history books, and French Catholic candidates could use textbooks entirely different from those used by English Catholic and Protestant candidates. Although there was no curricular or teacher textbook demarcation (before March 1888) similar to the wall of separation between the Protestant and Catholic inspectoral staffs, the differences may have been sufficient to lead the opponents of separate schools to conclude that, as long as the Board of Education was evenly divided between Protestants and Catholics, sectarianism and separatism would grow unless controlled at some other point. Hence the limitation on the ease with which separate school districts could be organized.

The tug-of-war between the board and the council was even more pronounced in 1887. Although the 1886 Ordinance again placed each section in complete control of examinations (including subjects and textbooks) for teachers in designated schools[94] (see Table I), in practice only the actual examinations were completely divorced in 1887. The point is important, for in 1887 the law created 'a general Board of Examiners' and teacher examination and certification were returned to a single body.[95] One would have expected the board's regulations to recognize this move in the direction of greater uniformity. In fact, however, the opposite followed from the regulations adopted in March 1888.[96] The books used by Protestant and Catholic candidates in 1888–9, as we have seen, were different in all subjects except 'The Science and Art of Teaching,' and even here the Catholic candidates used different texts in history, geography, grammar, and arithmetic, and were not required to read Browning's *Educational Theories*. It would appear that the 1887 exception granting each section exclusive jurisdiction over 'any additional subjects' prescribed[97] was given a very liberal interpretation.

This and the fact that by 1888 the French Catholic teachers' candidates were responsible for only five books, two less than the English Catholic candidates and five less than the Protestant candidates, underlined the fact that 'general' boards made up of members specifically nominated by the sections were just as prone to promote diversity as uniformity in educational practice, without regard for the intentions of the legislators.

The first interest in normal schooling was shown in July 1886, when the Board of Education and Thomas White, minister of the interior, discussed the possibility of attaching normal school classes to the public high school contemplated for Regina.[98] Several months later John Secord, a member of both the board and the council, tried to introduce legislation for 'one or more training schools for teachers.'[99] Nothing came of either move. In 1887 the board urged the federal government to furnish funds for 'one or more High Schools and a Central Training School.'[100] In January 1888 it passed a resolution requesting federal funds for 'a normal school principal, whose duty it would be to hold normal school sessions in different parts of the country.'[101] The resolution, although pointed enough on the surface, raised two important questions. In asking for a *single* normal school principal for a *dual* school system, did the board have a Protestant or a Catholic in mind? Moreover, in view of the clergy's prominent role in the territorial school system, the appointee could conceivably be a clergyman. How easy would it be to agree upon a candidate? Although Forget and Leduc supported the resolution, Leduc informed Taché that he disliked the visible tendency towards uniformity in the board's policies by attempting to bypass the sections.[102]

With professional training imminent, Grandin and Leduc took steps to have religious teaching personnel excluded from normal school examinations. In March 1888 the Board of Education approved Leduc's motion to grant priests first-class teaching certificates without examinations. The Reverend Baird was prepared to extend the privilege to the teaching sisters, but Judge Wetmore's strong opposition prevented this. Although Leduc was extremely pleased with the results,[103] Grandin had his reservations. The sisters, who had been writing non-professional examinations since January 1887, were beginning to complain that the examinations made them very tired and that the material on which they were examined was ridiculous, with many of the questions based on Protestant authors.[104] Numerous complaints on the subject followed, but the earliest at least were of doubtful validity. In 1888 the two Catholic members of the board of examiners set separate examinations for Catholic candidates in history and religious instruction; where the examinations were 'for All Candidates' the papers were set by all the examiners.[105]

By 1888, then, the basic outlines of the dual system were clear. Amid curricular similarities, textbook differences prevailed and were most marked in the early years of school. For the teachers' examinations English Catholic books were closer to those used by the French Catholic candidates than by the Protestants. Inspectoral staffs were entirely separate, but it was not unusual for teachers to write common non-professional examinations in subjects removed from history and religion. Professional teacher training was desired by both sections of the Board of Education, although neither seemed aware of the problems in establishing normal schools for a divided school system. Several elected members of council openly opposed church control of the territorial school system, and a virtual tug-of-war developed between the council and the Board of Education over whose school legislation would prevail. On the whole, however, relations between the Catholic church and the territorial government were friendly during the conciliar period (1873–87).

How much this friendliness reflected a general support for Catholic separate schools in the Territories is very difficult to say, however. Outright public criticism was rare, but the fact that most elected members of council and most non-Catholic newspapers favoured 'non-sectarian' schools would indicate that overall support for Catholic schools was not marked. That the Catholic church had its own school system was due primarily to Judge Rouleau's persuasive powers in council and the dualistic model of school administration in Manitoba. Even so, Catholic education in the Territories had already sustained several important setbacks, most notably the restriction on the proliferation of separate school districts, the appearance of religiously undesignated public schools, and the predominance of Protestant members on the Board of Education. Significant also were the first signs of the minority's reliance upon the federal authority to protect it from hostile local legislation. This was particularly true with respect to the status of French-language teaching, and this mixture of linguistic and religious issues made the North-West school question the most volatile of territorial problems in the next decade.

3
On the brink of
educational conflict, 1888-9

In 1888 the North-West entered upon a new political era – one teeming with educational difficulties for the Roman Catholic church. A legislative assembly replaced the North-West Council and held its first session. It contained twenty-two elected members and three legal advisers appointed by the federal government from among the five judges of the territorial Supreme Court. In 1886 the Territories had been given parliamentary representation, four seats in the Commons and two in the Senate. These changes, the result of numerous representations, did not necessarily improve the federal government's image, and criticism in the assembly increased as it became obvious that representative government did not entail responsible government. The governor was required, 'on matters of finance,' to consult a four-man advisory council selected by him from among the elected members,[1] but Ottawa restricted the council's authority to the management of local revenues, approximately 17 per cent of the total budget in 1887–8.[2] Thus executive authority remained with the governor, as did control of the annual parliamentary grant. The unhappy assembly voiced strong objections to the continued denial of financial autonomy. Also symptomatic of the assembly's tutelage was its lack of control over schools and therefore over separate schools and French-language instruction.

The federal government was in a difficult position. It had introduced separate schools in 1875 and was required by the BNA Act to protect them. The French language, too, received constitutional or official status in 1877, and Ottawa was bound to defend it. But political circumstances also required the federal government to guard the educational interests of Catholics in the

Territories. Since the 1840s an alliance had been growing between the Conservative party and the ultramontane section of the Catholic hierarchy in Quebec. So obvious was the alliance by 1870 that Bishops Bourget and Laflèche, its two chief architects, no longer concealed it.[3] In 1885 the alliance was severely tested on the gallows at Regina, for in the controversy over Louis Riel's execution the Catholic hierarchy rallied to the government's side only after Taché and Grandin, who appreciated the religious heresy that accompanied Riel's political agitation,[4] refused to defend Riel. Taché regarded the latter as a 'miserable madman and a fanatic.' Grandin, always suspicious of Riel's movements, saw the rebellion as one against God and the church as well as against the government.[5] But to criticize Riel was one thing; to blacken his popular image was far more difficult. To the French-Canadian press, Riel was a patriot, the victim of Orangeism, who had brought the Conservative government to its knees. Early in 1887 Honoré Mercier, the energetic *nationaliste* strongly opposed to Ottawa's treatment of Riel, carried the provincial election in Quebec, largely on the wave of anti-Conservative feeling generated by the French-Canadian press. In the federal election that followed in March Macdonald barely held Quebec, and that largely on the strength of Taché's counsel that the hierarchy support the Conservatives.

In the circumstances it was easy for Taché and Grandin to conclude that the Conservatives did indeed owe their retention of power to the influence of the western hierarchy.[6] Accordingly, fresh from his trying experiences at Regina, Grandin, in October 1887, approached Ottawa with several grievances, including the controversial school bill. The government, however, was either unimpressed or moved too slowly. In any case, when the ultramontane *La Vérité* (Quebec City) got wind of Grandin's difficulties, it derided the hierarchy for supporting a government that was now trampling its defenders under foot.[7] Grandin absolved the hierarchy and placed the blame on the absence of a united national movement in Quebec for protecting French-Canadian interests in the Dominion.[8] This did not, of course, hide the fact that, as an ally, the federal government was not reliable. It was easy to invest Ottawa with constitutional and political obligations, but something else again to have the obligations met.

Catholic leaders in the Territories, however, could take comfort from the fact that a devout Catholic, Joseph Royal, had succeeded Dewdney as governor shortly before the assembly met in 1888. Educated by the Jesuits in Montreal, Royal was one of 'a little phalanx of young men, able and true,' whom Taché had brought west after 1870 to uphold French Catholic interests (others recruited were Senator Girard, Judge Joseph Dubuc, and

Alphonse La Rivière, member of Parliament).[9] As the member of Parliament for Provencher (Taché's constituency) after 1879, Royal had served the church well on numerous occasions. His appointment was a political favour to the Catholic clergy in the North-West for not exacerbating the Riel question during the federal election. Grandin had requested a French Catholic governor in an earlier memorandum, and Judge Rouleau had pressed the matter in Ottawa after the council had threatened the French schools in October.[10]

Royal's arrival was, of course, eagerly awaited by those who shared his religious and ethnic origin. The Métis were hopeful he would usher in a new era in which suspicion and hatred of the government and the English would disappear. Forget thought Royal's mere presence would give him 'immense support' and he could always benefit in private from his experience. Father Leduc expected the appointment to enrage the 'francophobes,' to whom a French-Canadian governor would be as welcome as the devil himself.[11] Royal himself was not slow to give his co-religionists proof of their good fortune. Having drafted Manitoba's first school legislation and served as that province's first superintendent of Catholic education, he promised, in his reply to the Board of Education's welcome in September, to watch the school system's development with 'an increasing zeal.'[12] The Catholic church therefore expected much of the new governor. If Royal understood his duty, Grandin wrote Leduc, he would put all things on a good footing.[13] Royal's position, however, was not enviable. Judge Rouleau was the only Catholic member in the assembly, and he had no vote.

II

The first session of the Legislative Assembly opened late in October 1888. Much was expected of it. The *Regina Journal*, in a series of editorials on non-sectarian education, had called upon the legislators to abolish separate schools and the Board of Education,[14] and the *Qu'Appelle Vidette* had advised them to accept 'one nation, one language' as the territorial motto to make Canada a united country in which 'every language but one' was removed from the legislatures and common schools.[15]

As the session approached, Taché, having learned of Sir John Thompson's 'just views' on the use of French in the North-West, wrote him of the threat to French-language instruction in 1887 and of the amendments that had made the law more acceptable.[16] Thompson, a former member of the Nova Scotia Supreme Court and a convert to the Roman Catholic faith, had thought more amendments were in order, and had only refrained from 'pressing any remonstrance on the assurance that the Catholic clergy were satisfied with the Ordinance as it was.'[17] Surprised, Taché gave Thompson the following additional 'word of explanation':

The school ordinance, as passed last year at Regina, is not what we desired and, for my part, I was far from being satisfied. I wrote to Sir John A. Macdonald, pointing out some clauses, to which I objected and did not receive a reply. I inferred from that it was useless for me to seek redress and the Ordinance, prepared by authority [Dewdney], was so obnoxious that in reality we felt a relief in accepting the amended one.

I assure you that you cause me great pleasure when you state that you yourself 'had much fault to find with it' 'and drew up a memorandum showing the point in which (you) thought it should be amended.'

Now, dear Sir John, there may be a chance of renewing your efforts against anti-Catholic and anti-constitutional legislation, in the North-West.

There are several newspapers at work to endeavour to bring about the *abolition* of our separate schools. I am afraid there will be efforts made in that direction, in the coming sitting of the Council [*sic*] of the North-West.

A word to the Judges, who are the advisers of the Government there, may prevent mischief.[18]

When the session opened the Board of Education held the usual prominent place in the debates on responsible government. Royal, after consulting the assembly, had chosen Haultain, Jelly, William Sutherland (North Qu'Appelle), and Hillyard Mitchell (Batoche) as his advisory council.[19] This raised the question of the latter's political status. Was the governor obliged to consult the council when making appointments to bodies such as the Board of Education? Hugh Cayley (Calgary) thought the assembly should advise the governor because the new council had no more knowledge of the Territories than the new governor. Moreover, with the governor summoning both the council and the assembly to Regina, it was really the governor who governed and made the appointments. Oliver wished it clearly understood that the assembly had the power to control and revise executive acts,[20] but nothing came of these efforts to enhance the assembly's powers. The Board of Education remained independent of the assembly and was periodically criticized for the kind of irresponsibility which, it was alleged, indefinite lines of political responsibility made inevitable. At the same time Rouleau's continued opposition to responsible government[21] did little to strengthen his position as spokesman for Catholic educational interests when these came up during the session.

To counter the opposition of 'bachelors and malcontents' to the formation of school districts,[22] the assembly's first school ordinance introduced compulsory education, a full twenty-eight years before its adoption in Manitoba.[23] All children seven to twelve years of age had to attend school for at least twelve weeks in each year and negligent parents were subject to a nominal fine (ss. 181–5). Opposition to the change was considerable and the vote in favour only ten to eight.[24] Although compulsory attendance could lead to forced mixing of Catholic and Protestant children in districts where Catholics were too few to organize separate schools, the minority did not challenge the change. The clause, Royal wrote Taché, contained 'exceptions' and was 'acceptable.'[25]

Catholic educational interests were also seriously affected by other changes in the ordinance. The movement, led by John F. Betts (Prince Albert), to tax churches for educational purposes was partially successful when the size of church-site exemptions was cut from one to one-half acre (s. 98(6)). The ordinance also exempted only two acres of the land on which a school was situated (s. 98(4)) and omitted the exemption in the 1887 Ordinance on the grounds and buildings of 'universities, collegiate institutes or incorporated seminaries' (s. 100(4)), the St Albert Seminary included. Another amendment, however, freed separate school supporters of all responsibility for debts incurred by the public district once a separate district was established (s. 41). All Catholic property owners, in turn, were obliged to support the separate school that was established, a change which became a major issue in 1892.[26]

Even more controversial were the changes that involved separate school boundaries and French-language teaching. The minority, having finally noticed the 1886 limitation on boundaries,[27] urged the Board of Education to recommend changes in the separate school clause and these found their way into the school bill before the assembly. With several members surprised that the wording of the clause in the bill and the ordinance was 'materially' different,[28] Royal wired Thompson to ascertain whether section 14 of the NWT Act secured to the minority the right 'to establish schools even in districts wherein majority neglects getting organized or to join with persons of same faith resident outside of an organized district.'[29] The section, Thompson replied, 'does not enable minority to combine with persons of the same faith outside the district. Ordinance may do so.' This was explicit enough, but it only repeated the obvious. What Royal undoubtedly wanted to know was whether the ordinance *had* to 'insure' the minority an opportunity to combine with other Catholic ratepayers outside the district. The right to establish separate schools, Thompson continued, 'could be exercised under such ordinances [as were passed under section 14] even though minority did not organize.'[30] The point at issue, however, was not whether the right lapsed if the minority did not organize, but whether it could be invoked if the *majority* failed to act. Royal, undoubtedly disappointed by the exchange, did not request further clarification, and the assembly voted not to modify the separate school clause.[31]

The minority experienced another setback when the discretionary power of trustees over the school curriculum was repealed. The change imposed no specific restriction on the teaching of French, but it was now more difficult to encourage it. At the same time it became 'incumbent' upon all trustees 'to cause a primary course of English to be taught.'[32] Thus some English instruction in French elementary schools became mandatory, while the sole legal base for instruction in French disappeared. The change was introduced by Mitchell of Batoche and was supported by a petition from the Métis of Carlton requesting that English be compulsory in all schools.[33]

Governor Royal kept Taché and Grandin fully informed of developments at Regina. News on the school bill, he confessed to Taché, was very bad. The leaderless assembly had an exaggerated view of its own importance, and outside financial matters the advisory council had no influence on the members, who were free to undertake the most silly and obnoxious schemes.[34] To Grandin he confided that he did not mind compulsory English instruction because the teaching of English was already universal in the Territories. The taxation of church property for school purposes, however, exasperated him, but what could one expect from a legislature entirely Anglo Protestant? With Rouleau's and Forget's help he managed to defeat two other even more monstrous changes. One would have prohibited religious instruction in all schools in the Territories. (He threatened to reserve the whole bill to prevent the anti-Christian amendment.) The other would have replaced the Board of Education with an irresponsible minister. The proposed appointee was James Brown, the author of the amendments. Once Forget explained the absurd and selfish side of the proposal to several members, Rouleau had only to ridicule it to secure its rejection without discussion.[35] Taché alerted Thompson immediately, relying on his 'fair disposition ... to prevent the misfortune in store.' A veiled threat followed: 'You easily understand that the Catholic hierarchy will not remain silent in such an emergency and it is not difficult to foresee also what commotion would be the unavoidable result of our appeal to the Catholics of all the Provinces.'[36]

After the assembly prorogued Grandin wrote Taché that the amendments were samples of the Protestant persecution that was steadily increasing. Royal could do little to protect them. There were no Catholic representatives in the assembly and there would be none until the electoral boundaries were changed (or, he might have added, the Catholic population increased). (St Albert disappeared as an electoral district in 1888.[37]) Perhaps, he concluded, if Quebec made the study of French compulsory in all its schools, Ottawa would be more careful about the politics it encouraged at Regina.[38]

Lacking numbers, political strength, and funds, the territorial minority was, in fact, in no position to face the combined opposition of press and government to French-language instruction and separate schools, the two pillars of dualism in the territorial school system. Yet the attacks on both were in the infant stage; the worst was still to come.

III

Newspaper opposition to separate schools and the French language reached a fever pitch during the first half of 1889. The parliamentary debates on the Jesuit Estates Bill, led by the Irish-born D'Alton McCarthy and a group of Ontario Protestant Conservatives close to the Orange order, were the immediate cause, but the territorial newspapers required little urging. Since 27 September 1888, the *Regina Journal* had been crusading for a non-sectarian school system and its torrent of words soon engulfed practically every newspaper in the Territories. By the time McCarthy came west in August 1889 public opinion was well-prepared for his appeal to settle the school and language questions 'by the ballot,' or the next generation would have to do so 'by the bayonet.'[39] The *Lethbridge News* urged the territorial legislators to study developments in Manitoba,[40] where Thomas Greenway's Liberal government had announced its intention to replace the Board of Education with a department in charge of a cabinet minister at the next session of the legislature. In the wake of the announcement publication in French of Manitoba's official gazette was discontinued.[41]

In the campaign against denominational schools the newspapers (in particular the *Regina Journal*) developed the 'national schools' philosophy, the basic premise of which was that 'our age and circumstances as a mixed people' required a non-sectarian or national school system. Non-sectarian schools, the *Journal* insisted, did not ignore God, religion, or morality; they only eschewed church dogma, creeds, and 'creed makers.' Theoretical doctrine found in Board of Education examination questions on papal infallibility, the Blessed Virgin, the saints, the true church, and the forgiveness of sins was excluded; practical ethics which stressed obedience to parents, respect for superiors, truthfulness, honesty, loyalty, and man's duty to God and his fellowman were not. All Christians could agree upon the latter; those who wanted to teach specific religious tenets could do so at their own expense. To hold that the standard of public morality would be lowered by non-sectarian schools was unfair to Christian parents and devoted clergy whose influence, joined with the school's, made up 'the full measure of symmetrical education, each acting its part at the proper time and in the proper place since all cannot act at once.' The state, 'an organism independent and complete in itself,' required schools to preserve and perpetuate it by providing each child with the opportunity to become an intelligent and loyal democratic citizen. 'That which was formerly left to chance or charity, we secure by law. In order to subvert anarchy, communism and their kindred evils; in order to deliver from the power of the professional agitator and enable all to read, think, yea and vote aright, we educate.' The day of church school systems was at an end because the day of state-supported worship had passed. 'An eternal divorcement of state and church has been secured.' The resulting religious liberty was the same for all, and no church should seek the benefits of 'religious favoritism and class legislation' under 'the guise of religious instruction and in the name of education.'

There was no reason, the *Journal* continued, why section 14 should be 'tamely submitted to.' With Ottawa all-powerful, the public had to be educated to the 'evil' of propagating sectarian doctrines with public funds. If public sentiment were awakened before the granting of responsible government, 'a Provincial school system ... free of the "separate school" feature' would follow. To argue that the products of national schools would be less amenable to their religious guides or less susceptible to religious truth was to cast 'a foul and unwarrantable aspersion upon religion itself.' But non-sectarian systems in other countries had had no such results; the fears were unjustified. In fact even Roman Catholic laymen, 'left to themselves,' preferred national schools. It was true that teachers, like any public officials, could abuse their trust and transform national schools into distinctively Protestant or even anti-Catholic schools. However, the law in a national school system assumed that the teachers were 'all honorable,' and those in the Territories were possessed of 'such common sense and professional honor as precludes the possibility of their engaging in proselytism.' To suggest that the problem would disappear if all denominations were given separate schools was an 'imaginary project' of the Catholic church, which would do 'anything and everything to the end that the doctrine of the Church of Rome may be taught at the expense of the public.'[42]

A more searching version of the same philosophy was presented by Frank Oliver in the *Edmonton Bulletin*. A Protestant himself, Oliver was impatient with Protestants who insisted upon catechism instruction in public schools and then opposed separate school privileges for Catholics. On 27 July 1889, he said that until Protestants 'give up the idea of teaching Protestant doctrine in the public schools at the public expense ... they are only fighting against the object which they desire to accomplish – a uniform school system.' He favoured Manitoba's decision to replace the Board of Education with a responsible minister as in Ontario. Where politics and education are mixed, he continued on 24 August, 'abuses of any kind stand a far poorer chance of holding their place when subjected to the white heat of political debate than they would if kept out of sight by a board whose irresponsible control is the greatest abuse of all – protected from the public scrutiny by a board fence, so to speak.' Strongly committed to responsible government, Oliver criticized newspapers like the *Regina Journal* for speaking of responsible government and the abolition of separate schools in the same breath. To link the two, he argued on 31 August, was to ensure the failure of both movements: 'First catch your hare, then cook it. First secure control of your own affairs, then dispute as to how they shall be controlled.'

For Oliver, the question of religious instruction would be solved ideally if the various Christian churches could unite on a common form. But, if past experience were any criterion, he agreed (14 September) that there was little room for optimism. At bottom the problem was one of providing security for minority rights. The majority had to rule, but it was 'only right to consult the feeling of the minority to a reasonable extent.' Both should advocate changes in the interests of education, 'free from the remotest suspicion of a spirit of religious intolerance or disregard of the feelings of the religious minority merely because it is a minority.' Struggling to be objective, Oliver finally concluded there was no solution satisfactory to all. To do away with religious instruction was 'a sweeping not to say dangerous procedure'; to allow the will of the majority to reign supreme was 'simply ... religious intolerance and therefore most injurious to the state'; to perpetuate the separate school system, however, was to cause 'injustice to individuals who may from location happen to depend on the school of the opposite faith for the education of their children, a most frequent case in this Northwest.' A slight note of exasperation attended his concluding remarks on the subject (7 December):

In probably nine cases out of ten, the so called religious exercises in our public schools foster irreverence, instead of reverence, in the child, and do in this way more harm than they do good. The religious life of Canada would certainly be very low if it depended on the religious instruction given in the school. We have to thank Godly mothers and fathers, and live church agencies, for the high position

Canadians take as a religious people. The work properly belongs to the home and church ... What is required in Canada, and what will yet prevail, is a purely national secular school system where the children of the land will be trained in mental culture, and useful practical knowledge; either that, or else Separate Schools not only for Roman Catholic, but for any church or class that demand the privilege of massing their children in schools, where their peculiar views and doctrines can be instilled into their minds, to the neglect of the training and knowledge necessary to equip for the hard, practical duties of life.

The newspapers complemented their opposition to denominational schools with attacks on French-language teaching, particularly in the southern Territories where the English-speaking element predominated. Bilingual education, the *Qu'Appelle Vidette* maintained on 22 November 1888, perpetuated 'the division of the races' in Canada; moreover, there was no need for French where the majority of the French-speaking people, 'except, perhaps, the half breeds,'[43] could read, speak, and understand English. Jingoism ran high on occasion. There was, the *Calgary Herald* declared (24 February 1890), an 'absolute necessity of securing for the English language in Canada that supremacy which British arms, British blood, British courage, British ideas, British institutions may fairly claim at the close of this nineteenth century in a country over which the British flag has waved for a century and a quarter.' A further observation was irresistible. Some ratepayers in French-speaking districts were anxious to learn English but were 'refused' by their leaders.[44] The view that French-language teaching imperilled national unity was common:

If we are right in supposing that the official use of only one language will help to accomplish this desirable result [a homogeneous population], even our French-speaking friends will admit that that language must be English; and we confidently count on the liberality and enlightenment of the French population of the northwest to appreciate the justness of our arguments in this matter, as well as on their loyalty to Canada and Great Britain, to aid in amalgamating the people of Canada and in building up, not a French, not an English, but a Canadian nationality.[45]

The newspaper attacks brought varied reactions in the Territories. Despite repeated requests by the *Qu'Appelle Progress* for the people to 'speak out,'[46] Catholics and non-Catholics alike said little; letters to the editor were few. The *Regina Leader* hosted five, four opposed to the *Journal*, three from Protestants and one from a person of unknown religious origin.[47] The *Journal* itself received only three letters, all favourable,[48] and the *Qu'Appelle*

Progress none. In Alberta the *Journal*'s articles brought no lay reaction, but a *Lethbridge News* editorial on 13 February 1889, critical of the separate schools established at Lethbridge and Macleod, was followed a week later by a vigorous and lengthy defence of Catholic education by Father Van Tighem, parish priest at Lethbridge. D'Alton McCarthy's campaign, on the other hand, prompted a favourable letter from 'A Loyal Citizen' in the *Calgary Herald* (14 August 1889), balanced by an unfavourable one from plain 'Citizen' (proper names were rarely used) in the *Lethbridge News* (23 October 1889).

Catholics were no more responsive. At St Boniface the first council of the ecclesiastical province of St Boniface, held in July 1889, ignored the agitation in official pronouncements. Taché declared in a pastoral letter (July 1892) that, when the decree on the education of children was passed, the council had not envisaged the storm that would engulf Catholic educational interests in western Canada.[49] *Le Manitoba,* which had succeeded *Le Métis* in October 1881 as the voice of the French-speaking half-breeds, took no notice of the school or language agitation until 1 August 1889, almost a year after it had begun. It placed its faith in constitutional guarantees, which presumably made editorial comment unnecessary.

Equally hopeful, but at loggerheads with the *Journal* as early as mid-November 1888, was the minority's only other newspaper, the *Northwest Review*, 'The Only Journal,' as its weekly masthead declared, 'Devoted to the Interests of English Speaking Catholics West of Port Arthur.' The *Review* met the *Journal* squarely on both practical and theoretical grounds. In a common school system it was 'practically impossbile' to teach history acceptably to a mixed class of Protestants and Catholics. Was Queen Elizabeth, for example, ' "Good Queen Bess" or the "Ezabel of England?" ' The harmony between Protestants and Catholics sought by non-Catholic editors already existed – the result of 'a spirit of liberality *on account of their* separation.' A sectarian school system might be more expensive, but honest and fair-minded legislators would not allow the idea of spending a few dollars less to influence them 'a hair's breadth' towards prejudicing the rights and liberties which Catholics and many others desired. The *Journal*'s view that a non-sectarian school could teach a ' "free, tolerant, universal, general Christianity" ' was the claim of the ' "sect of no religion," ' which when realized in the average non-Catholic school was 'practically always anti-Catholic and often agnostic.'

On the theoretical level the argument revolved around the meaning of education, liberty of conscience, the scope of civil authority, and toleration. With education defined as physical, intellectual, and moral development, a non-sectarian school system could only attend to the first two because there could be no teaching of morality without religion. For the Catholic, liberty of conscience ('involving what Protestants profess to respect most highly') required that the religion be Catholic, otherwise faith and morals would be endangered. Not that the non-sectarian schools necessarily produced immoral men; where the home and school were supportive of each other all was well. But '... the necessity to look for an outside agent to complete the work left partially undone by the public schools, compels us to conclude to their deficiency.' And where outside agents failed, the pupil was '... without a proper governor to regulate his motions. He is skilful but his skill is apt to aim at evil as well as good, and even more so because of the human depravity. He is a shrewd and expert business man, but his chances to be dishonest or honest are even, to say the least.' Catholics, in turn, did not need to show that they were a *'higher* class' of citizens to enjoy *'equal* rights.' The Catholic church, however, did produce 'far greater compliance with the Commandments of God as epitomized in the Decalogue' than any other religious organization, 'and there are no true statistics in existence which show the contrary.'

A system of non-sectarian schools was, moreover, 'beyond the moral competency of the state.' Although in charge of temporal affairs, the state was restricted by 'a superior law,' the law of nature, which gave parents the right and duty to feed, clothe, and educate their children. To have moral force, state law had to be in harmony with natural law. Disharmony resulted from compulsory attendance in state schools; harmony followed when the state gave compulstory powers to the church to ensure the discharge of parental duty for the state's own protection against the rise of an ignorant population and for the protection of children against 'evil or neglectful parents.' For the common good, the state had to be as tolerant as was the Catholic church itself. Although the latter did not approve of evil, it tolerated it as long as the public welfare was not endangered. Leaning heavily on Pope Leo XIII's 1888 encyclical on 'Human Liberty,' the *Review* concluded:

... Catholics have never punished Protestants as such – that is for *being* Protestants, but for *apostatizing* from the faith; for wilfully perverting and blaspheming the truth of God, obstinately persisting in their heresy and *seducing* others from the true Church. The same cannot be said of Protestants. When they have persecuted Catholics, they have persecuted them for *being* Catholics and *remaining* Catholics.

Examples dating back to the sixteenth and seventeenth centuries followed and the whole separate school issue once more bared the watershed of Christianity's crisis – the Reformation.[50]

The *Review* paid far less attention to the language question, though it reacted with vigour to the *Calgary Herald*'s opinion that Canada's lack of unity would only end with a national school system and a single language from coast to coast. To the *Review*, American unity was not the result of a particular system of education but of 'feelings common to all – *a hatred of tyranny, and a love of justice and freedom*' born of a struggle which had 'reddened every plain from Maine to Florida.' One language would not reduce Canadian tensions, as the continuing prejudice towards Irish Catholics, whose language was 'dead,' had shown. State documents in German, Scandinavian and 'even Bohemian' were published on occasion in Minnesota.

And because one official paper is published in French in this country all this din is raised about our ears. Where was the Calgary *Herald* when that humble Frenchman, Fr. Lacombe, was quieting the Blackfeet Indians in each and every language that was needed during those days of anxiety a few years ago. *That was the time to protest against the use of any but the English language* ... It is not the language, nor the separate school system that is at the bottom of this uncalled for agitation, but the object evidently is to strike a blow at the Catholic Church. This being the case we have no alternative but to stand or fall by the side of our coreligionists.[51]

The *Review*'s vigilance brought only six letters to the editor (all favourable) before the territorial assembly met in 1889. Two referred to the school question, one to language, and three praised the paper for upholding the Catholic position in general.[52] There can be no doubt that newspaper editors and clergy, both Catholic and non-Catholic, paid far more attention to the school question than did the general public. This is not to imply that a gap existed between the clergy and people on either side, though it may be significant that three and possibly four letters opposed to the *Journal*'s articles were from Protestant laymen, not clergymen, and that upon Archbishop Taché's return from eastern Canada in November 1889 much emphasis was placed on the unity between laity and clergy in the French and English addresses of welcome.[53] However, there is no evidence that the Catholic clergy and laity (with the exception of some Métis) were out of step at the early stages of the school question; whatever differences existed were not publicly apparent until 1896.[54] Public apathy was undoubtedly the result mainly of economic depression after 1873, which, except for a brief period between 1879 and 1881, continued until 1896,[55] when anticipated settlement finally materialized, prices rose, and the struggle for survival no longer ended in exodus to the United States.

Activity at the political level, however, was considerable as the territorial session approached. At Regina the advisory council (chaired by Royal) decided in August not to honour the Catholic section's request for five hundred French copies of the 1888 School Ordinance.[56] In a dispatch to Taché, Royal surmised that the assembly would petition Parliament to abolish the use of French in the courts and in the printing of territorial documents (authorized in section 110 of the NWT Act). Unlike Father Leduc, however, he did not think the schools would be touched.[57] Reports to Ottawa also indicated that a serious crisis was brewing. Dewdney and Royal, after separate tours of the west, informed Macdonald that Haultain and the advisory council were considering amendments, which, Dewdney believed, Catholics would oppose strongly.[58] However, the people themselves, Royal observed optimistically (perhaps unduly swayed by the rhetoric of the numerous complimentary addresses he had received), were 'unequivocally loyal to Canada, lawabiding and willing to live and let live.'[59] Macdonald had a memorandum prepared on the school and language legislation in Manitoba and the North-West,[60] and asked Royal for a report on the assembly's attitude towards the language question: 'I fancy that our Parliament would be very much guided by the opinion of your Assembly.'[61] After considerable delay Royal replied that, as a question of fact not policy, the printing of all public documents in French was in most cases a useless expenditure of public money. The French printing of school ordinances and related documents, however, should be continued, at least for some time to come. Royal minimized the significance of territorial 'McCarthyism,' notwithstanding newspaper efforts 'to boom the movement in their immediate locality.' On the other hand, it was not very safe to infer that there was nothing to fear from the assembly: 'Hot heads, politicians in quest of cheap popularity are to be found in every legislature, and our Assembly may not altogether prove to be free from them.'[62]

When the assembly met on 16 October 1889, the influence of McCarthy and the newspapers showed itself immediately in Hugh Cayley's motion to appoint a committee to draft a resolution to the governor-general to repeal the French-language clause in the NWT Act.[63] After noting that others were preparing a similar resolution on separate schools, the *Edmonton Bulletin* predicted on 2 November that '... the educational question will be the most important one the members will have to deal with during the session.' 'One significant fact,' it added, 'was that the governor's speech was read in English only, while last year it was read in both French and English.' On 18 October a special committee – Cayley, Haultain, James Clinkskill (Battleford), Thomas Tweed (Medicine Hat), and James Neff (Moosomin) – was named to draft the resolution for the repeal of section 110,[64] and on the twenty-fourth B.P. Richardson (Wolseley) and Dr R.G. Brett (Red Deer) moved that the assembly address the governor-general and both houses of Parliament to repeal section 14, the separate school clause in the Act.[65] On the twenty-eighth Cayley reported the draft resolution expunging the French-language section. After a lengthy debate an amendment by Rouleau and Mitchell for a six months' hoist was defeated seventeen to two.[66] Next day the Richardson-Brett separate school motion was debated and carried unanimously, and A.G. Thorburn (Whitewood), Richardson, Secord, Betts, and Neff were named to the special committee appointed to draft the address.[67] On 6 November the committee reported a draft resolution against the separate school clause, which passed without amendment and apparently without debate.[68] Finally, on 19 November both resolutions became part of the assembly's memorandum to the federal government.[69] Thus, in one forceful move, the assembly made its bid to control two subjects of vital concern to the Catholic church.

In the debate on the language resolution Tweed alone referred to bilingual education. The primary English course introduced in 1888, he believed, reflected the sentiments of the country as well as of the assembly.[70] In the lopsided vote only Mitchell and James Hoey (Kinistino), an Orangeman whose daughter's attendance at St Ann's Convent, Prince Albert, provoked a sarcastic exchange between the *Qu'Appelle Vidette* and *Northwest Review*,[71] supported Rouleau's amendment. Clinkskill of Battleford, where the Métis influence was also significant, did not vote.[72]

On the school resolution Rouleau again led the opposition. He did not wish to see the federal government embarrassed as in New Brunswick, where it had found itself powerless to protect the minority against the 1871 Common Schools Act.[73] No changes were needed; the existing system worked remarkably well and a more powerful majority would likely abuse its power. Betts reminded Rouleau that he was only an appointed member and criticized him for always advancing distasteful arguments and throwing doubt on the liberality of the people in the Territories. Several speakers denied that the resolution was a declaration for or against separate schools. It committed no member on the question; it only asked for 'full power in every particular' (Brett). The minority had nothing to fear: Oliver promised to uphold the rights of the majority only 'as long as they were right and not wrong (Hear, hear.).' Brett, too, hoped the members had 'sufficient confidence in this House, and in future Houses, to believe that their power would not be abused.'[74]

Neither side presented much of a case. The Protestants asked the Catholics to believe that separate schools would survive the repeal of section 14. But a struggling minority could hardly be expected to take the argument seriously, especially as 'the Jesuit business,'[75] following hard on the heels of Riel's execution, had already raised religious and ethnic tensions to a high level in the nation. Rouleau, on the other hand, asked the Protestants to spare the federal government by retaining the status quo. Yet a majority struggling to win responsible government could hardly be expected to pity a distant government whose ignorance and neglect of the Territories was entering its third decade.[76]

The debate on sections 14 and 110 was followed by a consideration of two school bills, both with provisions that belied Protestant professions of goodwill. Betts's private bill sought to abolish the board's sections and decrease the number of board members.[77] It was defeated eighteen to three, with only William Plaxton (Prince Albert) and G.S. Davidson (South Qu'Appelle) supporting Betts.[78] The school committee's bill, however, did transfer the appointment of commissioners, who reported on the condition of schools, from the governor to the lieutenant-governor-in-council (s. 10). Difficulties at Bellerose Catholic public school near St Albert, where the trustees were accused of receiving more money from the board for the teacher's salary than they paid,[79] and at St Patrick's Catholic separate school at Prince Albert, where three families with a total of eight children had established a school,[80] probably prompted the change. Changes in the ordinance, however, would have been more numerous if Betts and Cayley had had their way. The former wanted to transfer the appointment of inspectors from the sections to the lieutenant-governor-in-council, and the latter wished to abolish the Board of Education when its two-year term ended in 1890. Both changes ran into considerable opposition and neither became law.[81]

The federal government and the Catholic church both kept a close watch on developments at Regina in 1889. Bishop Grandin had dreaded the session's opening.[82] When the assembly passed the language and school resolutions, Royal announced them to Macdonald without comment[83] and Rouleau reported them to Grandin and Taché, recommending that petitions be signed before the opening of Parliament early in the new year.[84] Leduc blamed Orangeism, Freemasonry, and Protestant fanaticism (its initiates, its ministers, and its bishops) for Catholic difficulties in western Canada. It did not help that Rouleau was not an elected member or that Royal had read his opening address only in English or that at least two Catholic school districts were suspected of financial irregularities. He was disappointed that neither Taché nor Grandin had gone to Regina during the session and annoyed that the priests in the Territories were insufficiently disturbed by recent events.

It seemed to him that the minority behaved too much like sheep among wolves. If Quebec did not aid them, the consequences could be disastrous.[85]

Royal explained to Grandin that he had omitted the French reading to remove any pretext for a strong, immediate protest and to save (perhaps) the minority's schools; besides there was no reason '[d'] agiter un drapeau rouge devant les yeux de ces —.' All members, however, were of one opinion when they arrived, and the outcome on the school question was a foregone conclusion.[86] Before the session prorogued Grandin was ready with a petition to the governor-general-in-council,[87] phrased so as to win the support of Protestants.[88] Rouleau and Royal gave their approval,[89] but Royal himself would have preferred a good letter, full of facts, dates, and names, published in some moderate newspaper. The governor-general, after all, would only send the petition to the prime minister, where the matter would end.[90]

A petition to the government was one alternative; another was an appeal to the church itself. Accordingly, Grandin undertook what he himself termed a very serious and delicate work: a letter to Cardinal Taschereau and the Quebec hierarchy designed to divert the flow of French Canadians from New England to the North-West in hopes of increasing the minority's strength there.[91] If it also led his episcopal colleagues to reappraise the policies of a government whose territorial subordinate was multiplying the hierarchy's difficulties, then well and good. How else could the federal authorities be convinced that to ignore Catholic grievances was politically dangerous? The letter, dated 20 November, attributed most of the minority's difficulties to the poor position of Catholics, especially French Catholics, in the North-West. Because electoral boundaries were drawn unfairly, men like Royal and Rouleau worked in vain to protect the French language and to ward off the 'so-called secular schools' ('nothing else' than anti-Catholic schools, even admitting they were not 'Godless'). Petitions to the governor-general in the name of the people were ignored because Catholics 'counted for nothing' in the eyes of the legislators at Regina. The situation could become dangerous. The Métis, after all, were quite sensitive to this indifference. Nothing at the moment would be easier than 'to fire the powder ... because our Catholics have no longer the same reliance in their clergy. They have been told so often that we are paid by the Dominion Government to work for it against them, that they now believe this.' The government, as any constituted authority, had been supported, but the clergy had been 'very badly requited and those who have found fault with us on this account are partly justified.'

Without the funds to stimulate a movement of Catholic peoples westward, Grandin, in a bitterly supplicatory passage, begged the bishops to send 'at least the crumbs which fall from your tables,' the New England expatriates. 'If even one-fourth of those who emigrated ... during the past ten years had come to us, we would still constitute the majority, or would at all events be a powerful minority which would have to be taken into account and against which none would think of enacting extraordinary laws.' Here, too, the federal government was not blameless. In a land discovered by French Canadians and opened by them and the Métis to religion and colonization, the federal government not only allowed men from every nation ('men without faith and without religion') to settle, but brought Mennonites from a great distance and even Mormons, who were 'seemingly held up as examples to the Blackfeet.' Yet each year 'a multitude' of French Canadians were allowed to depart for New England. The only recourse was an appeal to the charity of the clergy and people of Quebec. Perhaps the latter could persuade the federal government and the railway companies to help re-direct French-Canadian colonists. Quebec would not be impoverished; on the contrary, it would acquire strength and extend its influence by protecting 'the poor Canadians who are threatened with the fate of outcasts on their own lands.'[92]

The letter spared neither the government nor the episcopate. It indicted the former for neglecting its political colony and the latter for neglecting its home missionary work. The government for the moment said nothing. Several bishops, on the other hand, extended their sympathies and showed some contrition, but held out little hope for aid in the immediate future. Cardinal Taschereau thought it was difficult enough to dissuade the emigrants from going to New England; it would be even more difficult to persuade them to give up a familiar way of life for another hundreds of miles away. Moreover, reports in Quebec newspapers of coercion suffered by Catholics in the North-West did nothing to help the situation.[93] Archbishop Duhamel of Ottawa did not think a collective letter on colonization signed by the episcopate in the ecclesiastical provinces of Quebec, Montreal, and Ottawa would have much effect. The French Canadians already had too many relatives in the United States to change the course of migration.[94] Taschereau agreed: such a letter would only spur the Ontario Protestants to greater efforts. It was better to rely on the fecundity and courage of the French Canadians already in the North-West: the approach, although slower, would be more reliable.[95] The strongly Conservative Bishop Laflèche was concerned that *L'Electeur*, the leading Liberal newspaper in Quebec, had recently published Grandin's letter and provided the opposition with a windfall. Its natural impact was to dispose the government unfavourably towards episcopal goals. At a recent meeting therefore he could not persuade his colleagues to help Grandin, even though they understood his predicament well. Without praising the Conservatives he reminded Grandin that recent events in Manitoba had shown well what the minority could expect from a Liberal government at Ottawa.[96]

From eastern Canada Governor Royal summed up the reaction of Quebec newspapers to the letter and noted that Dewdney, minister of the interior since 1888, was not pleased with the publicity.[97] Father Lacombe, in turn, was quite critical. While the letter had its merits, it contained a few things that were perhaps a bit exaggerated. He did not wish to minimize Catholic difficulties with English Protestant officials, but the minority itself was not blameless because church leaders, in their missionary zeal, occasionally mistook official acts for injustices. Explanations followed, but the French Catholics, as a minority, always believed they were being persecuted. He did not believe the government's administrative policies in general were designed to extinguish the French in the North-West. The English there were like the English in Africa and elsewhere. Through perseverance and commercial enterprise, they first became the economic masters and then the rulers of the country. The only antidote was French Catholic colonization, but unfortunately Archbishop Taché preferred to concentrate on settling Manitoba with the habitants from Quebec.[98]

According to Leduc, Forget liked Grandin's letter, Royal disliked the publicity, and Taché was much disturbed that Grandin had sent a copy to Mercier[99] but not to Macdonald. Mercier undoubtedly was responsible for its publication; Grandin now had to prove all he had written, and that (Leduc paraphrased Taché) not with generalities but with clear facts which avoided all digressions and vague references to those at fault.[100] Taché himself informed Grandin that all of them suffered great difficulties and were much troubled; God alone knew what was the best course of action. Not surprisingly, one did not always see matters in the same light.[101] Grandin, under strain, accused Taché (with some justice) of not giving his long letters sufficient attention: What he wanted (and had a right to expect) was positive direction, yet Taché's replies tempted him to conclude that his letters had not even been read.[102] Taché insisted (with less justice) that he was usually consulted only when it was too late and cited Grandin's controversial letter to Dewdney in 1888 as a case in point.[103] Of Grandin's latest letter he said nothing; he did not wish to meddle in the affairs of other dioceses.[104]

Public reaction to the letter in the Territories was confined to non-Catholic newspapers. In an editorial, 'A Dark Outlook,' the *Calgary Herald* compared Grandin to McCarthy, the 'firebrand' at Ottawa. The *Macleod Gazette* thought the letter was 'impolitic and ill-advised,' and the *Lethbridge*

CAMROSE LUTHERAN COLLEGE LIBRARY

News referred to it as 'a most remarkable production.' The equally Conservative *Saskatchewan Herald* at Battleford insisted there was 'nothing in the circumstances of the country to justify the letter.'[105] But it was the Liberal *Edmonton Bulletin* that voiced the strongest objections. All reports, it declared (15 February 1890), had to be scrutinized and '... the Assembly and its officials would be doing less than their duty if they did not find fault when the occasion demanded.' St Albert disappeared as an electoral district 'to secure the assistance of the French half breeds to defeat a certain English speaking Protestant [Oliver].' The assembly was not anti-Catholic; amendments to school laws were necessary to meet changes in 'the circumstances' of the country, and to demand the right to make changes was not to enter into the relative merits of religious or secular schools. A bold statement, full of unexplored constitutional implications, followed: 'Had they been desirous of amending the school laws so as to impose anti-Catholic or Godless schools, there was nothing in the Northwest act to prevent their doing so – they did not need to appeal to Ottawa for power in the matter – therefore they did not show the prejudice charged against them.' The French Canadians were not held in contempt; to print all documents in two languages was 'to waste the public money.' It was only natural that a minority should exert less influence, but no reasonable person would oppose a larger French immigration. The threat of Indian and Métis unrest was unwarranted. The last rebellion was the result of federal 'bad faith'; to assert that 'spiritual and sentimental' matters had anything to do with it was 'to tread on very dangerous ground.'

At Ottawa the first to react to Grandin's letter was Alphonse LaRivière, Royal's successor in Ottawa from the riding of Provencher, who complained to Taché of the publicity in Quebec newspapers.[106] The federal government itself said nothing until 29 January, when Guillaume Amyot, a Conservative *nationaliste* from Bellechasse, Quebec, placed the entire letter on record and asked the government to state its intentions. The government, Macdonald replied, had not received the letter, but would 'attend to the complaints of Monseigneur Grandin, and those of any other clergyman or person in Canada who has any complaints to make.'[107] During the extensive Commons debate in 1890 on the status of French in the Territories Grandin's letter was mentioned briefly by only two members, one opposed to the abolition of French, the other in favour.[108] No commission was appointed to look into the charges of unfair treatment by government officials and, contrary to the *Calgary Herald*'s expectations, none was requested by 'the Nationalist members of the Commons.'[109]

Bishop Grandin himself, of course, regretted the publicity.[110] The fault, he confided to Sir Hector Langevin, was probably with some lay secretary hired to make copies. However, he did not regret the letter. He wished to believe that the federal government was not responsible for the abusive language at Regina, but he had to conclude that the Catholics were victims of real hostility. Langevin and several others in the cabinet were, of course, not to blame, but unfortunately they alone did not constitute the government.[111] The government's embarrassment troubled him little. He told Laflèche he was most indifferent towards the Conservatives. Each Protestant government supported the interests of its co-religionists and granted the minority only as much justice as fear required. He inclined towards the Conservatives only because Laflèche supported them, as did undoubtedly most bishops, above all Taché.[112] He had nothing against the government; he only wanted justice and he would do his utmost to obtain it. Though the government suffered, though it even died, though he himself died as a result, he would at least be doing his duty.[113]

Thus the battle between church and state was properly joined as the nineteenth century entered its last decade. A confrontation was probably inevitable, once the hoped for Catholic (in particular French Catholic) immigration had failed to materialize. The outcome early in 1890, however, was still very much in doubt, not so much because the church was strong (though its connections in Quebec could not be minimized), but because the federal government had still to react to the demands of the pesky territorial assembly. That the territorial politicians were in earnest about responsible government cannot be doubted; that most also strongly disliked separate schools and the French language is also true. And on both counts they could be said to reflect the popular will, judging by the slight public outcry in the non-Catholic press. From the minority's viewpoint, the fate of its educational interests became inextricably linked with the most contentious of political issues – responsible government – which could easily lead to the abolition of separate schools and French-language instruction. And for most politicians responsible government *was* the basic issue, though it did provide an opportunity for some to vent pent-up religious and racial feelings.

4

The establishment of
state control, 1890-2

The Legislative Assembly's 1889 memorandum requesting the repeal of
sections 14 and 110 in the NWT Act was the first direct challenge to the
federal government from the North-West on the school and language questions. In January 1890 D'Alton McCarthy followed with a bill to repeal
the French-language clause.[1] Of the four territorial members of the Commons (all Conservatives and non-Catholics) – Nicholas F. Davin (West
Assiniboia), Edgar Dewdney (East Assiniboia), Donald W. Davis (Alberta), and Day H. Macdowall (Saskatchewan) – only Davin and Dewdney
participated in the long and heated debate on McCarthy's bill. When Davin
and Davis moved to give the Assembly power to deal with the language
question after the next territorial election, Thompson restricted that power
to regulating 'the proceedings of the Assembly and the manner of recording
and publishing such proceedings.'[2]

Thompson's vague amendment was a compromise and LaRivière recognized it as such. Without it, however, he told Taché and Grandin, all might
have been lost. He accepted it to win recognition for French and to prevent
its abolition in the schools.[3] Grandin was grateful to all, Davis and Davin
included.[4] Taché, however, could not understand how Sir Hector Langevin
could support an amendment that would inevitably undermine all Catholic
rights in the North-West. It was better to lose everything under the malignant
inspiration of McCarthy than to suffer the same fate under the bad vote of
the minority's ostensible defenders.[5]

McCarthy's bill dealt only with language and, as Edward Blake observed,
merely opened the campaign to repeal other provisions in the BNA Act. To

David Mills, it was just 'the first step towards the unity of the population of the North-West from a linguistic point of view.' To succeed, McCarthy had, among other things, to prohibit 'the use [of French] in the schools public and private.' McCarthy was 'glad' to report that the North-West Assembly was itself dealing with that question, 'perhaps, the most important of all.' LaRivière quoted the *Moosomin Courier* on the need for 'One People, One Country, One Religion' and expressed grave concern about the future.[6] However, references in Parliament to the North-West school question were generally brief during the language debate. W.D. Perley, a senator since 1888, admitted he had changed his mind about giving the assembly power to make 'all necessary ordinances in respect to education' after the next territorial election. The Conservative McCarthy and the Liberal John Charlton, an American-born Presbyterian with strong sabbatarian views who had supported McCarthy on the Jesuit Estates question, intended to raise the matter in the Commons, and it might be opposed, even defeated, if first carried in the Senate.[7] James A. Lougheed, the other territorial senator, did not comment.

Nevertheless, the territorial school question was not entirely out of sight at Ottawa. On 10 January Thompson, in a report to the governor-general-in-council on the legality of the 1888 School Ordinance, found the compulsory school clause within the powers of the assembly but termed the clause restricting the boundaries of separate school districts 'objectionable': '... the provisions of the North-West Territories Act, before cited [s. 14], cannot be abridged by the Ordinance, and must be considered as still in force, notwithstanding the restrictive terms of the Ordinance.' He refrained from recommending disallowance because the latter was 'merely a re-enactment of an earlier Ordinance [1886] ... which was allowed to go into operation, probably because attention was not called to this provision.'[8] As the federal government had only one year within which to disallow an ordinance, Thompson, in 1890, was powerless to affect the earlier change. The Catholic leaders took no notice of Thompson's report and there is no evidence the clergy even knew it existed. They could, of course, do little, but the report itself would return to haunt several politicians in 1905.[9]

The opposition in Parliament also kept a close eye on the question. Three days after the language debate ended Blake wrote Laurier that the school question would present still greater difficulties than had the question of language, because of the tone and temper of the Liberals in the recent debate. It was important that Laurier consult his leading supporters for their views, though Blake himself could see no basis for united action. Too many English Liberals treated the Territories as if they were already a province, and the resolution of the language question had only strengthened this view. French Liberals treated 'the doctrine' of provincial rights as a variable quantity, disallowing acts of provincial legislatures if the majority in Parliament thought the local majority had disregarded the interests of the minority. The transition state of the Territories made it unnecessary still to disturb the provisions of 1875. But the abolition of separate schools was 'almost inevitable,' because the vast majority of Protestants in Canada would never agree 'to fasten' them on the North-West against the will of the people there. Parliament could either preserve the status quo and eventually allow the people themselves to decide the question before the Territories became provinces, or ensure that the provincial constitutions left the people free to settle the question after attaining provincial autonomy. The great weakness of both alternatives, Blake said, was that it 'forces on the locality for an indefinite period a system repugnant to their feelings, consoling them only with the prospect that at some future day they shall have freedom to get rid of it.' Blake was seeking 'a common ground, based on reason'; he wished to see 'the extremists on either side' checked. He was not, however, optimistic: '... it is impossible to reconcile opinions on this subject ...'[10]

In the North-West only the newspapers continued to agitate the school and language questions; the politicians said little. In toasting D.H. Macdowall at a Métis banquet at Batoche on 10 December 1889, the politically ambitious Charles Nolin complained of the very unjust and false course pursued by the legislators at Regina on both questions. Macdowall assured his hosts that, with men such as Langevin, Chapleau, and Caron in the cabinet, their rights would be respected.[11] A few miles away James Clinkskill, another Conservative, told a Battleford audience a few days later of his objections to the dual school system and to the 'compulsory' use of French. D.L. Clink, Clinkskill's opponent in the 1888 election, also spoke, but supported 'the retention of the French as an official language, the maintenance of separate schools, and the establishment of Provincial autonomy and Responsible Government.'[12]

In northern Alberta Frank Oliver discussed the same subjects at a series of public meetings six months later. Although reluctant to raise 'divisions among the people of the Territories at a time when it was particularly necessary that they should be united on matters of greater and more pressing material interest,' he approved the action of the assembly on the school and language questions on grounds of economy and responsible government. Those entitled to control must do so in the name of 'the public good – the good of French as well as English.'[13] At St Albert J.U. Prieur, whom Grandin favoured as that district's next representative, warned Oliver to watch his vote in the assembly or be prepared to answer for his 'mistakes' at the next election.[14]

When the 1890 session opened late in October Governor Royal again read his address in English only and had bilingual copies printed.[15] On 5 November Richardson of Wolseley gave notice of motion to confirm the 1889 resolution on separate schools.[16] Ten days later he asked that the notice stand; he wished to see whether 'the majority' would give it the prominence it deserved among the resolutions regarding the last session's ungranted memorials. Rouleau objected that the separate school resolution was too important to be drowned among the other items; it ought to be voted on separately.[17]

The objection was premature for 'the majority' was in no position to act immediately. Politics overwhelmed the assembly and the school question became enmeshed in the contest for political leadership between the Brett-Betts and Cayley-Haultain factions after the Haultain council (formed in 1888) resigned late in October 1889 'to bring about a more definite understanding with regard to the various powers and authorities of the Territories.'[18] A new council (Brett, Betts, Jelly, and Richardson) failed to survive Clinkskill's want-of-confidence motion on 9 November. The governor replaced Jelly with Secord in January, but as none of the four council members had supported 'the majority' on Clinkskill's motion, Royal was, in effect, attempting to rule with a minority government. Shortly after the new session opened (18 November) the new council re-introduced the school question with Richardson and Brett reaffirming the assembly's stand in 1889 and condemning Parliament for failing to act.[19] Opposition was immediate. The resolution, Cayley declared, was put up 'simply for buncombe'; neither he nor the House would enter into its merits. Moreover, all such resolutions would fail as long as the council did not command the confidence of the House.[20] Betts attacked Cayley personally, accusing him of swallowing his convictions for the sake of party and of trying to 'right' himself with his constituents for favouring the school and language resolutions the previous year.[21] Ottawa, too, was probably watching: 'If the House voted down his colleague's motion, they would be putting a powerful weapon in the hands of the opponents of the motion in the House of Commons.'

Judge Rouleau found himself in the unenviable position of manoeuvring between two lines of fire, one prepared to dispatch him immediately and the other wishing to delay the blow, only to deliver it another day. With the minority in a poor position to introduce motions, he scolded Cayley for thinking that majorities 'could do as they liked.' Why were the members so opposed to separate schools? 'There were no petitions before them asking for such a move. It was all a matter of idea.' J.H. Ross, a member of the Cayley-Haultain faction, showed that the opposition to Richardson's motion, spearheaded by Cayley, was purely political. The House would yet pass resolutions 'that would show the Dominion Government how they stood.' On division the government's motion was lost fifteen to six, with Jelly and Joel Reaman (Wallace) alone supporting the council.[22] Cayley and Haultain then followed with a similar resolution,[23] which expired when Royal prorogued the House abruptly after 'the majority' defeated Brett's attempt to move it into committe of supply.[24]

With the North-West Assembly stymied temporarily by political wrangling the initiative on the school question passed to Ottawa. In March 1891 the Territories returned all four incumbents to Parliament. The school and language questions, discussed extensively in Macdowall's constituency,[25] had little effect on the final electoral result. Macdowall, who openly supported separate schools and the French language, lost one Métis poll and had only slight majorities in the others,[26] an indication of how unreliable the Métis vote could be.

On May 13 D'Alton McCarthy introduced his first combined bill calling for repeal of the language *and* school clauses.[27] Brett and Betts, in Ottawa since early May, discussed both issues with the territorial representatives and several government members, including the titular prime minister, Sir John Abbott, who had succeeded Macdonald on the latter's death early in June, Dewdney, minister of the interior, and Thompson, *de facto* head of the administration.[28] The resulting government bill brought the language clause in line with the amendment of the previous year, but left the school clause untouched. Responsible government, too, was denied. The advisory council and the three stipendiary magistrates were abolished and the assembly's powers increased in several directions, but no provision was made for an executive.[29] Colonel O'Brien, the Conservative member for Muskoka who had helped McCarthy found the militantly anti-Catholic Equal Rights Association in 1889, criticized the government for not amending section 14. There was nothing final about constitutional arrangements in the Territories: '... all our dealings ... have been so far tentative, and experimental rather than absolute.'[30] LaRivière objected to representatives from Ontario trying to impose ideas outside their province. The earliest schools in the Territories were separate schools protected by section 93 of the BNA Act whose spirit favoured them. Parliament's enactment in 1875 'only continued the system that was already in existence, and a system already under the protection of the constitution. The British North America Act provided that what existed in the provinces that were then united should be extended also to the provinces afterwards taken into the Union and to-day form part of Confederation, and that provision applies also to the territories we have acquired since.'[31]

LaRivière was treading on difficult ground. The mission schools prior to 1875 were separate only in the sense that they were distinct from other private denominational schools. They were not separate in the sense of being apart from 'majority' schools brought into being by a school ordinance passed by a local government, as the 1875 Act required. LaRivière also defined the date of union as 1870 and argued as if the Territories entered Confederation as provinces on the same footing as did Canada, New Brunswick, and Nova Scotia in 1867. This was the usual French-Canadian position. Laurier would argue in like manner in 1905, giving the latter as the date of union.[32] In 1891, however, LaRivière overlooked the fact that the union in 1867 included three provinces, with four school systems. Therefore 'what existed in the provinces' could not be extended automatically, unless one were prepared to take the impossible position that *all* four school systems were thereby extended.

Macdowall and Davis, the only territorial members to comment, argued against disturbing the status quo, because the people were neither opposed to separate schools nor much interested in the school question. 'When those territories are divided into provinces,' Macdowall declared, 'then they may be given control of their schools; but while they continue to be territories it is better to leave the school question as it is.'[33] Thompson, in a leading statement, assured Amyot, anxious about the future status of French in the Territories, that the whole system of territorial government, 'as it is established either by the original Act or by this Bill,' was temporary: 'Parliament will have complete control over the whole subject when it lays down the constitution which may be given to any provinces which may be created in the North-West.'[34] In this way final settlement of the school and language questions was shelved. Lougheed and Perley did not participate in the Senate debate on either question. Perley, however, did oppose Senator Bellerose's move to prevent the territorial assembly from altering the status of French, and in a letter to the East Assiniboia newspapers in June he maintained that both questions should be controlled locally.[35]

II

The Catholic clergy passed no comment on the political situation at Regina. They also ignored the 1891 federal election, even though James Reilly of Calgary, Davis's Catholic opponent, had written Grandin sympathetically about the minority's difficulties late in 1889.[36] Although Leduc congratulated

Davis for speaking 'like a gentleman true to his word and conviction,'[37] the clergy generally concentrated their attention on Manitoba and on the need to secure French Catholic representation at Regina, in view of the forthcoming vote on the French language. Girard and Macdowall had raised the matter of French-speaking electoral districts in 1890, and in 1891 the government created three: St Albert, Mitchell, and Cumberland.[38] This gave French-speaking electors the majority (or the balance of power) in four districts (including Batoche) and a substantial influence in Battleford, Prince Albert, Kinistino, and North Qu'Appelle.

At St Albert, Bishop Grandin pinned his electoral hopes on J.U. Prieur, whom he judged more capable than Samuel Cunningham,[39] St Albert's former representative (1885–7). The frantic search for a successor that followed Prieur's sudden death of a heart attack ('while listening to the result of the general elections'[40]) led Royal to suggest that Grandin run Leduc or Father Lestanc as a last resort.[41] Grandin preferred Lacombe, but Taché rejected the very idea of a clerical candidate.[42] In the election on 7 November Antonio Prince, a French-Canadian lawyer from Edmonton, opposed Daniel Maloney, St Albert's Irish Catholic businessman. Grandin promised to support Prince if it could be shown that Maloney had indeed criticized the French language, but in the end he cast no ballot and allowed the mission clergy a free vote.[43] The latter took a keen interest in the election and Grandin was obliged to lecture the community on verbal indiscretions at political meetings.[44] In the balloting Prince narrowly defeated Maloney (210–183), with most of the clergy, Grandin believed, supporting Prince.[45]

Elsewhere in Alberta the election caused little stir as the seven other members were returned by acclamation. Anticipating opposition, Oliver restated his position on the school and language questions and made no promises.[46] Haultain, at a public meeting at Pincher Creek nine months before the election, confessed to a strong dislike for religious instruction and the separate school system and (to loud applause) promised to 'work and vote against it as hard as he could.' An angry Father Lacombe returned the challenge in a letter to the *Macleod Gazette*: ' "I will work and vote against him as hard as I can." Yes, sir, to the last we will fight for our religious system and privileges in our schools. We may be overwhelmed, but will never surrender.'[47]

In Saskatchewan, where only two of the six members, Hillyard Mitchell (Mitchell) and Thomas McKay (Prince Albert), received acclamations, the school and language questions were lively issues. Religious animosity showed itself at Cumberland, where the solid French vote at Cumberland House went against the victor, Betts, a strong opponent of French Catholic interests in the assembly.[48] At Battleford, where Clinkskill and his opponent both favoured separate schools and the French language, efforts were made to show that Clinkskill's assembly record did not support his platform stand.[49] Clinkskill was vulnerable, for he had abstained on the French-language vote and joined in the unanimous support given the Richardson-Brett motion against separate schools. Although he won the election, the opposition drew well in Métis centres, cutting his margin to thirty-two votes.[50]

In Assiniboia the Orange-tinted *Qu'Appelle Vidette* and the Catholic clergy played prominent roles in the bitter contest at North Qu'Appelle. The *Vidette* strongly supported William Sutherland, the incumbent, and used every opportunity to criticize vociferously French and/or Catholic interests.[51] When Father J.P. Magnan of the Lebret mission (near Fort Qu'Appelle) challenged Sutherland by letter to state his policy on the school question, the *Vidette* gleefully embarked upon an extended campaign to show that Sutherland's opponent, A.D. Stewart, a 'well-to-do' Protestant farmer, was a Catholic candidate, who, unlike Sutherland, had pledged himself to support separate schools in order to reap the benefits of church influence with the Métis.[52] Sutherland carried the election by a slim five votes, largely because of Stewart's strong showing at Lebret (63–18) and Dauphinais (12–3), 'almost exclusively half-breed settlements and largely under the control of the priests.'[53] That Stewart had given the church a pledge is doubtful: 'On being asked [at a political meeting] whether he endorsed the action of the majority in the late Legislature, he said that he did.'[54] That the church probably supported him is understandable. As 'A Lebret Voter' declared in a letter to the *Vidette*, '... after Mr Sutherland's refusal to reply straightforwardly to the Rev. Father Magnan's letter, no Catholic could conscientiously vote for him.'[55] When all territorial returns were in, Catholic influence in the assembly had risen from 14 to 19 per cent (an accurate reflection of the population ratio in the Territories), the main supporters being Clinkskill, McKay, Mitchell, Prince, and Charles Nolin (Batoche).

The educational issues that faced the legislators at Regina in December 1891 were all subordinate to the main political question: How much power did the new territorial act really give the new assembly, especially its executive branch? The 1891 Act did concede the most contentious point of all – control of the annual parliamentary grant – but it was, as L.H. Thomas has said, 'provokingly indefinite'[56] about the executive. The advisory council was abolished and the governor was to spend funds with the advice of the assembly or 'a committee thereof,'[57] but the new act made no provision for a committee.

When the assembly met, the Cayley-Haultain group took immediate control by naming Ross speaker. After a brief discussion Haultain's bill to provide for a four-man executive committee (appointed by the governor) passed unanimously. Haultain, on Royal's invitation, then chose Clinkskill, Tweed, and Neff to assist him on the first executive committee. With Haultain from Alberta and the others from Saskatchewan, West Assiniboia, and East Assiniboia respectively, there was at least an implicit understanding that the committee would represent the four main regions.

The committee took no immediate action on the school and language questions. Initiative on the first was left to Daniel Mowat (South Regina), who had given notice of a school bill on 11 December.[58] Progress was slow. The school committee was large, 'practically a small parliament,' Mowat complained.[59] As news of impending changes reached Taché,[60] he relayed them to Grandin, noting sarcastically that their learned legislators were threatening them with the benefits of their wisdom.[61] From Calgary Bishop Pinkham, chairman of the Board of Education, asked Royal to convene a special meeting at Regina,[62] and on 29 December Leduc, Forget, and Prince made impressive representations before the school committee.[63] The executive committee, Neff wrote Dewdney, had made up its mind to sit on the school bill; Mowat was 'a little to [*sic*] fast.'[64]

On 19 January the language question came to the fore, as Haultain and Tweed moved to publish the assembly's proceedings in English only.[65] Prince found it 'most extraordinary that the first avowed act of the first responsible Government of the Territories should be to attack the privileges of the French people.'[66] The change, his amendment protested, was not in the public interest.[67] One language, Tweed insisted, was imperative, for the large number of German and Scandinavian settlers already in the Territories 'might justly claim that their language should not be ignored.' Nolin denied that the Germans had the same right to consideration as the French, a loyal people who had done 'so much' to open up the country.[68] On division, Prince's amendment was lost twenty to four, with Nolin, McKay, Mitchell, and Prince alone supporting it. Haultain's original motion then passed on an identical vote.[69] The possible impact of the change on bilingual education was not considered.

The assembly now turned to the much-delayed school bill. Mowat admitted there were certain features that the school committee did not approve and said that he brought the bill in as an individual member. The most important change abolished the Board of Education and established the executive committee as the Council of Public Instruction. The latter would cut costs and bring school finances under executive control. The separate school system was written in 'word for word ... as in the old ordinance'; other changes envisaged a superintendent of instruction, two or more examiners, and four inspectors, all appointed by the lieutenant-governor-in-council. No clergyman could serve as superintendent, inspector, or trustee. Finally, English was to be the language of instruction in all schools. The school committee, Mowat admitted, had 'struck out' the last provision.[70]

The debate was brief. Clinkskill thought the bill required more discussion in committee; in its impact on separate schools it 'leans towards a certain class in the country.' At Haultain's request Mowat agreed to withdraw the bill for a year. It involved 'radical' changes that could be discussed during the recess. Next day Haultain, in a surprise move, introduced his own school bill and, with House rules suspended, had it passed in the last two days of the session.[71] Its principal provisions, the ones 'considered necessary at the present time,' were taken from Mowat's bill.[72] All affected the Board of Education: members would hold office during pleasure and the lieutenant-governor-in-council which appointed them would direct the time of meeting; the same council would also appoint the inspectors and a general board of examiners, but the Catholic section of the Board of Education would continue to select textbooks for examinations in history and science and prescribe additional subjects as it wished, for which purpose it could appoint examiners to a number fixed by the lieutenant-governor-in-council.[73]

Mowat did not object to the changes. Prince, of course, disliked them all, especially that governing school inspections. With Clinkskill's support he made a determined bid not only to preserve denominational inspection, but to secure the additional principle that a knowledge of French be required of school inspectors where instruction was in that language.[74] Haultain stressed the need for 'power to appoint men we pay; ... as a business transaction if they were responsible for officers they should have the control of their appointment.' The House had to give the executive committee 'credit for being willing to exercise a certain amount of common sense and unwillingness to do anything that would call forth the condemnation of every fair-minded man in the House.' The Prince-Clinkskill amendment was rejected ten to five, with ten abstentions, Prince, Clinkskill, McKay, Nolin, and Davidson supporting it. Haultain's motion for third reading was then approved by the same vote. Clinkskill was prepared to resign from the executive committee immediately, but Haultain insisted that the bill only amended previous legislation and was not one on which the committee had to stand or fall as a whole.[75]

III

The School Ordinance of 1891–2 was the most important school legislation since 1886. The Ordinance of 1887 had returned the appointment of school inspectors and teachers' examiners to the sections of the board, where it had remained until 1891–2 (see Table I). Under the new ordinance the sections continued to control and manage their own schools, select school textbooks, cancel teachers' certificates upon sufficient cause, examine teachers in history and science and additional subjects, and determine appeals from the decisions of inspectors. But the retention of these powers could not hide the fact that the status of Catholic schools had changed considerably. Choice of textbooks in some teachers' examinations could mean little if the examinations themselves were read by unsympathetic, or even prejudiced, non-Catholic eyes. Moreover, the concession – additional Catholic textbooks and examinations in history and science and other subjects – was really a minor one. Early in July 1891 Father Leduc had asked the board to adopt 'only one good textbook on each subject for teachers' candidates,' the 'same text-books only to be used by the Board of Examiners.'[76] The board, in September, drew up three lists of textbooks, one each for the three types of non-professional certificates, and directed non-Catholic and Catholic candidates alike (the special category of French candidates was not mentioned) to use the same textbooks in all subjects, except reading (third- and second-class candidates), 'History of Literature and Poetical Selections' (third-class), and dictation (third-class).[77] According to Cayley, '... Father Leduc and Dr McLean, being a Committee for the purpose, drafted the regulation of which the former had given notice and which is now in existence.'[78] Leduc's initiative in this important departure from the principle of dualism (without objections from either Taché or Grandin) was probably the result of his many administrative duties.[79] He may have wished to escape the numerous inquiries that differences in curricula and textbooks for Protestant, English Catholic, and French Catholic candidates undoubtedly encouraged. In any case, the new school law only conceded what the Catholic section had already given up voluntarily. Of course, the right to additional texts and the discretionary clause permitting additional examinations could be useful. Neither, however, could compensate for the loss of control over inspections and the partial loss of control over examinations.

Bishop Grandin saw the School Ordinance of 1891–2 as the hellish strategy of the Freemasons and Orangemen to secularize the separate schools they could not abolish.[80] Leduc saw it as a temporary reprieve for the board. But to benefit from it, he wrote Grandin, the minority had to find a Catholic thoroughly conversant with the territorial curriculum and the English language, whom the government could appoint as a school inspector. He could suggest no one.[81] Early in March Taché learned from the Reverend Joseph Caron of Regina that only five inspectors and four examiners would be appointed, all on a permanent basis.[82] On 21 March, J. Hewgill, W. Bothwell, the Reverend James Flett (Anglican canon at Prince Albert), and the Reverend David Gillies (Irish Catholic priest at Wapella, East Assiniboia) were appointed inspectors by the executive committee, and on 13 July they became 'permanent officials of the North-West Government.'[83] Annual salaries probably implied an understanding of full-time employment from the beginning. Gillies, who found the dual role of parish priest and school inspector exhausting,[84] resigned in April 1894 and was succeeded by a non-Catholic, James Calder,[85] a Moose Jaw teacher who became Saskatchewan's first minister of education in 1905.

For the minority to accept a single Catholic school inspector was one alternative. Another was to ask Ottawa to disallow the new school ordinance. On 5 March, therefore, Grandin and Bishop Albert Pascal, newly appointed vicar-apostolic of Saskatchewan (northeast of the attenuated Diocese of St Albert: Fig. 2), asked Thompson for his confidential opinion on the assembly's right 'to impose' Protestant inspectors on Catholic schools.[86] Refusing to commit himself, Thompson suggested that the prelates submit a petition if they thought their rights had been encroached upon in any way.[87] Grandin left the matter to Taché,[88] who apparently decided against the petition, for none was sent to Ottawa in 1892.

In fact, the territorial school question was dormant at Ottawa in 1892, as McCarthy's second bill to repeal the language and school clauses was overwhelmed 132 to 33, Dewdney and Davis supporting the majority and Davin and Macdowall abstaining.[89] A motion to give the assembly power to deal with all matters relating to education and dual language after the next territorial election, providing 'no school section, as at present constituted, shall be interfered with without the consent of the parties composing such section,' dropped out of sight, after a short exchange of arguments which would be more fully developed in 1894.[90] And in the Senate the school question was not even discussed.

At Regina, however, the same question reached a climax in 1892. The Board of Education, disliked by both council and assembly, was finally replaced by a council of public instruction and policy-making in education passed from the board's sections to the executive committee. That it took two sessions to make the change was not due so much to the resistance encountered, as to some adroit political manoeuvring by Cayley to replace Haultain as political leader in the North-West. School issues did not play an important role in the mounting political turmoil; they were, however, frequently used to mask motives in the struggle for political power.

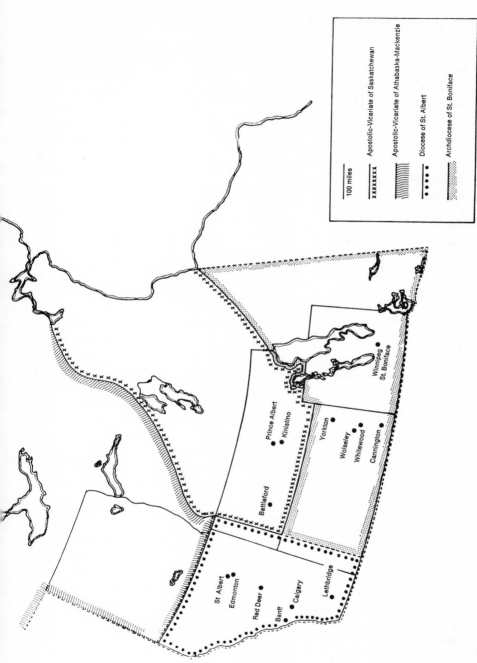

Figure 2 Boundaries of Roman Catholic dioceses, 1891 (Source: D. Benoit, *Vie de Mgr Taché*, 2 vols, Montreal 1904)

Mowat re-introduced his school bill on 4 August, indicating that its contents were unchanged.[91] Prince and Clinkskill, in amendment, insisted that the provisions respecting the council of public instruction did not commend themselves to the House.[92] Betts approved Mowat's bill in principle, but, in a surprise move, sided with Prince because the Board of Education was the minority's last protection. J.P. Dill (Wolseley) dismissed Prince's contention that national schools and a single language would discourage immigration: the experience of the United States did not support it. Cayley, having fallen out with Haultain, now favoured Prince. He personally opposed separate schools, but the House should respect them 'as long as things remained as they were.' The executive committee's pedagogical knowledge did not impress him and the uniform textbooks for all public and separate schools threw 'doubt upon the constitutionality of the Bill.' Haultain agreed that uniform textbooks were unconstitutional, but denied that the Board of Education had had that 'paramount experience and ability which some seem to regard as necessary.' Respect for minority rights did not necessarily require that all the educational machinery be duplicated. The 'horrible' predictions made last year for uniform inspection, for example, had not been fulfilled. When Prince pointed out that lots of people were dissatisfied but had to endure, Haultain declared that for a lot of people they had not made a great deal of noise. On division Prince's motion was defeated fifteen to eight and the main motion carried by an identical vote. The political jousting had increased the minority's strength. Besides Clinkskill, Betts, and Cayley, Prince was supported by McKay, Mitchell, W.F. Meyers (Kinistino), and C.E. Boucher, who had unseated Nolin as the member for Batoche after the territorial Supreme Court ruled their disputed election in his favour.[93] Clinkskill's important motion, three days later, to add four denominational members to the council of public instruction (two of them Catholics with full voting rights) passed after Brett moved to deny the vote to the religious representatives.[94]

The next contentious point reversed the bilingual arrangements of 1888. All school instruction was to be in English, with trustees free 'to cause a primary course to be taught in the French language.'[95] Prince's strong defence of the amount of English taught in Catholic schools in the Edmonton inspectoral district led Oliver to observe that the French-Canadian public school trustees at St Léon (southwest of St Albert) had to 'struggle,' and the English-speaking separate school ratepayers at St Joachim (Edmonton) had to take 'strong steps,' to get English taught 'in this English country.' Prince parried the thrust facetiously. There was not in Edmonton 'a single French child of the age of five who could not speak English as fluently as the hon. member who represented that district.' But it was Cayley's stand that probably aroused the curiosity of most members, for it was he who had so eagerly introduced the resolution to repeal section 110 in 1889. The crafty Calgarian now saw no need for a compulsory English-language clause because French-language instruction would gradually cease under the new system of inspection. As support he cited Leduc's letter to James Brown (3 July 1891) asking that teachers' examinations be uniform. This showed 'the anxiety of the French people to have their children learn English and therefore no change was required.' Haultain, in turn, used the same letter to *support* the compulsory English clause. The latter was 'in perfect harmony with the regulation introduced by Father Leduc and no one could be injured by it.' On division Prince's amendment to delete the clause was defeated fifteen to seven, with Meyers abandoning Prince.

Religious instruction, the opening of school with prayer, and separate schools were next on the legislative agenda. Haultain's motion to confine religious instruction to the last half-hour of the day in public *and* separate schools was carried without discussion. Oliver and Mitchell followed with an attack on the morning-prayer clause and it was deleted, again without discussion. When Dill criticized the 1886 limitation on the organization of separate school districts, stressing the minority's predicament when the majority failed to open a school, Oliver declared the principle of the school bill to be a 'voluntary' one. 'It recognized the right of the majority to rule and a school opened against the will of such majority could not be satisfactorily conducted.' Despite pressure from Betts, Davidson, and Mitchell, Oliver insisted that Dill's objections were 'not in harmony' with section 14 of the NWT Act and the subject was dropped.[96]

On 24 August the session was suddenly thrown into disarray by a want-of-confidence motion introduced by Betts and Mowat, criticizing the executive committee's 'conduct ... towards the district of Saskatchewan and in other respects.'[97] At the root of the trouble was Clinkskill's resignation from the executive committee on 6 February 1892 on the issue of Catholic school inspection.[98] When McKay, a Saskatchewan member, rejected Haultain's invitation to serve, Cayley joined the committee temporarily on the understanding that a Saskatchewan member would replace him after Haultain's return from Ottawa. Cayley resigned on 18 June and on 29 July, a few days before the session opened, Mitchell joined Haultain, Tweed, and Neff on the committee.[99]

Surprised and annoyed by the motion, Haultain accused Betts, 'the whilom opponent of separate schools,' and Mowat, 'mounted on his white horse' apparently from the same stable as Betts's, of duplicity. '... The present critical position of the Executive Committee was due to our school legislation of last year ...'; Clinkskill, 'that lineal descendant of John Knox,' had criticized it and Betts and Mowat were now playing into his hands. Cayley accused Haultain of high-handed action on the school and language questions, insisting that Haultain had not consulted Clinkskill during the 1891–2 session, and denied any connection between Mowat and the separate school supporters: 'Mr Haultain and the so-called separate school crowd were in perfect accord on many points of the School Bill.' Oliver accused Mowat of ingratitude to Haultain, 'to whom he was indebted for valuable assistance in connection with the School Bill.' On division, however, the Betts-Mowat motion carried thirteen to twelve,[100] and on 29 August a new committee took office: Cayley, Mowat, McKay, and Reaman. When Ross, the speaker and a long-time supporter of Haultain, resigned in protest, Cayley moved that Sutherland, also a Haultain supporter, succeed Ross, and a deadlock resulted when Ross and Sutherland both sided with Haultain. Royal then prorogued the House on his own initiative, presenting Haultain, Tweed, and Charles Magrath of Lethbridge, a Haultain supporter, with a *fait accompli* when they proposed Magrath as speaker.[101]

With the school bill inadvertently once more a legislative casualty, the Board of Education gained a further reprieve of four months. The embattled Haultain certainly erred when he accused Cayley's supporters of favouring Catholic educational interests. Only four members, Clinkskill, Prince, McKay, and Boucher, had supported the minority's cause consistently. Betts and Cayley were recent 'converts,' and Cayley's support was left-handed, to say the least. Even though Betts defended the minority's interests with considerable zeal (especially the Board of Education), this may have reflected his dislike of Mowat's intemperate language towards the clergy.[102] He had, of course, an old political score to settle with Haultain, who initiated 'the majority's' stalling tactics against the Brett-Betts council in 1889. The opposition of Brett, Reaman, and Jelly probably had similar roots. The last two had supported Haultain on the school and language votes and their opposition could not be attributed to his educational policies. Brett abstained on the school question, but supported Haultain on the language vote. Davidson abstained on the language question, but supported him on the school vote. Meyers opposed Haultain on the latter, but supported him on the former. None could be considered consistent opponents of Haultain's educational policies. The most puzzling votes were cast by two of Haultain's closest followers, Mowat and J. Lineham (Calgary), the latter's support going back to the days of 'the majority' in 1889. It is possible that, with Cayley also from Calgary, geographic loyalties weighed more heavily with

Lineham than ethnic and religious loyalties. Mowat's chance to serve on the executive committee probably determined his vote. But whatever their motives, most of Haultain's opponents were not hard-core supporters of Catholic educational interests, as their votes four months later showed.

Royal thought the school question contributed little to Haultain's downfall: '... the School Bill before the House had emerged from the Committee of the Whole in a shape, which rendered it unobjectionable to every one.'[103] Nevertheless, it was easy for Haultain to suppose that the French Catholic governor welcomed the delay on Mowat's bill.[104] Although Royal may be criticized for 'precipitate and injudicious action,'[105] there is no evidence of deliberate intent to kill the bill. The clergy, in turn, said little about developments at Regina, probably because the news from Manitoba, where Catholics were faced with double taxation to maintain their schools after 1890, was so grave.[106]

Eager to right the political situation Governor Royal called another session for 7 December. Thompson had ruled in September that Haultain's bill creating the executive committee in 1891–2 was unconstitutional and suggested the assembly amend it to avoid 'confusion and misinterpretation.'[107] The assembly's own political crisis was resolved after Joel Reaman, a member of Cayley's executive, died early in October[108] and Frederick R. Insinger, Haultain's supporter, defeated Thomas McNutt, Cayley's supporter, in the by-election at Wallace (near Yorkton) on 12 November. The school question was an important issue in the campaign, as Haultain upbraided Cayley and McNutt for supporting separate schools and the accused paraded their preference for national schools.[109] With Ross again in the speaker's chair Mowat introduced his school bill for the third time. Apart from Insinger's concern that Jews and Mormons did not qualify for separate schools,[110] the bill moved along without incident until 19 December.

Before the executive committee could replace the Board of Education it had to be recognized as the territorial executive by the federal government. This Thompson refused to do[111] and Haultain therefore had to proceed with care. On 12 December his resolution calling for the appointment of four members to advise the governor passed without incident. The next day two of his supporters moved that Haultain, Neff, Tweed, and Mitchell resume office as the executive committee. A crucial amendment by Clinkskill and Betts to have both parties represented was narrowly defeated on a straight party vote (fourteen to twelve), and the first major hurdle was passed. The second hurdle (the definition of the committee's powers) involved the federal government and victory here was less certain. On 19 December the House passed Haultain's resolution asserting the assembly's right to advise the governor through its executive committee on 'all Executive Acts and Appointments made necessary by Territorial Ordinances.'[112] Haultain then informed Royal that a bill recognizing the executive committee as a permanent four-man body was needed: one member would reside in Regina and constitute a quorum; the others would help when available.[113] Royal referred the matter to Thompson, who had succeeded Abbott as prime minister on 24 November. Thompson consulted Thomas M. Daly, the new minister of the interior, who saw no need for immediate action.[114] Haultain, however, pressed on. On 29 December a bill incorporating the earlier resolution on executive acts and appointments passed without difficulty.[115] The next move was up to the federal government, whose mood had grown more conciliatory. Haultain's bill, Thompson had informed Royal shortly before Christmas, did not 'seem' to encroach on federal authority. While the prime minister reserved the right of review, the government was 'most anxious to meet the views of the Assembly in any reasonable way.'[116] This was the all-important breakthrough; passage of a school bill that would substitute the executive committee for the Board of Education was now practically assured.

The school bill had advanced with only sporadic, minor exchanges until 19 December, when Haultain declared that all Catholic ratepayers in a separate school district were not bound to support the separate school. The earlier summer session, over Haultain's objections,[117] had disposed of the issue by retaining the 1888 law: '... all property within such Separate School District belonging to or held by ratepayers of the religious faith indicated in the name of such District, shall be liable only to assessments such as they impose upon themselves in respect thereof.'[118] This did not indicate clearly whether a Catholic ratepayer *had* to support the Catholic separate school; on the other hand, it was not easy to exercise a choice, as long as all property was liable. Haultain argued that the 1888 law placed 'an interpretation' upon section 14 of the NWT Act, even though a 'difference of opinion' existed in the assembly on the matter. The exact language of the federal act should be used, leaving 'interested' parties free to consult the courts as to its meaning. Prince and Clinkskill opposed any change. Oliver, who had drafted the separate school section in the first school ordinance, reminded the House that the evident intent of the NWT Act to promote minority rights 'would be violated if the majority of any minority were allowed to coerce the minority of a minority.'[119] Haultain's amendment carried twelve to five, and the following clause became law: 'The minority of the ratepayers in any organized Public School District, whether Protestant or Roman Catholic, may establish a Separate School therein, and in such case, the ratepayers establishing such Protestant or Roman Catholic Separate Schools shall be liable only to assessments of such rates as they impose upon themselves in respect thereof.'[120] Double taxation of the minority was impossible, but the section did not necessarily bind the property of minority members who did not wish to support a separate school. Prince and Clinkskill failed to re-instate the deleted clause ten days later and Mowat's motion for third reading was finally carried eighteen to five.[121] Assent for the school bill was certain after Thompson wired Royal on 27 December to agree to Haultain's bill creating the executive committee: 'Assembly is entitled to exercise large powers as to appointments under Territorial Ordinances.'[122] On 31 December, with Royal's assent, dualism in education ended at Regina. Only the government at Ottawa could restore it by disallowing the new ordinance.

The ordinance created a formidable new body to administer the territorial school system. The Council of Public Instruction assumed all powers formerly held by the Board of Education and those transferred to the lieutenant-governor-in-council in 1891–2. The ordinance made provision for a superintendent of education appointed by the lieutenant-governor-in-council (s. 6). It stipulated that secondary education would be 'non-sectarian' (s. 184d); decreed that every teacher's certificate granted by the Council of Public Instruction would bear the signature of the superintendent (s. 168), who could suspend for cause the certificate of any teacher awaiting council's investigation (s. 9e); relieved inspectors of responsibility for the examination and certification of teachers;[123] and required school trustees to appoint a truant officer 'invested with police powers' (s. 191). To ensure that the ordinances and regulations of council were observed, each inspector was required to make a full report of each school inspection to the superintendent and to the trustees of the district inspected (s. 91(3)). The ordinance gave the churches one slight concession: all church land in use as a public cemetery (not exceeding twenty-five acres) was exempted from taxation for school purposes (s. 103(6)). There could be no doubt that the development of the school system had entered a new era.

5

Church opposition at its height, 1893

Catholic leaders in the North-West Territories paid little attention to the 1892 School Ordinance before September 1893. It was, of course, a long time in coming and probably contained few surprises. Then, too, the even greater difficulties in Manitoba continued to overshadow territorial developments. On 19 January an ailing Bishop Grandin had left for Europe, not to return until 13 March 1894. Father Leduc accompanied him until midsummer 1893. Archbishop Taché was thus the sole episcopal leader as church-state relations entered their most difficult period. Suffering, like Grandin, from a chronic inflammation of the bladder, an illness which soon ended his life (22 June 1894), the aging archbishop was hard pressed to provide the energetic leadership required.

The deadline for disallowance of the ordinance was 7 February 1894, a year after the governor-general-in-council had received it. The first Catholic petitions reached Ottawa on 2 November 1893. Earlier petitions in themselves would not have hastened a decision, but the onus for delay would then have been upon the federal government, not the church. As it was, once disallowance was refused, further discussion was pointless as the time limit had expired.

The territorial school question was not discussed in Parliament in 1893, even though D'Alton McCarthy introduced his third bill in February to repeal the school and language clauses.[1] The lengthy debate on the Manitoba school question overwhelmed even the redoubtable McCarthy, and nothing more was heard of the bill. McCarthy's move, however, did yield forty-seven favourable petitions, thirty-five from Assiniboia, eleven from Alberta, and one from Saskatchewan.[2] On 30 May Judge Rouleau urged the ultramontane Senator A.R. Angers, minister of agriculture, to disallow the *ultra vires* ordinance. Absolute control by the majority of the minority's schools and compulsory English instruction were both contrary to the spirit of federal legislation, and the controversial minority-within-a-minority provision limited Catholic school rights more than was intended by section 14.[3] For several months, however, Rouleau's was the only voice demanding relief from an ordinance whose troublesome nature was becoming more and more apparent.

In July, for example, Sister Truteau, a teacher at St Albert, informed Taché that the new system of school inspection was jeopardizing the teaching of French. After visiting the school at St Albert, Inspector Hewgill complained that the time devoted to French impeded progress in English. The teachers were concerned that French might be curtailed to please the inspectors and a few Irish families, who were leading the school by the nose.[4] The Protestant Hewgill, however, was not the only critic of French teaching. The Reverend Gillies had expressed the hope in April 1892 that the teaching of both languages at St Joachim separate school in Edmonton would be 'discontinued' and the pupils taught 'either English or French.'[5] And the following July Sister Gibson, on tour of the convents of the Faithful Companions of Jesus, the most important female teaching order in the Diocese of St Albert, asked Grandin whether French children at St Joachim could answer in English 'according to the wish of the Inspector,' it being understood that French was not 'being *in any way put aside*.'[6] Even before the new ordinance passed therefore, irritating observations and requests had been on the increase; once it became law the ordinance, and in particular the regulations of the Council of Public Instruction, multiplied both.

The eight-man Council of Public Instruction was largely a political body. The non-voting members were appointed by the executive committee and the entire council met only at the committee's discretion. The latter's quorum consisted of the single resident member at Regina, who, since early in 1892, was 'Premier' Haultain.[7] On 4 January 1893, the committee appointed Haultain chairman of the Council of Public Instruction and James Brown superintendent of education. The council's quorum consisted of the chairman and one other member of the committee. On 4 April Haultain, 'a Sub-Committee of one for the transaction of all ordinary business,' appointed David J. Goggin of Winnipeg chief inspector of schools and 'Director of Normal School and Teachers [*sic*] Institutes.' On 1 December Goggin replaced Brown as superintendent.[8]

Neither Haultain nor Goggin had the background to win the confidence of French Catholic leaders. As French Huguenots, the Haultains had fled to

England in 1685 and came to Canada in 1860, after several generations of distinguished service in the British army. Haultain's father, Peterborough's representative in the Canadian legislature, made a strong plea in the 1865 confederation debates for legislation to protect the English-speaking Protestants of Quebec from a recent papal encyclical denying emigrants to Catholic countries freedom of worship.[9] In his early teens, Haultain lived in Montreal, where his father was secretary of the French Canadian Missionary Society of the Presbyterian church. After attending the Montreal High School and the Peterborough Collegiate Institute, he enrolled in the honours classics programme at the University of Toronto, where he came under the influence of the Anglican Reverend Dr John McCaul and became a good friend of McCaul's son, Charles. In 1884 the latter, in need of a legal partner, persuaded Haultain to come west. Once at Macleod, however, Haultain, sensing the opportunities before him, established his own flourishing practice and in 1887 was elected to represent that centre in the North-West Council. He was then a Conservative in federal politics, an Anglican, and a confirmed convert to non-denominational education, the result of Dr McCaul's dislike of denominational influences in higher education and Haultain's own familiarity with the struggle to free the University of Toronto from such influences. In 1888 Haultain became an executive member of the Macleod branch of the Upper Canada Bible Society and in 1891 he joined the Freemasons.[10]

Haultain's background made him an easy target for the French Catholic clergy, especially as his growing influence in territorial education in the 1890s was accompanied by a corresponding decline in their own power. The clergy criticized him severely in private, but on personal contact were usually surprised to find him amiable and friendly. To them, as to most of his political colleagues, he was something of an enigma. He could be exceedingly charming (especially when he had the upper hand) or cold and aloof (even arrogant), the image of one completely dedicated to his public responsibilities with few doubts about his own intellectual abilities. In the assembly he was masterful in debate, unexcelled in his command of facts or in his ability to organize them. His persuasiveness, like his administrative effectiveness, rested upon an intimate and thorough knowledge of the workings of government. A contemporary described his speeches as 'models of logic, precision and lucid expression.'[11] To him, it was illogical that a dwindling religious minority should have such a prominent role in the territorial school system; it was even less logical that an even smaller ethnic minority should enjoy equal status with the ever-growing English-speaking element in the west. That he affected 'English' ways in speech and dress is clear,[12] but in the absence of private correspondence, it is difficult to say whether he was personally prejudiced against either group. To Father Leduc, of course, Haultain's prejudice was surpassed only by Goggin's. But significant also were Haultain's later rulings as chief justice of Saskatchewan's Supreme Court (1912–17), requiring all Catholics to support a separate school, once established.[13] Conceivably, a confirmed anti-Catholic might have been less generous.

Of Goggin's national and religious sentiments much more is known.[14] Born and educated in Ontario, whose educational system he greatly admired, Goggin became principal of the Manitoba Normal School in 1884, completing simultaneously his BA and MA degrees at the University of Manitoba. Haultain hired him at a salary of $3000 per year ($400 above his own) and defended the move in the assembly by declaring that Goggin would 'train teachers, inspect schools, act as chairman of the Board of Examiners, and the government was not in a position to pay a man for each of these functions.'[15] Goggin was much more prominent as an Anglican and Freemason than Haultain. Regularly a delegate to Anglican synods, he served on occasion as lay secretary of the Synod of Rupert's Land. Of more consequence to the Catholic clergy was his rank as a thirty-third degree Mason, an honorary status achieved through distinguished service to the community, nation, or to Masonry itself in posts such as provincial grand master, which Goggin had held in Manitoba.

To the French Catholic clergy the Masons were a secret society, only ostensibly in favour of non-sectarian education. Masonry's true sectarian nature, they believed, revealed itself on occasions such as the opening of the public school at Virden, Manitoba, in August 1892, where, according to a dispatch from Virden to Winnipeg (included in Archbishop Taché's essay on the history of Manitoba schools, excerpts from which were sent to Sir John Thompson by Taché late in 1893[16]), the cornerstone was laid ' "with impressive Massonic [sic] ceremonies ... conducted by Grand Master D.J. Goggin," ' assisted by D. McLean, minister of education, and the Reverend H.L. Watts. That McLean and Goggin 'alluded to the admirable union prevailing between masonry and State Education' and that Watts was present showed that 'Free-Masonry, State Education and Protestantism' were in accord on the question of non-sectarian schools and that 'the triple alliance' was anti-Catholic.

That the report from Virden incriminated Goggin can hardly be denied, but there is no evidence of similar incidents in the Territories, probably because Haultain's own Masonic ties were not marked.[17] On the other hand, the Anglican, Masonic, and pro-British and imperial sentiments of the Goggins (Mrs Goggin was a prominent member of the patriotic IODE in

Regina, and Goggin, a charter member of the British Empire Club, became its national president in 1908 and secretary-treasurer in 1922;[18] in 1897 Goggin gave the major address at Regina's public commemoration of Queen Victoria's Diamond Jubilee) made the territorial superintendent of education a formidable threat to French Catholic clergy troubled by the assimilative powers of Great Britain's prestigious empire and unable to distinguish between Masonic lodges in France, Italy, and Spain, which were 'the rendezvous and the hotbed of an utterly militant anti-Catholicism,' and lodges in Germanic, Scandinavian, and Anglo-Saxon countries, which were 'fraternal and social organizations for humanitarian purposes or for business connections' minus the spirit of militant anti-Catholicism, though 'tainted with the rationalist spirit of the Enlightenment from which the lodges originated.'[19] As paranoid as were the French clergy on the Masonic question, their fears that territorial Anglo Protestants, unlike comparable elements in Manitoba, would use more subtle means to arrive at similar ends, were more justified. Goggin was certainly not as impetuous as Manitoba's attorney-general, Joseph Martin, who openly supported D'Alton McCarthy, and Haultain learned much from the national furore created by Premier Thomas Greenway's legislation denying financial aid to Catholic schools. In the Territories administrative rather than political measures would gradually alter the status of Catholic schools, and that, as Taché correctly observed, with less noise and 'more facility and more certainty.'[20]

After Goggin's appointment Haultain had approached Leduc and Forget to represent the minority on the Council of Public Instruction, but both declined ostensibly because of projected trips to Europe.[21] Both, however, were undoubtedly piqued by recent developments and quite possibly preferred not to be associated with schools in which church influence was minimal. Nevertheless, on 8 June Forget was appointed without his knowledge,[22] along with the Reverend Joseph Caron of Regina, Bishop Pinkham, and A.H. Smith, principal of Moosomin Union School.[23] The first and only meeting of the whole council in 1893 (soon the centre of much controversy) was held the next day. Forget, having just returned to Canada, did not attend.[24] The only official record of the meeting is the following minute:

Mr Haultain, in opening the meeting, stated that the appointed members had been summoned to meet the Executive to discuss certain changes in the Regulations which seemed desirable. The Executive Committee did not, at the present meeting, intend to pass any formal resolutions, but notes of the suggestions offered by the appointed members, or arising out of the discussions of the day, would be made, and these would have due weight when the Executive, at a later date, resolved on the Regulations it would issue.

The Chairman then submitted propositions under the following heads for discussion by the Council: (a) Subjects for Teachers' Examinations, (b) Text-Books (Teachers' Examinations), (c) Percentage for passing, (d) Training of Teachers, (e) Relative value of Certificates, (f) School Text-Books.[25]

The deliberations and precise agreements (if any) are not known. Haultain submitted later that, with Caron's approval, 'a uniform series of text-books for all schools was prescribed, with one exception.'[26] Caron's version was rather different:

... Mr Goggin, having expressed the idea that it would be desirable to render uniform the use of books in the schools, I said, in a general way, that in fact, on account of our system of inspection, it would be very advantageous if all the school children could use the same books.

Should those books be the catholic or protestant books? That question was not on the tapis, and consequently, I did not think that I should fully express my views by saying that if the members of the council wished for the uniformity of books for the good management and for the efficacious inspection of the schools they could adopt our series of catholic books.

Later on, in the course of my remarks, Mr Goggin, it seemed to me, wished to insinuate that catholic books could be left aside and replaced by the Ontario readers, and then I said that 'the younger the children who attend the schools the more do we urge that the books put in their hands should be perfectly catholic.'

And, on account of the special composition of the council of public instruction, and knowledge that, by the ordinance of 1892, that council has absolute power to impose upon us books of its own choice, I thought proper to add that 'if we were obliged to put aside the catholic reading books, we would more willingly abandon the books used for the scholars of the 4th degree than to abandon the books used for younger scholars.'[27]

The school books authorized by the Board of Education in March 1886, as we have seen, were entirely separate. In reading, the Protestant section adopted the Canadian Readers and the Catholic section adopted the Metro-politan Readers,[28] in use in the province of Quebec.[29] In September 1890, when the Protestant section adopted the Ontario Readers, the Catholic section made no change.[30] Even in September 1891, when both sections adopted the same subjects and textbooks for high school entrance and teachers' examinations, the readers for second- and third-class examinations were separate.[31] Since teachers' examinations were based on the work of the elementary schools, it followed that the readers in the schools would also be separate. In history, however, Buckley and Robertson's *High School History of England and Canada* (soon also the centre of much controversy) became, in September 1891, the single text on which all teachers' examinations were based.

On 15 August 1893, the executive committee, with all members present,[32] adopted a uniform set of readers, and 'on or about' 16 August the council informed the Catholic schools that after 1 January 1894 Ontario Readers would be prescribed in all standards above the second. In Standards I and II (the 'one exception' noted earlier) either the Metropolitan or Ontario series could be used. In reply to 'inquiries' the council's quorum (Haultain and Neff[33]) passed a 'minute' on 13 September reaffirming the earlier decision and permitting trustees, where French was the vernacular and the inspector's consent in writing had been obtained, to use 'the Ontario series of Bi-lingual Readers, parts i, ii and the Second Reader' in Standards I and II in place of the Metropolitan or Ontario Readers.[34] The change above Standard II was justified, Haultain said later, because the Catholic committee of the Council of Public Instruction in Quebec, chaired by Cardinal Taschereau, had recently 'struck' the Metropolitan Readers from its list of approved books.[35] Moreover, Ontario Readers were allowed in Ontario separate schools and had already been used in some Catholic schools in the Territories.[36] Taché, unimpressed, pointed out later that the committee in Quebec had replaced the Metropolitan Readers with 'another series of catholic readers.'[37] He ignored Haultain's references to Ontario and the Territories.

The change in readers was preceded by a new set of regulations governing teacher certification. On 10 August the council (Haultain and Neff) declared that 'a non-professional certificate was invalid as a license to teach.' First- or second-class professional or non-professional certificates issued in Ontario or Manitoba since 1886 were acceptable, but those from other Canadian provinces, the British Isles, or 'institutions other than those mentioned' would be exchanged only at the council's discretion.[38] The changes, designed to lay the foundations for normal schooling, meant that certificates from Quebec and the British Isles, where the ranks of the Faithful Companions of Jesus were frequently replenished, would be carefully scrutinized. The changes were undoubtedly prompted by the earlier failure to introduce normal school sessions. In 1888 the Board of Education had been authorized to establish a 'Normal Department' in schools with a high school branch (usually called union schools).[39] In March 1889 the board adopted regulations to facilitate normal schooling,[40] but the results were very disappointing. By September 1890 there were six union schools (including a Catholic one in Calgary), but only Moosomin had held a normal session.[41] The board therefore established normal departments in the union schools at Regina and Moosomin and 'invited' teachers with non-professional certificates to attend.[42]

To stimulate attendance it made non-professional certification more stringent. Since 1888 no certificates had been granted without prior academic examinations in the Territories or 'elsewhere.'[43] In September 1890 the board required all imported teachers with non-professional certificates to write the territorial examinations held annually since early in 1887. Only graduates in arts were excluded. For Protestants the examination subjects for third- and second-class certificates were Standards v and vi; for Catholics the equivalent subjects were the Intermediate and Superior courses. In this way the academic background of teachers was strengthened and made more uniform, at least within each section. The board also tightened professional certification by raising the amount of teaching experience for second- and first-class certificates from two to three and five years respectively. Moreover, all imported professional certificates were made 'good' only until the next examination of teachers.[44] As a result all teachers had to submit to territorial examinations, regardless of previous preparation or experience.

Again the results were disappointing. No students enrolled at Regina and only six attended Inspector Hewgill's classes for third-class professional certificates at Moosomin in 1890. In 1891, neither centre held classes.[45] With voluntary normal sessions clearly a failure the board ordered all Assiniboia teachers with non-professional certificates to attend the sessions[46] and revived its earlier request for a peripatetic normal school principal.[47] Inspectors Hewgill and Rothwell conducted normal sessions for Assiniboia teachers in 1892 and 1893, but no Alberta or Saskatchewan teachers accepted the board's invitation in November 1892.[48] Haultain and Neff therefore invalidated all non-professional certificates in August 1893, and on 1 September James Brown announced a three-month session at Regina for teachers with first- and second-class non-professional certificates, followed by similar sessions at Calgary and Regina for teachers with third-class certificates.[49]

As might be expected the Catholic minority reacted vigorously to these changes in teacher certification. A test case was provided immediately in the person of Sister Bond, mother superior of the convent in Edmonton and a teacher at St Joachim with nearly thirty years' experience 'in England and elsewhere.'[50] On 1 September 1891 Sister Bond had received a second-class non-professional certificate after passing the academic examination at Regina. She expected to exchange it for a professional certificate on 1 September 1893,[51] in keeping with an 1890 regulation granting a first-

or second-class professional certificate to anyone who passed the required examination and held 'a Normal School Diploma or the Inspector's endorsements approved by the Board of three years' successful teaching.'[52] Sister Bond had no normal school diploma and expected to gain professional standing on the basis of four inspectoral endorsements.[53] If her certificate had been endorsed at each of the two annual visits required of the inspector,[54] by the fall of 1893 she could have had the four endorsements required. What she may have lacked was three years' teaching experience in the Territories, though of course she had taught for many years elsewhere.

On 1 September 1893, however, James Brown sent Sister Bond the following communication:

Inspector Hewgill had no power to endorse certificates when he visited Edmonton last spring. Endorsation ceased when Normal training was instituted. There has been but one way to secure professional certificates since midsummer 1892, viz., by undergoing training at a Normal School.

Certificates issued in 1891 come practically under the same rule since it was impossible for the holders to secure the required four endorsements. As these certificates expire today they have been extended till the opening of the Normal School in Regina, 2nd Oct., 1893.

Beyond that date no non-professional first or second class certificate is valid as a licence to teach.[55]

Two points in the letter are open to question. First, Inspector Hewgill did have the power to endorse certificates in 1893. Under the 1892 Ordinance inspectors had 'to endorse all Teachers' certificates in accordance with the regulations of the Council of Public Instruction.'[56] Secondly, there was more than one way to secure professional certificates after mid-summer 1892. The regulation on endorsements, quoted above, applied as long as the board existed and it was not repealed by the council in 1893. The point on which a professional certificate might have been denied – the years of teaching in the Territories – was not mentioned by Brown.

Father Leduc, aware that the assembly (then in session) was about to repeal the endorsement clause,[57] left for Regina early in September.[58] After consulting Lacombe at Calgary[59] he and J.K. Barrett, who had challenged Manitoba's school legislation in the courts in 1890, conferred with Taché at St Boniface and returned with instructions to declare solemnly that teaching sisters would never attend normal sessions which required them to mingle with Protestants. Barrett interviewed Haultain and Goggin as Taché's representative and told Leduc he could expect little sympathy from either. Goggin was a thirty-third degree Mason and Haultain did nothing without him. On

15 September Leduc, accompanied by Caron and Forget, insisted in a meeting with Goggin that the sisters would only attend special normal courses in their own convents. When Goggin suggested that the minority employ lay teachers or import only sisters with professional certificates, Leduc countered that the minority preferred devoted sisters to salary-conscious laymen. Moreover, did Goggin really think that sisters could be imported like so many sacks of grain? A normal session in the public school at Calgary, where the minority had a convent, was then proposed, but Leduc only promised to discuss the matter with his superiors. Goggin also suggested that the pope be petitioned to modify the rules of the female teaching orders, 'a most singular and original bit of advice,' according to Leduc.[60] He told Taché he had made it clear that normal sessions would be in the convent, with the instructor (presumably Goggin) the only male present, provided he always conducted himself like a true gentleman.[61] Forget presented Sister Bond's case vigorously and was directed by Goggin to submit his evidence to the Council of Public Instruction. Haultain, polite, even affable, promised to get her a professional certificate and to do everything he could to settle the normal school question according to the minority's views. (Forget later presented a memorandum to council and the case was settled in Sister Bond's favour.[62]) The textbook issue was not raised, but Caron, Forget, Prince, and Boucher discussed it with the executive committee later in the same month.[63] Leduc came away from Regina completely convinced that the council was prepared to carry out the programme of the Freemasons: godless schools, banishment of all Catholic religious education, and warfare against all convents and teaching orders without regard to congregation.[64]

On 21 September, three days after returning to St Albert, Father Leduc launched the minority's campaign to have the 1892 School Ordinance disallowed. In letters to Thompson and Senator Angers he compared the 1884 and 1892 Ordinances to show how everything had gradually been lost.[65] Thompson sent a copy of Leduc's letter to Haultain and noted unofficially that the school ordinance did not appear to be *ultra vires*. Leduc, too, only claimed that in the course of administering its provisions separate schools were 'being extinguished.' Thompson wished to ascertain the facts, for 'the policy of the Ordinance' would 'no doubt' be raised in Parliament.[66] For the moment Haultain said nothing. On 15 October Fathers Leduc and Léon Fouquet preached Sunday sermons on the school question at St Albert and Edmonton respectively,[67] and by the end of October Nicholas D. Beck, a lawyer and chairman of St Joachim Separate School Board, whom Leduc had converted to Catholicism in 1883,[68] had prepared a petition to the governor-general-in-council which Catholic school trustees were to send to

Taché for transmission to the secretary of state.[69] In the two-month period before 7 January Taché sent nineteen identical petitions to Ottawa[70] From Lethbridge Father Lacombe solicited the influence of his personal friend, Lord Aberdeen, the governor-general, on behalf of the petitions.[71] Beck, in turn, urged Taché to have some one ('for instance one of the Fathers at the Ottawa College') take the matter in hand in Ottawa to prevent its being 'pigeon-holed' and 'to press preferentially for disallowance.'[72]

The petitions raised the following points against the ordinance and the regulations of council:

1 The educational system under the board had operated with entire harmony and to the general satisfaction of all connected with the active work of education in the Territories.
2 The teaching sisters, well-trained in their own houses with extensive experience in the art of teaching, did not require normal sessions. Moreover, their living in community according to rules made it practically impossible to comply with regulations requiring attendance.
3 The prescribed textbooks were highly objectionable to Catholics, either asserting many things which Catholics had always repudiated, or entirely ignoring, greatly minimizing or misrepresenting the part the Catholic church and its members had played in history, including the contributions both had made to science and literature.
4 Separate Catholic normal schools were not provided and normal school textbooks were open to the same objections as books in the ordinary schools.
5 The ordinance and particularly the regulations which followed destroyed the distinctive character of separate schools, rendering them separate in name only.
6 Passage of the ordinance had been strongly opposed in the assembly in the name of the Catholic minority.
7 Father Leduc, on behalf of clerical and lay Catholics, had recently placed the minority's objections before the council without result.
8 By giving non-Catholics the absolute control and management of Catholic separate schools, the ordinance surpassed in spirit, intention, and effect the powers of the Legislative Assembly in relation to education.
9 If the ordinance were not disallowed, repealed, or amended, it would greatly disturb the peace and harmony between Catholics and Protestants in the Territories and in other parts of the Dominion.[73]

With the first petitions before him Thompson wrote Haultain again. Catholic separate schools, he submitted, could not be properly governed by a body composed wholly of Protestants or vice versa. Complaints had already been lodged and he wished to co-operate with Haultain to prevent any unnecessary feeling manifesting itself on the subject.[74] Haultain replied late in November and enclosed Leduc's letter (3 July 1891) and the regulations adopted by the Board in September 1891,[75] but none the council had passed in 1893. The documents showed how little the situation would change if the 1892 Ordinance were disallowed: '... the more important points in question ... [were] largely a reenactment of earlier legislation which has been allowed to go into operation.' To support his thesis he discussed, in order, teacher certification, the appointment of inspectors, and school textbooks.

The examination and licensing of teachers had been vested in the whole Board of Education since 1888. In 1891, on Father Leduc's suggestion, 'a uniform course of study and a practically uniform series of text books' were prescribed for all teachers' candidates, even in controversial subjects such as history and science. In view of this, he observed correctly, 'the practical necessity' of the 'safeguarding' clause on the choice of textbooks in the 1891–2 Ordinance could be 'estimated.' Regarding inspectors, the 1892 Ordinance 'simply' re-enacted the 1891–2 Ordinance, which had provided for their appointment. Moreover, the Reverend Gillies was one of the four inspectors, a fair ratio, he thought, as there were 286 Protestant and only 44 Catholic schools in the Territories. The only change in school textbooks had been made at the June meeting of council in 1893, when, 'with the consent and on the suggestion of' Caron (a statement for which no evidence was provided), a uniform series of textbooks was prescribed, with the 'optional' use of Catholic readers in the primary classes. The history text was Buckley and Robertson's, 'considered unobjectionable by the Roman Catholic Section and ... in use in the Territories before our late Regulations or the Ordinance ... came into force.'

Even if the Council of Public Instruction had replaced the Board of Education, Haultain continued, there were still two Catholic members on council. The council, in any case, did not govern the individual school absolutely: '... the domestic concerns of the School, including religious teaching, choice of Teacher and generally the denominational tone of the School rest entirely in the hands of the ratepayers, acting through the Trustees.' Complaints by the teaching sisters were also unwarranted. Sisters with 'scholarship and professional skill' could obtain certificates without attending normal classes, but no exceptions could be made for those without 'equivalent qualifications.' Moreover, those already teaching in the Territories were 'not affected by this regulation' (a curious statement in the light of Sister Bond's case), even though in the future '... we expect Religious Communities wishing to engage in teaching in Schools drawing public money to conform with regulations of which they have full notice.'

Protestants, Haultain objected, would not govern Catholic schools: '... our Educational system as a whole can be and should be administered by a non-sectarian body. The Policy of our law is to give a good plain English Education to every child in the Country, and so far as is possible, in the same way.' The religious complexion of the school was a local matter and a duplication of the educational machinery from top to bottom was both impossible and unnecessary. Territorial school legislation met both the letter and spirit of the act and no real grievance existed:

There has been no practical wrong alleged truthfully and I venture to assert that the Roman Catholic Laity of the Territories, the parents, trustees and teachers have no complaint to make. We have been until lately able to boast that we have achieved a most desirable uniformity in our School system, without friction, without the sacrifice of a principle or the foregoing of a conviction on the part of anyone.[76]

This ended the 'unofficial' discussion. A week later Taché discussed Goggin's Masonic background with Thompson and put the school question to him squarely: 'If there is no possible protection for Catholics in this country, it is just as well that the fact should be known at once. On the contrary, if our rights are to be safeguarded let a check be put to the attempts directed against such rights.'[77] With official documents slow to arrive Thompson wired Taché for the regulations passed by the council in 1893. Taché minimized the regulations as 'an instance of what can be done' and stressed the ordinance, which, he said, placed Catholics 'altogether in the hands of the open adversaries of their schools.' Conscious that no petitions opposing it had been sent until November, he declared its 'dangers ... so obvious that at first we thought it was unnecessary to petition for its disallowance, and that the government would prevent its coming into force.' It had seemed impossible that the ordinance would escape its notice.[78]

On 4 January Governor Charles H. Mackintosh, who had succeeded Royal on 1 November 1893, sent Thompson his first report on the situation in the North-West. Haultain, he said, was 'an honest fellow, very vain and extremely crochetty and self-confident,' 'the very personification of delay, the high priest of procrastination,' the cause of 'much' of the discontent in the Territories. 'Statesmen' of Mowat's order were 'as plentiful as gophers, but not quite so intelligent – for the latter know at least when to go to their holes and stay there.' Although the school ordinance was 'within the letter of the Constitution,' the assembly had acted 'unfairly' in 'pressing' new applicants for certificates among the sisters to attend normal sessions and in refusing the minority at least two votes on council. In the textbook controversy the Irish Catholics did not care 'a pot' about readers. Disallowance, he believed, would 'create a bitter feeling here, and might imperil even the rights now enjoyed.' Rather, the territorial government would have to make concessions once 'the clamor and agitation now noticeable in Old Canada' disappeared.[79]

Haultain's official reply (4 January) to the Catholic petitions contained few new points. On teacher education he cited the board's resolutions in 1888 and 1891 recommending the appointment of a normal school principal, and the 1891 regulation establishing compulsory normal sessions for Assiniboia teachers, and noted that at the 1888 meeting Leduc and Forget were 'present and approving' and that at the 1891 meeting Forget moved the compulsory regulation and Leduc and Rouleau were 'present and approving.' On offensive books he observed that 'a general charge ... can only be met by an equally general denial, or by putting the books in as evidence.' He went on to expand on the dilemma of religious dualism in education:

Granted the right of Roman catholic inspection and Roman catholic management and control, the further necessity will arise for a Roman catholic assembly to make ordinances for the government of Roman catholic schools, and a Roman catholic lieutenant governor to assent to such legislation, and a Roman catholic governor general to allow the law to come into operation, on the advice of a Roman catholic council, possessing the confidence of a Roman catholic house of commons.

The legislative assembly, he asserted boldly, 'cannot be ordered to repeal or amend its own legislation by any power or authority.' Disallowance would only change the name of the governing body and cause that '"great disturbance of peace and harmony"' to which the minority had referred.[80] The territorial government clearly had no intention of easing the federal government's task.

To strengthen the minority's case Beck sent Thompson a copy of Oliver's editorial in the *Edmonton Bulletin* (11 January 1894), which defended the 1892 Ordinance but criticized compulsory normal sessions as 'a piece of intolerable bureaucratic impertinence, if it be nothing worse.' These sessions, the *Bulletin* added, were expensive and unnecessary and 'not contemplated in or by' the school ordinance. To Beck, these remarks supported disallowance.[81] Oliver's criticism of normal sessions, however, found no echo in the rest of the territorial press. All newspapers opposed disallowance, even though a few Conservative ones criticized some of the recent educational changes. The *Moose Jaw Times* and the *Moosomin Spectator* thought the Liberal *Regina Standard* was generally too strident in its criticisms of the old school system.[82] The even more Conservative *Regina Leader*, Davin's organ, believed the assembly should reconsider the deletion of morning prayers, out of deference to an 'old established rule.'[83] It termed the Council of Public Instruction 'an anomalous and unduly ponderous body.'[84] Goggin's appointment was well received, as was the change in school inspectors, although the *Standard* and the *Bulletin* editorialized strongly against the retention of 'clerical gentlemen.'[85]

What the school system of the Northwest needs ... now perhaps more than ever [Oliver declared], is the services of inspectors who have made first-class public schools and a first-class public school system their life study and have found in them their life's work, not men who, having given the best of their lives and minds to another calling, now undertake a work for which their whole training and experience renders them unfit.[86]

Several papers echoed the *Standard*'s view that Goggin himself should conduct all normal session, with short sessions in several centres for third-class teachers 'who cannot afford to go a great distance.'[87] The *Saskatchewan Times* and the *Spectator* suggested normal schools at Battleford and Moosomin respectively.[88] The *Spectator*, in commenting on Leduc's sermon in Calgary opposing normal classes for teaching sisters, declared that the council could not 'in justice to all concerned make fish of one and flesh of another in dealing with teachers.'[89] But the *Standard* wondered how Haultain and others could consider the present school system satisfactory when the teaching sisters, 'upon the advice of their spiritual advisers,' refused to attend the normal sessions at Regina.[90]

In the assembly itself the only reference to the school question in 1893 was Haultain's statement that the school system had progressed well in recent years 'without the slightest feeling of dissatisfaction on the part of any minority, or any set of people in the Territories (loud applause).'[91] No one challenged the statement. Outside the House, C.A. Magrath of Lethbridge explored the issue in February in a long letter to the editor, 'National vs. Separate Schools,'[92] and Haultain declared in Toronto in March that 'expediency' made it 'unwise' for McCarthy and others to agitate the school question 'just now.' He assured the east that the west could take care of itself.[93]

At Ottawa, Senator Angers, Daly, and G.E. Foster, minister of marine and fisheries, were the Privy Council's committee assigned to reach a decision on the ordinance.[94] The textbook changes apparently gave the committee the most difficulty. When Daly wired Regina for the textbook regulations adopted in June 1893,[95] Haultain sent the explanatory circular of 30 September 1893, containing, he said, the only changes made. He also indicated that a uniform series of textbooks was 'determined upon,' not 'prescribed' in June.[96] The change in wording did not, of course, change the fact that the council did eventually prescribe the books. Haultain only admitted that the change was not made on 9 June, without divulging when and by whom it was made. Dissatisfied, Daly wired Mackintosh for the regulations that would show 'fully' the changes made in June.[97] Mackintosh referred Daly to Haultain's recent letter (12 January) and added, '... that letter appears to show all changes made in text books.'[98]

Governor Mackintosh tried hard to effect a church-state compromise in January. After a serious talk with some members of the executive committee he wrote Thompson of 'an evident desire to somewhat relax the regulations of the School Ordinance – should it be allowed.' He had 'no doubt' Catholics would be given a vote on council and teaching sisters would be certificated without attending the normal sessions.[99] In another dispatch to Thompson he attributed much of the discontent over schools to the tight money market and depression, which gave people 'fads which they imagine to be grievances.' 'Trouble-mongers' would find 'more healthy employment' when better days returned, and 'P.P.A.'s and Patrons'[100] would discover there were 'other beings than themselves in the world.' The settlers themselves were tractable and reasonable; they only needed 'something cheerful to think about,' like a North-West Exhibition – a 'dish' for which he knew 'precisely the condiments likely to tickle the delicate palates of these lusty western pioneers.'[101] Thompson revealed himself delighted with the prospect of compromise at Regina,[102] and the reported tractability of government and people may have had an important influence on the government's decision in February not to disallow the controversial school ordinance.

The officious Governor Mackintosh misread the situation and was much too sanguine. The Catholic minority was in a poor bargaining position. Having given away so much by chance, it was numerically too insignificant to command political respect. Moreover, the rapid changes following hard on the Council of Public Instruction's establishment were fundamental and largely unprecedented. The new administrative order was too young and inexperienced to hazard compromise. It was also politically ambitious and too poor to ignore the high costs of frontier education (in 1891–2 the average teacher's salary was $620 in the Territories, compared to $469 in

Ontario and $282 in Quebec, outside Montreal[103]). Economies, it was confidently maintained, would result from the abolition of separate schools and bilingual education. Without minimizing the general antipathy towards all things Catholic and French, the economy argument carried much weight with most members of the assembly. Haultain, we have seen, was determined to control the 'men we pay' and Oliver was convinced that a responsible executive in control of education, as in Ontario, would be cheaper and more efficient.[104] Provocative headlines like the *Regina Standard*'s (29 July 1891) deliberately placed the Board of Education in a bad economic light: 'Half Yearly Meeting, Nothing to Do – A Two-Hour Session at an Expense of Three Hundred Dollars.' Prince insisted that the board was inexpensive, but it was also true that each elected member was free to dispense patronage in his constituency,[105] and it was a matter of no small consequence to know that the policies of an independent board regarding teacher certification, for example, might upset local arrangements for the support of schools and teaching personnel. Control of the educational dollar by the assembly became the *sine qua non* of most members, for it would not only mark the triumph of responsible government, but secure the combined blessings of efficiency and economy, and that at a time when education, as we shall see, was rapidly becoming the most important charge upon the territorial treasury.

6
The triumph of state control, 1894

The long-awaited report of the Privy Council's committee, released on 5 February,[1] regretted that recent educational changes should have caused, 'even unwittingly,' dissatisfaction and alarm on the part of the petitioners, and advised careful inquiry and review by the executive committee and the assembly 'in order that redress be given by such amending ordinances or amending regulations as may be found necessary to meet any grievances or any well-founded apprehensions which may be ascertained to exist.' In the light of the assembly's deliberate and sustained efforts (going back to 1889) to assume complete control of the territorial school system, the final recommendation is rather remarkable. Protestants could accuse the committee of ignoring political realities in the North-West; Catholics could censure it for inviting the state to do nothing. The committee, however, may have concluded it could do little more, as both the majority and minority held naive expectations. The Protestants had asked to be trusted and the Catholics had asked to be tolerated. Yet the assembly had already shown how much the Protestants could be trusted, and the emphasis of the church on complete dualism and separation made toleration difficult. In its dilemma the committee suggested that perhaps all was not well in the remote regions of Christendom and asked the assembly to furnish the remedy itself.

In its report the committee leaned heavily on Haultain's thesis that the school law and regulations before and after 1892 were not 'materially' different. It contrasted the educational systems under the board and council and concluded that, even though the systems did differ 'materially,' complaints were not justified because '... it was under that system [the board system] that the regulations now objected to were made,' and the petitioners themselves had admitted that that system had operated to the general satisfaction of all. Comparing the duties of inspectors under both systems, the committee concluded they were 'practically the same,' ignoring the fact that the inspectors now served a different master. It recognized that the formation of the board of examiners was different under the new law, but it was unable to ascertain that the Council of Public Instruction had 'in any way altered or restricted the mode and manner of examining teachers.' Apparently it was unaware that examinations in the future could be set and marked entirely by non-Catholics. It quoted Haultain to show that, with equivalent qualifications, attendance at territorial normal sessions was not compulsory. It ignored the council's arbitrary rejection of teaching certificates from all provinces except Manitoba and Ontario, and the equally arbitrary distinction between normal school certificates and those issued by convents and religious teaching orders.

The abolition of Metropolitan Readers above Standard II, although recognized as an exceptional fact, was accepted without comment. However, the committee did note correctly that no objectionable teachers' textbooks had been cited, and that the complaints were primarily against uniform curricula and textbooks, for which Leduc had to accept some responsibility. On separate normal schools the committee interpreted the board's 1888 resolution to favour 'one normal school for all.' It ignored the reference in the same resolution to normal sessions 'in different parts of the country,' which could mean several normal schools, Protestant and Catholic.

The committee quoted the ordinance (ss. 32 and 36) to show that separate schools continued as legal entities, but avoided details, probably aware that the separate school clause was a general proposition, which did not commit the territorial government to particular administrative arrangements regarding schools. It noted that the status of religious instruction had undergone a 'material' change between 1888 and 1892, but suggested no remedy, probably because the school curriculum, too, was not governed by the separate school clause.

Finally, the committee invoked Haultain's thesis to dispose of the petitioners' main concern: inadequate representation on the Council of Public Instruction. So similar were the regulations of board and council that the petitioners themselves 'could hardly ask with confidence for disallowance,' adding the alternative that assembly and council be ordered and directed to repeal or amend the ordinance and regulations. The committee was prepared to approach the assembly, but it preferred inquiry and review to edict and directive.

The Catholic minority was, of course, bitterly disappointed by the government's report. On 6 February Father Leduc left St Albert to help Archbishop Taché prepare an appropriate rejoinder. The resulting memorandum, dated 7 March, contained Taché's extensive criticisms in two parts, with supporting letters from Caron, Forget, and Leduc, in four appendices.[2] Focusing on Haultain's thesis, the memorandum detailed how the 1892 Ordinance and subsequent regulations had altered the status of Catholic schools; it naturally ignored the equally significant fact that the separate school clause did not necessarily guarantee a board of education at the centre of the educational system.

Comparing the school systems under the board and council, the memorandum concluded, correctly, that 'here lies the whole separate school question,' for the board had indeed offered 'guarantees' to both Catholic and Protestant schools. For example, control of teachers' examinations by the whole Board of Education had not endangered Catholic interests because 'good understanding and mutual concessions' had characterized the work of the board. And in any case had any member proposed a regulation 'antagonistic to the views of the members of the other section, surely the latter in their individual capacity would have opposed the motion.' Leduc's 1891 agreement had grown out of the fact that each section had 'exclusive choice of their authors, on certain matters, and the exclusive conduct of the examination of their candidates on certain special subjects.'[3] This view of the board's activities was, of course, a true one. Concessions had been agreed upon, not imposed, and were therefore not irrevocable. Moreover, the selection of school textbooks remained 'altogether' in the hands of individual sections. However, it was equally true that, apart from the readers, the Catholic section had accepted a common school curriculum and textbooks (including Buckley and Robertson's history) in 1891 without complaint, a development which would seem to make separation of little practical value.

The memorandum was on firmer ground when it turned to the arbitrary substitution of Ontario and Metropolitan readers above Standard II.[4] Forget, in his letter, reminded Haultain of his earlier declaration in the assembly that he 'could not agree to the clause making uniform text-books compulsory, it was contrary to the constitution.'[5] However, Leduc's complaints that teachers' examinations in French had been 'abolished'[6] were less valid because he must have known that the regulations he had 'provoked'[7] in 1891 made no mention of subjects or textbooks for French candidates, and his two translations of the examination papers in French[8] were therefore not required. To censure only Inspector Hewgill for criticizing French-language instruction was also unfair because Inspector Gillies had criticized the system of bilingual teaching as well.

In discussing normal schools the memorandum pointed out correctly that each union school, Catholic or Protestant, could establish a normal department.[9] It also quoted Leduc to good effect:

All the members understood, or at least could understand, by Mr Forget's remarks and mine, that when the time to act would come, we could claim our right to one or several catholic normal schools. And, in fact, every time that the question has been brought before the board of education since January, 1888, until our last session in the summer of 1892, I have always supported by my colleagues Hon. Judge Rouleau and A. Forget, Esq., claimed catholic normal schools, if ever the board should pass a resolution making compulsory the attendance at those schools.[10]

Nevertheless, when the first regulations for normal departments had been adopted in March 1889, the professional curriculum and textbooks were identical for all candidates. These and the board's resolutions in 1888 and 1891 that a single normal school principal be appointed gave at least tacit support to the idea of common normal school sessions. That the sessions were to be held 'in different parts of the country' did not *necessarily* mean separate sessions in Catholic institutions. The resolutions were admittedly vague, but it would not be surprising if Leduc's, Forget's, and Rouleau's support led Protestants to believe that dualism in education would not be extended beyond the high school. The minority itself, then, was partly responsible for the development of common normal school sessions. The Catholic union school in Calgary had existed since 1889, but there is no evidence of a normal session before 1893. Unable to lay the foundations for its own normal school, the minority had no vested interests in professional teacher training. Most Protestants had also ignored the voluntary sessions, but Catholics could ill afford to follow the Protestant example if they hoped to set precedents for the future. In a report to Taché in 1890 Leduc himself did not appear disturbed that voluntary normal sessions in union schools would be difficult to organize. Localities with union schools which wished to establish normal school departments at their own expense could do so by approaching the Board of Education, which probably would not result in too many applications.[11] There is nothing in the statement to suggest disappointment. Yet precedents would have been valuable in claiming the separate facilities described in the memorandum.

The 1892 Ordinance did lessen clerical influence in education, and the Reverend Gillies, 'though a catholic priest,' did have to inspect schools 'in a very different way' as an appointee 'under the ordinance of 1892.'[12] It is significant, however, that neither Grandin nor Taché had petitioned to disallow the 1891–2 Ordinance under which Gillies was first appointed. Despite the archbishop's pointed objections, therefore, there was some evidence to support Haultain's thesis that disallowance of the 1892 Ordinance would change little, especially where school inspection was concerned.

Separate schools, the memorandum concluded, were now separate in name only. To Leduc, the recent changes reflected Goggin's gradualistic policy, leading to the complete abolition of separate schools.[13] Forget used history to emphasize 'the strange spectacle of catholic schools managed and inspected by protestants, and in which the programme of studies is fixed and the text-books are carefully selected, according to the advice of a protestant superintendent of education.'[14] The memorandum wondered whether Catholic parents and clergy could really be accused of 'an excessive sensitiveness' in objecting to school regulations made by a Council of Public Instruction and a superintendent who 'may be protestant, freemason, Jew, agnostic, infidel, materialist.'[15] On religious instruction the memorandum dismissed the last half-hour of the school day as inadequate because children were 'most tired' at that time and, on short winter days, 'restless and anxious' to return to worried parents who urged them to leave at the earliest possible time. Moreover, with no religious instruction required to secure a licence, teachers for Catholic schools could be 'entirely ignorant' of the religious instruction they were expected to impart.[16]

In sum, the Privy Council's report, the memorandum stated, was largely an endorsement of Haultain's views and the minority should not have been kept in complete ignorance of his submissions. It was hard to believe that missionaries who had grown old 'amidst the dangers, fatigues and privations unavoidable in a country in which they entered as pioneers of faith and civilization' could be treated as if they were 'incapable of appreciating the nature of their complaints.' The report even 'went so far as to ridicule them in stating that they themselves had approved what they condemn to-day.'[17]

Taché took it as a personal affront that he, who had been hurriedly summoned from Rome to help establish federal authority on the Red River in 1870, should now bear 'ridicule' at the hands of the same authority.[18] Taché had specifically asked for disallowance on 15 November 1893.[19] While recognizing that section 93(3) of the BNA Act, which sanctioned an appeal to the governor-general-in-council, did not apply, his memorandum questioned the wisdom of asking relief from 'the very men who [had] caused the whole difficulty' and whose leader had already asserted that the minority had 'no "grievances or any well founded apprehensions." ' 'Time alone will show what will be the result of such an indefinite and uncertain policy.'[20] He felt he had a right to expect more, and to support that view he presented a closely reasoned argument on several constitutional points in the second part of the memorandum.

In the writer's opinion the recitation of imperial and federal legislation, guarantees, and assurances to establish the constitutional argument in the memorandum's second part, while perhaps significant in relation to the Manitoba schools, was immaterial in the North-West. In the Territories the basic issue was neither legal nor constitutional, for no fundamental or superior law had been violated. The 1892 Ordinance had certainly affected the administration and curricula of Catholic schools, but the schools themselves were not abolished; nor were their supporters confronted, as in Manitoba, with the burden of double taxation. The basic issue in the Territories was the establishment of the political principle that in a representative democracy the majority must rule, exerting popular control over the institutions of society. A divided school system with a prominent role for the clergy was an institution foreign to the majority from Ontario, even though it was familiar enough to the minority from Quebec. The majority, of course, had to respect the well-defined rights of the minority, but in the Canadian west the rights of the minority were poorly defined, as the memorandum itself sadly recognized: 'The diversity of opinion between the tribunals and between the members of some of them[21] is not an inducement for the minority to view with satisfaction a result depriving them of rights guaranteed by the negotiations and which have been recognized as certain during twenty years after the creation of Manitoba. One is compelled to acknowledge that human justice is very uncertain and that human laws are often badly defined.'[22] Even with well-defined rights, the minority's situation would still have been precarious. By the 1890s the struggle for control of the western hinterland had been resolved in Ontario's favour. The latter's influence was reflected in the fact that 73 per cent of the members in the first territorial assembly were born in Ontario.[23] Once the English-speaking non-Catholic settlers from Ontario and the British Isles outnumbered the French-speaking Catholic settlers from Quebec and New England, agitation to bring social institutions in line with demographic facts followed as a matter of course.

Handicapped by indefinite constitutional guarantees and lacking numbers, the minority had looked to the federal government for protection. When the latter failed, the memorandum naturally attacked 'the sacrifice of federal autonomy' 'under the pretense of respect for provincial or territorial autonomy.'[24] It was easy to berate the federal authority, but it was also true that a number of factors, some French Catholic in origin, had greatly restricted the scope of that authority by 1894. The architect of a strong federal government, Sir John A. Macdonald, was dead, and his centralist Conservative party, in power for all but five of the twenty-seven years since 1867, was riddled with corruption and internal dissension. It was therefore in no position to take heroic stands against impertinent legislators or administrators in the west. Moreover, in the 1870s and 1880s Sir Oliver Mowat, Ontario's Liberal premier, had taken the lead in re-defining the scope of federal power. He carried federal-provincial disputes to the Privy Council in London, until both governments emerged as co-ordinate powers, each sovereign in those areas that the BNA Act had allocated to it. And, according to section 92, jurisdiction over 'property and civil rights' belonged to the local legislatures, limited in education by the as yet uncertain status of the right to denominational schools in section 93.

But if Ontario had led in re-defining the nature of Canadian federalism, Quebec was not far behind. A powerful central government, which encouraged the habitant to identify with the larger Canadian nation, threatened not only the French language, but, according to the logic of Quebec, the Catholic religion as well.[25] Yet a weak central government was pregnant with difficulties for the French-speaking Catholics outside Quebec who looked to Ottawa for protection. Quebec therefore soon found itself torn. On the one hand, it espoused a separate, even isolationist, point of view; on the other, it saw itself as a religious and national fatherland within North America, which together with the federal government would protect French Catholic interests in the rest of Canada. The first view neutralized the second, and Quebec and Ontario gradually weakened the central government to the point where it was either powerless or reluctant to act. To heed the pleas of Quebec on the school question was to antagonize Ontario; to give in to pressures from Ontario, as in the earlier Jesuit Estates question, was to antagonize Quebec.

Even in more favourable political circumstances, the federal government would have found it difficult to rule in the minority's favour. The situation in the Territories was changing rapidly. Even though depressed economic conditions had held back the anticipated influx of population, the majority who did come expected the shortest possible passage through the pioneer stage, followed by the establishment of improved versions of institutions experienced elsewhere. It was only a matter of time before impatience with full-time, non-professional educational personnel, let alone non-professional personnel able to devote only part-time attention to school needs and costs, would arise. Professionalism in education was beginning to spread in the American midwest, and both Regina newspapers had already suggested a greater role for the teaching profession in the management of schools.[26] But professional personnel would undoubtedly increase school costs, necessitat-

ing increased state aid and more irksome questions about teachers' qualifications and academic standards from tax-conscious politicians. The *interna*
of schools managed by an independent denominational board with a large
annual budget would then be a perennial source of church-state tension.

A fundamental issue – ignored in both the memorandum and the minority's
petitions – was being raised: How was a democratic society to establish
effective popular control over public school expenditures? It could not be
maintained that the separate school clause determined the administrative
arrangement for territorial schools, and merely to insist on a return to the
status quo of an earlier period was not sufficient. The Board of Education
and most of its administrative personnel had not been specialists. As conscientious parents and politicians, as businessmen and tradesmen, as priests
and ministers, all were educators in their own right. But for them schools
were institutions they supervised, inspected, and administered on a part-time
basis. It may be that the territorial legislators who opposed religious and
non-professional influences in the schools were insufficiently grateful to the
Catholic clergy for their services on behalf of education in the early days.
But the ingratitude of the legislators was not the substantive issue.

Substantive was the steady growth of educational expenditures from 1888
to 1892 (Table 2), until approximately one-half of the federal grant supported schools. Abolition of the Board of Education and an increase in
professional personnel were perhaps inevitable to make the best use of the
available funds. A larger Catholic population might have delayed the step,
but continued denominational influence in education, once school costs rose,
would have required a 'blending of State and Church control'[27] similar to
that in Quebec, a system which was alien to the temperament of most
Canadians outside Quebec ever since the days of the Family Compact in
Upper Canada. The territorial situation therefore was not the simple picture
of broken promises and political expediency the memorandum presented.
But the men who wrote it were intense participants in the drama unfolding
in Manitoba and the North-West and in no position to advance balanced
points of view. 'I feel how unpleasant I may be considered in urging so per-
sistently the rights of our people,' Taché wrote Thompson, 'but I am their
Archbishop and I must look for the salvation of their souls and mine.'[28]

Whatever the federal government's decision, either the majority or the
minority would obviously have been disappointed. Obviously, too, the government would have to justify its decision before Parliament, and Wilfrid
Laurier and his lieutenant in Quebec, Israel Tarte, carefully prepared the
opposition's case: 'It is evident,' Laurier wrote to Senator Scott, 'that the
Government are now in a serious quandary and have their hands full.'[29] To

TABLE 2

Federal expenditure on territorial schools as percentage of total federal 'supply' in the North-West Territories, 1888–9 to 1894–5*

Year	Federal expenditure on territorial schools	Total federal 'supply' in the North-West	Per cent
1888–89	$ 71,025.73	$161,269.39	44
1889–90	70,320.15	150,044.01	47
1890–91	126,922.49	233,824.00	54
1891–92	100,941.76	228,011.06	44
1892–93	88,177.30	245,378.53	36
1893–94	42,903.50	261,026.19	16
1894–95	83,751.01	287,184.54	29

*SOURCE: Reports of the Auditor General of Canada for the years 1888–9 to 1894–5, *CSP*, sessions of 1889 to 1895 inclusive

soften the blow Sir Adolphe Caron sent Taché a long letter defending the government's decision, saying he had reason to hope the assembly would heed the committee's request, but that calmness and prudence had to prevail or the future would be darker still.[30]

The government had reason to be concerned. Bishop Grandin (back from Europe) and Father Lacombe were busily preparing the ground for a new petition, this time from the Catholic hierarchy in Canada.[31] Taché's memorandum was distributed *en masse* and won Bishop Laflèche's immediate approval. Many would now realize, he wrote Taché, that the strife was not between Catholics and Protestants, who had hitherto always been on such good terms, but between Christians and free thinkers or atheists, who wished to impose their systems of godless schools on Christians.[32] Bishop J.M. Emard of Valleyfield, designated to represent the Quebec hierarchy at St Boniface, arrived on 5 April and together with Taché and Grandin drew up the petition.[33] By 20 April all bishops in Quebec and Ontario had signed it and Archbishop Joseph Duhamel of Ottawa was ready to present it to Parliament. The government, Lacombe reported to Grandin, was in very hot water. But the hierarchy, too, had to be careful. If it were checked, Duhamel confided to Lacombe, it would lose what little influence it still retained.[34]

Meanwhile, on 20 March McCarthy introduced in Parliament his fourth bill to give the assembly control of the school and language questions,[35] and next day Tarte, in requesting copies of all correspondence bearing on the school question in the west, berated the French-Canadian cabinet members for supporting a government that had rejected disallowance. The minority could expect little from Regina, for Haultain had already indicated no changes would be made. Davin, the only territorial member to debate the school question in 1894, countered that Haultain could not commit the assembly because the North-West was still without party government. Moreover, in view of the strong sentiment for local autonomy, disallowance would have led to agitation for Manitoba's school legislation.[36] From the exchange it would be difficult to say whether Tarte was more disturbed by the territorial minority's fate or by the perplexing fact that the Conservative government had still not fallen on the school question. Davin, on the other hand, leaned heavily on the government's report, and from the outset political considerations were very much in evidence.

Senator Lougheed made his only statement on 5 April. Senator Perley did not speak. The grant of additional powers to the assembly had enabled the executive committee to dispense with the Board of Education. Regulations of a more modern and advanced character followed, which the territorial superintendent assured him had made no change in the separate schools. The 1892 Ordinance was within the assembly's rights, as the committee had shown, and to disturb it 'might create greater animosity than at present exists.' The appropriate time for federal interference, he suggested, was 'where a province has clearly exceeded its powers or where so manifest a wrong has been done that it must be obvious to the entire public, as contradistinguished from those controversial questions which are constantly arising in the provinces between different sects.'[37]

Debate in the Commons resumed on 18 April, with Davin introducing a mysterious letter, dated 4 April 1894, from an anonymous 'gentleman from the North-West.' The letter reported an interview between Goggin and the sisters at the Lacombe separate school in Calgary:

The Readers are not objected to by the Roman Catholic teachers in the schools I have visited. The Sisters in the Calgary Convent pronounced them very good Readers; and Sister Greene, the mother superioress, said the history was an excellent book. She spoke quite strongly in its favour ... I asked each whether any change in the work had been caused through the action of the Legislature of the session of 1892 or 1893; and each said that there was no change except that of the Readers in the higher class. They said it was not what had happened, but what may happen that they feared.

Davin, an Irish-born lawyer and journalist who emigrated to Canada when twenty-nine and eleven years later (1883) established Assiniboia's first newspaper, the *Regina Leader,* found himself in a difficult situation and with a reputation as the North-West's most brilliant orator-politician appealed to all sides at once. First, he was disturbed by the lack of trust shown by the letter in 'the powers that be.' The North-West would not stand for other parts of Canada (Ontario or Quebec) being used as a 'fulcrum ... to move a weight for us in the North-West Territories.' As an Anglican and a good friend of Archbishop Taché, he was also personally convinced that the best education was 'shot through and through with religious teaching,' and was disappointed that the four religious representatives on council had no vote. (En route to Ottawa he had confessed similar views to Taché at St Boniface.[38]) As a strong Conservative, however, he insisted that the 1892 Ordinance had changed little, as Haultain, the committee's report, and even Taché's memorandum had shown, and thus the furore in Quebec and in the House had 'the paltry purpose of trying to snatch a party victory.'[39]

The debate rapidly degenerated into a contest for political advantage. On 26 April Sir John Thompson entered the fray to make four main points in support of the Privy Council's report. First, the petitioners had 'obviously mistaken views' of the regulations in force before and after the 1892 Ordinance was passed. Haultain's letters showed how little disallowance would have changed the situation. Second, with 'assertions ... made on one side and denied on the other,' it was no help to be told that 'we produce such [regulations] as have been made; but do not look there for our grievances, because our grievances may arise in the future.'

Upon every one of these points there is a positive disagreement as to the facts. Surely the onus lay upon those who raised the objections; and, although we would not let the question turn upon the rule as to the burden of proof, where there was time for inquiry, let me call attention to the fact that ... not until November did we receive a petition, eleven months having elapsed since it [the school ordinance] was passed and ten months after it was received here ... There was barely time to investigate what appeared on the subject in half a dozen volumes of ordinances and half a dozen regulations, and there was certainly no time then to await an answer ... by His Grace of St Boniface, in response to the reply which had come from the Executive of the Territories ... Therefore, it seemed to me plainly the obligation of the Governor in Council to decline to disallow under these circumstances.[40]

The submission of petitions, then, was badly timed. The minority, however, had nothing to fear; Parliament had 'plenary powers' regarding the Territories. While the disallowance of provincial statutes was limited to the immediate exercise of power, in the North-West '... we have the power from day to day, and from year to year, to correct any substantial grievances found to exist there, if the Legislature should turn – though I am sure it would not – a deaf ear to those complaints.'[41] The government, then, based its decision not to disallow on Haultain's assurances, on insufficient proof of injury, on the delay in forwarding petitions, and on Ottawa's continuing plenary power. Wilfrid Laurier said little; Tarte's motion asked for a return of the very documents he wished to examine before going on record.[42]

The Catholic clergy were much involved in the political discussion in Ottawa from the beginning. Asked by an *Ottawa Free Press* reporter to comment on Davin's remarks that recent legislation had changed little, Father Lacombe replied 'with much vim: "It is a lie – we have schools in name but not in fact." '[43] Davin, in the House, refused to believe the Ottawa report: '... even if he said it, I would put it down to the anger of the moment, and it would not lessen my respect for that self-devoted and self-sacrificing missionary."[44] Father Leduc published an open letter to Davin, dated 6 May, and attributed Goggin's separate school visit to him, declaring it not to be in Goggin's interest to find grievances, but 'to surprise the noble religious simplicity of the sisters, incapable of suspecting any cunning designs.' He detailed the visit, quoting in full a letter he had received from Sister Mary Greene, the mother superior:

The person alluded to as having written ... to Mr Davin must be Mr Goggin, as he made an official visit on the 19th and 20th March and examined the school. He inquired, among other things, if any material change had been made in the school, while enforcing the late laws. We replied that we had made none except we were using the Ontario readers in the higher standards, there having been no other means for children to pass the approaching examinations.

He asked also if we had any objections to Swinton's History [required reading, in addition to Buckley and Robertson, of candidates for the second- and first-class non-professional teachers' certificates], and we answered that we did not know the work sufficiently to give our opinion for or against it. We told him that we liked Robertson & Buckley's history, as it was well compiled and less bigoted than other histories.

Mr Goggin did not question about any of the other books, but he concluded from what we said that we approved of all the others, both school and text books. Had he, for instance, asked what we thought of Browning's educational series[45] I would have answered that it was an infamous production fit only for the fire.

When Mr Goggin spoke of the good will of the Government I told him I had no confidence in their sentiments, that they were drawing a circle around us, and by pulling and tightening it gradually they hoped to ensnare us completely.

The books now used in the school, textbook excepted [?], are not objectionable, or very slightly so, but since we have no longer the power to choose our books or refuse those imposed on us we are, in a position, made to accept any book however much it may be in contradiction to our religious or moral tendencies, and this apprehension is the fear which Mr Davin makes so light of.[46]

Davin published Leduc's letter and his own reply in the *Leader* on 24 May. He denied that Goggin's visit was a trap for the sisters: 'That my informant truly reported what the Rev. Sister M. Greene said her letter quoted by you, confirms.' Davin's letter was generally conciliatory, however. Every profession produced its own habit of thought and the habit of the ecclesiastic was 'an absolute temper,' stemming from the fact that 'theology is the sphere of the absolute.' Men therefore may be great statesmen and poor theologians and ecclesiastics 'great in their own sacred walk, but yet, somewhat wanting when they come to act as statesmen.' Leduc did not comment; he had already told Royal that the minority was entitled to expect more from Thompson, whose speech was pitiful.[47]

Meanwhile Thompson presented the hierarchy's petition to Parliament on 9 May,[48] after interviewing Archbishop Duhamel at the episcopal residence.[49] The petition dealt mainly with Manitoba and was signed by Cardinal Taschereau, seven archbishops, and twenty-two bishops. As the assembly had still not reacted to the government's report, the petition merely asked the governor-general-in-council to transmit the hierarchy's views to the lieutenant-governor in order that, 'by amending ordinances, redress should be given to meet the grievances of which the Catholics of the North-West complain.' The petition was moderate in tone. It explained that Manitoba's school policies had been 'partly' followed in the North-West and that the 'compact' and 'promises' made when Manitoba and the Territories entered Confederation were 'broken' by both governments, even though the assurances and guarantees had been given 'in the name and by the authority of Her Majesty.'[50]

The reference above was undoubtedly to two documents. The first was Governor-General Sir John J. Young's Proclamation, 6 December 1869, which included this passage: 'By her majesty's authority I do assure you [the Catholics in the Red River settlement] that on the union with Canada all your civil and religious rights and privileges will be respected.' The second document – an 'autograph' letter given to Taché by Young on 16 February 1870, before he left Ottawa for the Red River – had instructed Taché to state, 'with the utmost confidence, that the imperial government has no intention of acting otherwise than in perfect good faith towards the inhabitants of the North-West. The people may rely that respect and attention will be extended to the different religious persuasions; ...'[51] But what the clergy considered a 'compact,' parliamentarians like David Mills viewed as 'policy.' In 1894, for example, the house heard the following exchange:

Mr AMYOT. Does the hon. gentleman attach no importance to the promises given by ... Sir John Young?

Mr MILLS (Bothwell). I attach no importance to any one's promises; I attach importance to the constitution itself ... We have decided at different times that this [the inclusion of a separate school clause] is the best means of securing the settlement of the country and its contentment, and of avoiding the differences and conflicting opinions on the subject of religion in this Parliament, and I believe we decided rightly. I see no reason why we should change that policy; I believe it is the proper policy to pursue; but it is not a compact under the terms of the British North America Act, as the terms entered into with the provinces of Ontario and Quebec constitute a compact. It is a matter of policy, as a matter of policy we have supported it ...[52]

The Thompson government did not reply to the hierarchy's petition until 26 July, three days after the session ended. Meanwhile Lacombe informed Taché that many in the east were of the opinion that Taché himself should make a supreme effort to come to Ottawa.[53] The archbishop, virtually on his death-bed, could not leave St Boniface. However, he did write two long letters, one to Davin[54] and one to Thompson,[55] in which he took strong exception to their remarks in the House. Davin prepared a twenty-page memorandum in reply[56] and Thompson made marginal notations on the archbishop's letter. The Thompson-Taché discussion is presented in Table 3.

The three men covered the old arguments again, Taché's letter to Davin differing only in its severe and lengthy criticism of Browning's *Educational Theories*, a history of educational ideas which the Protestant section had first recommended for its teachers in March 1886 and which the Catholic section had accepted in September 1891.[59] Concerned to provide that 'single page or extract' which Davin had found lacking in the minority's textbook complaints,[60] Taché censured Browning for eulogizing the Jansenists, for praising Luther, for exalting Rousseau for 'the very theory which is conducive to the destruction of religion and all social order,' for presenting Voltaire as 'a benevolent man ... who little deserved the bad reputation with which he is branded in history and society,' for acclaiming Rabelais and Montaigne, and for rejecting the Jesuit system of education as 'very inferior and undesirable.'

Davin read the book 'carefully' and devoted almost half of his memorandum to it, presenting Browning's treatment of each subject criticized by Taché to show that the letter was either mistaken or biased. His own opinion frequently followed, as in Taché's treatment of Voltaire:

The eminent writer [Taché] says further: 'Then comes Voltaire who is represented as a benevolent man ever ready to sacrifice himself in the defence of innocence or weakness and who little deserved the bad reputation with which he is branded in history and society.'
Only a few words are devoted by Browning to Voltaire (p. 134). They are as follows: 'The effect of Voltaire and Rousseau on the revolution was very different. Voltaire by nature a benevolent man ever ready to sacrifice himself in the defence of innocence or weakness *spent his energies in destructive criticism*, and has obtained the reputation of a cold heartlesness [*sic*] which he little deserved. Rousseau, weak, sentimental and selfish, poured out in his writings that universal philanthropy, that love for the human race and sympathy with its sufferings which he never showed in any action of his life. Thus his influence was much deeper and has been more lasting than that of Voltaire.' This is all that is said of Voltaire. Could a condemnation of Rousseau be stronger? If the writer [Browning] leans, it is to a condemnation of Voltaire as a thinker. His benevolence is a matter of history. Do we not see today, agnostics who are benevolent. That a Deist may and can be and often is benevolent is a fact. Strong believers are often wanting in benevolence, which is a natural virtue.[61]

In the heat of battle it was not strange to have churchmen condemn ideas out of context and politicians assume the role of moral theorists.

Debate in the Commons on the North-West school question resumed on 16 July.[62] When the House adjourned at two in the morning it had defeated two amendments and listened to thirteen speakers, including Laurier and Thompson. McCarthy triggered the discussion with the usual resolution to give the assembly control over education. In Calgary, he said, invoking the economy argument, the cost per pupil, based on daily average attendance, was $29.53 in Catholic separate schools and only $18.65 in Protestant public schools; in Prince Albert the figures were $48.58 and $33.55 respectively. Colonel Samuel Hughes, the Ontario Orangeman 'with a fighting look in his eye & a desperate opponent of all Separate Schools,'[63] wished a stronger resolution. The assembly should pass no laws 'permitting or authorizing or recognizing the teaching or the practising of any creed, or theology, or sectarian forms in any educational institution receiving public support.' Children should be educated entirely in a non-theological context. Hughes's lone

TABLE 3

Thompson's remarks in the House (26 April)	Taché's replies (30 May)	Thompson's marginal notations
1 Neither Thompson nor any of his colleagues had received any complaints until late in October 1893	1 Judge Rouleau had written 'to one of your colleagues'	1 'I never saw it until after passing the o. c.[57] in the Abp's reply. It was unofficial and merely stated the gratuitous & assumed position that the Ordinance was *ultra vires*'
2 Several of the complaints were based on regulations passed before the 1892 Ordinance was enacted	2 The regulations complained of were 'all the result of the Ordinance of 1892, either in themselves or in the radical change, brought by the new law, in their application.' The circumstances of the old regulations were 'so completely different' that after the 1892 Ordinance passed the same regulations 'lost their primitive character and restraint; the securities, by which they were surrounded, have been changed into real dangers for want of power of control on the part of Catholics ... Surely, passengers, on board of a vessel, will object to her crew throwing all the ballast overboard and removing the rudder; and will not be satisfied with the assurance, given by the captain, that the vessel, being the same, must be considered as safe as before and that there is no reason for complaint'	2 'False and Evasive.' 'A trick of expression' 'Then the change was not made by the Ordinance but by circumstances. Disallowance wd. not have changed the circumstances' 'They asked that the ship be condemned – not that the ballast be restored. I sought to have the ballast restored'
3 Catholic leaders, because of zeal or erroneous information, were misled in their complaints	3 'So, the House is advised, by its Right Honorable Leader, to consider, as over zealous and misled, the Catholic Bishops, Judges, priests, lawyers, members of the Legislative Assembly, school trustees, members of the old board ... and to rely only on the word of men who take no interest in the same schools from a Catholic point of view'	3 'Because their statements were found to be contrary to the fact'

TABLE 3 *(Concluded)*

Thompson's remarks in the House (26 April)	Taché's replies (30 May)	Thompson's marginal notations
4 No member of a religious order already teaching in the Territories was affected by the new normal school regulations	4 Sister St Lucie of Battleford had her second-class non-professional certificate, obtained at Nicolet, Quebec, in June 1893, exchanged at par on condition she taught with 'third class standing' until the next normal session opened in September 1894, presumably at Regina[58]	4 'These ladies are not teaching except under non-professional certif. They are not affected'
5 No objectionable textbooks had been introduced	5 Caron, Forget, Prince, and Boucher had complained to the executive committee because 'certain books were struck off and others were put on'	5 'When?' 'The books were changed at the instance of the Catholic members of the Board'
6 Taché's letters did not indicate any regulation that created a practical grievance	6 On 2 January 1894, he had referred to the 1893 regulations as an instance of what could be done, noting that delay would have proved nothing in favour of the ordinance. Oliver himself had complained about the regulations in the *Bulletin*, as the quoted extracts showed	6 'This is an expression anticipating what *may be done*. All that had been done was commended in that letter' 'The quotation is a wicked piece of garbling'
7 French was not abolished in the schools	7 French was 'virtually' abolished and was, in fact, abolished where 'the regulations are concerned'	7 No comment
8 Because Protestant parents in some districts might send their children to separate schools, school prayers could be waived and religious instruction deferred until the last moment	8 There could be no 'better proof that the Catholic schools have been practically abolished as such.' Schools for the benefit of Catholic children, supported by Catholic parents, were to lose their 'religious character' because ' ... per chance, there may be a Protestant child in the neighborhood'	8 No comment

supporter was Walter W. McDonald, who had succeeded to East Assiniboia early in 1893 after Dewdney became lieutenant-governor of British Columbia.

Laurier differed from McCarthy 'in toto': the issue was not the merit of separate schools; it was 'simply the question of carrying on our system of Confederation upon the basis which was adopted in 1864, and maintained in 1875.' During the confederation discussions the future legislatures of Ontario and Quebec were 'deprived' of control over education to protect the minority in both provinces. In 1875 the territorial legislature was placed upon 'absolutely the same footing,' 'without a word of dissent from any hon. member on either side of the House.' Thompson, Daly, and Laurier's fellow-Liberal, Mills, also opposed McCarthy. Mills, a participant in the 1875 debate, refused, however, to follow Laurier on the origin of separate schools in the North-West:

In these provinces [Ontario and Quebec] they are protected under the constitution; they cannot be interfered with by the Local Legislature. But in the North-West Territories, as the hon. Minister [Daly] has said, it has been a matter not of right, not of guarantee to any particular class of the population, but a matter of policy. They were introduced with a view of preventing conflict in this House upon the subject of separate schools and for the reason that they were introduced there they should be maintained as long as these Territories are under the control of this Parliament. When this Parliament has discharged its duties and when the people of these Territories have received the population to entitle them to enter the union they must assume the responsibility of deciding for themselves under the British North America Act how far they shall maintain the principle of separate schools or maintain the non-denominational system.

Thompson, after reminding McCarthy that 'toleration was expensive,' presented yet another interpretation of how the question would be settled in the future: 'What the constitution of the future provinces shall be, in view of the pledges which have been referred to, or in view of any other set of circumstances, will be for Parliament to decide when it decides to create those provinces.'

It was clear, then, that Laurier believed no change was possible in the status of territorial separate schools; Mills (and Daly) believed that the provincial legislature would have the final decision in the matter; and Thompson believed that the federal Parliament would have the last word. Davin, like McCarthy, would have had the assembly deal with the matter immediately:

I made a point of calling on an eminent ecclesiastic [Taché], whose recent death I deplore, to talk with him on this very subject ... His Grace said to me that if, as regards the schools of Manitoba, they had thrown themselves on the Local Government and the Local Legislature, they would have been better off. I will give the House my reason. I do not think there exists in the Territories any such feeling against separate schools as there is against being deprived of the power to which they believe they are entitled in accordance with the spirit of the British North America Act. It is not merely this Parliament depriving them of this power, but when they are deprived of that power ... because of an influence and force used by other branches of our federation, this irritates the Territories, just as it would irritate any province if menaced with the sentiments of another province.

On division McCarthy's amendment was defeated 114 to 21, the territorial members splitting their vote on a school or language issue for the first time: Davin supported McCarthy, Davis and McDonald voted with the majority, and Macdowall abstained. Thus the North-West school question was disposed of at Ottawa for a whole decade, even though it was always near the surface whenever debate on the Manitoba school question resumed.

With the hierarchy's petition still before it, the federal government passed an order-in-council on 26 July[64] transmitting a second Privy Council committee report to Regina. Catholic missionary work, the report declared, gave 'a strong claim for generous recognition' of Catholic rights in western Canada, and the assembly was again requested to take 'speedy measures' to provide redress, should 'any well founded complaint or grievance be ascertained.'[65] Archbishop Taché did not live to see the government's reply. His death late in June came, as Leduc remarked to Grandin, at a time when the minority seemed to need him the most.[66]

Bishop Laflèche, in his funeral oration, represented Taché as a martyr in the cause of Catholic education – the cause that the child belongs not to the state, but to the parents (as God's gift) in the natural order and to the church (the child's mother through the sacrament of baptismal regeneration) in the supernatural order. To claim otherwise was to fall into that

... erreur qui a été proclamée à l'époque de la grande révolution française au dernier siècle par les révolutionnaires qui avaient entrepris de détruire l'ordre social et chrétien dans notre ancienne Mère patrie, la France. Cette erreur découle de la proclamation de prétendus droits de l'homme qui n'allaient à rien moins qu'à chasser Dieu de la société et à constituer, pour l'avenir, l'ordre social exclusivement sur l'autorité humaine.[67]

In the Territories newspapers had generally taken the view that no government would dare to disallow the school ordinance. They were less certain, after the February report, that Ottawa would not pressure Premier Haultain into granting concessions in exchange for more liberal financial aid.[68] His movements therefore were carefully watched and his statements given wide publicity. On 5 March he addressed the Junior Liberal-Conservative Association in Calgary and denied that any outside pressure could make him alter the ordinance. 'This is a matter of Territorial right. I take my stand without dictation from anyone.' At Medicine Hat, on his way east, he dismissed 'the growling' in Quebec: '... I do not know that we need bother ourselves much about it. I, at least, am losing no sleep over it.' The territorial government's attitude, he added, was not negative: 'We don't say we will not remedy anything. We simply say there is nothing to remedy.'[69] If the newspapers had intended to commit the premier, his opposition to change could hardly have been more explicit. Nevertheless, Governor Mackintosh continued to assure Thompson that changes would be made. Goggin not only was prepared to recommend one or two Catholics 'with votes' to council, but was also willing to 'attend' the teaching sisters at their Calgary convent 'personally' if they came to his public lectures, 'where a special place would be reserved for them.' Mackintosh and Thompson agreed that behind the April resignation of Inspector Gillies was 'the hierarchy objecting to his acting under the present ordinance.' It was, Mackintosh thought, a 'foolish' move because it only opened the way for a Protestant successor, as Gillies was the minority's 'only' qualified candidate.[70]

A month before the session opened in Regina, Grandin appealed to Mackintosh to induce the members 'to change in their laws that which is contrary to the law of God and Nature and to the constitution of the Country.' Primary children from French and Indian homes could not answer inspectors who spoke only English, and the performance led some to accuse the sisters of incompetence. The minority could hardly acquiesce before such laws: 'We are not in any case a conquered people – we entered confederation by agreement ... To-day we form two parties, one being oppressed by the other, and what have we done, I ask, to deserve such treatment.'[71] On the eve of the session Leduc sent Taché's memorandum to Prince and advised him that, 'well penetrated with the document, you will find invincible arms' to uphold the minority's claims.[72] Leduc also appealed to Haultain's 'integrity' for justice. Taché's memorandum 'has never been refuted, and it never will [be], except by a radical amendment of the Ordinance 1892.'[73]

In his opening remarks on 2 August Governor Mackintosh asked the assembly to receive Taché's opinions 'with that moderation, that consideration, and that generous sympathy to which his life's works so well entitle him.'[74] The school question, however, was not raised until 24 August, when Prince asked whether the government intended to replace Caron, who had resigned from the Council of Public Instruction on 18 April 1894,[75] five days after Gillies left the inspectoral staff. Haultain replied in the affirmative, even though the need for a replacement 'was not felt.'[76] On 29 August, with dissolution a week away, Prince prodded Haultain into admitting that the minority's complaints were being considered and 'such changes as might be found necessary' would follow.[77] Next day Prince and Clinkskill moved that the school committee examine and report on the documents before the assembly, and that 'ample opportunity be afforded to representatives of the complainants for appearing and fully stating their case.'[78]

Accordingly, on 31 August Prince, Leduc, and Forget presented a memorandum to the school committee. It declared, for the first time, that *under section 14 of the* NWT *Act* the minority was 'guaranteed' the right to control, manage, and inspect its schools, license and certify its teachers, select its textbooks, use French as a language of instruction, and open its schools with prayer. The minority also had 'the right,' hitherto ignored in *official* protests, to establish schools 'with boundaries irrespective of those of Public School Districts already established.'[79] A council of public instruction 'with direct responsibility to the people' was acceptable, provided the Catholic members had a vote. Normal sessions were admissible, if held in one of the minority's schools in terms of a resolution by Mitchell and F.E. Wilkins (Red Deer)on 29 August, favouring sessions at Moosomin, Prince Albert, or Edmonton when six applicants for third-class professional certificates were available in any year, and at Regina and Calgary for second-class certificates 'when practicable.'[80] Moreover, the memorandum added, 'female lay candidates, Protestant as well as Catholic,' would be welcome. The regulations prescribing Ontario Readers and Buckley and Robertson's history were to be repealed. Finally, if Catholic inspectors were refused, then at least one 'of the two annual inspections required' was to be by a Catholic. To justify the latter Leduc presented[81] the complaints of the St Albert Catholic public school trustees to a recent inspection of their school.[82] It was clear that the desperate Catholics, realizing they had little to lose, had finally seized the offensive. How much of their former position they could recover remained to be seen.

In the evening the executive committee came in for a heavy round of criticism in the House. Even though the people received the school ordinance with 'apparent satisfaction,' there was, Brett said, 'a great deal of discontent' concerning its administration. Oliver's editorial on normal sessions 'reflected the sentiments of almost all intelligent people.' The committee, in addition, had still to modify the ordinance 'respecting the selection of four persons to deliberate with them on educational affairs.' Oliver defended Haultain, notwithstanding the severity of the *Bulletin*'s criticism, but McKay and Tweed advocated a more conciliatory policy towards the minority. The latter, a grand master in the Masonic order, was disturbed by the number of petitions opposing the ordinance sent to Ottawa by certain people in the Territories. Prince, Boucher, and Clinkskill criticized the council's membership and the manner in which its meetings had been held.[83]

Haultain said nothing in the House and little before the school committee. On 4 September the Reverend J.C. Sinnett, Reginald Rimmer, a lawyer, and John McCarthy, a merchant (all of Regina), and E. Bourgeois, a teacher from Duck Lake, criticized the readers and histories before the school committee.[84] Next day Haultain introduced three changes which became part of the school ordinance in 1894. In special cases the lieutenant-governor-in-council would allow school districts to exceed their boundaries, when 'all' the resident ratepayers had agreed to the change 'in writing' (s. 4); no general regulations respecting schools, teachers, textbooks, or normal sessions would henceforth be adopted or amended, 'except at a general meeting of the Council of Public Instruction duly convened for the purpose' (s. 2); and trustees could direct schools to open with prayer (s. 7). Leduc ignored the first change and described the second as 'futile and puerile.' The third was permissive, not obligatory, and children were still 'forbidden' to recite the Hail Mary, the Apostles' Creed, and the Ten Commandments.[85]

The school committee's report, submitted on 6 September, endorsed Haultain's changes and refused to sanction separate schools outside the limits of public school districts. Missing the point of the Catholic objections entirely, the committee declared that the law[86] already permitted any person not within a school district to apply to the trustees of any organized school district to have property not already included in any other district assessed for education. This only enlarged a separate school district until an adjacent public school district could be organized. It was 'inexpedient,' the committee also thought, to change the regulations governing the teaching of French. Nor would it recommend a change in the history text 'until a more desirable book for general use' was secured. Should any reasonable objections be raised against any selection in the readers, such selection 'shall not be prescribed.' To direct the council of Public Instruction on school inspections was inadvisable, but the council could 'accede' to the request for Catholic normal sessions under the Mitchell-Wilkins resolution, when practicable.[87]

Prince and Boucher, determined to take the issue down to the wire, countered with three additional amendments to the ordinance and three resolutions, which the minority would accept as a fair settlement of its grievances. It should be possible to create a separate school district outside the limits of a public school district; to use English as a language of instruction, 'except in schools where the Council of Public Instruction shall otherwise order'; and to recite prayers when school *and* classes opened. The resolutions recommended that 'any' regulation prescribing Buckley and Robertson's history and the Ontario Readers be withdrawn; that normal sessions, as in the Mitchell-Wilkins resolution, be granted to the sisters, allowing them 'in view of their peculiar circumstances' to teach with non-professional certificates until they had the required six candidates; and that every Catholic school be inspected alternately by a Protestant and Catholic inspector. The suggested changes were defeated nineteen to three, with Prince, Boucher, and Clinkskill alone supporting them.[88] Tweed's motion for second reading then passed on an identical vote. It remained for Oliver to add the last touch. With the school bill up for third reading, he and Magrath failed to delete Haultain's proposal that no general regulations be passed without the sanction of the whole council.[89]

Except in South Regina, the school question, despite the attention it had received at Ottawa and Regina, was not a major issue in the territorial election that followed on 31 October. Haultain took a very active part in the campaign at Regina, openly supporting J.W. Smith against Daniel Mowat, whom he continued to associate 'with parties opposed to the members having advanced ideas on the school question.'[90] Mowat blamed Haultain's defeat in 1892 on his own 'haughty, cold, and distant' manner, which resulted in his not consulting Clinkskill on the school bill.[91] Mowat resented the intervention deeply and accused Haultain of neglecting administrative duties for which he was paid 'so liberally.'[92] With Smith silent on the school question, the relentless attacks of the influential Haultain may have aroused electoral sympathy for the underdog Mowat, who defeated Smith handily (310–237).[93] Elsewhere in Assiniboia the school question, although discussed occasionally, had no apparent influence on the final results.

In Saskatchewan Betts boldly declared his support for national schools and taunted his opponent in Prince Albert East to declare himself. The latter refused but there is no evidence that this contributed to his defeat.[94] At Battleford, Clinkskill, who defended his support of separate schools on constitutional grounds,[95] won a narrow victory over Benjamin Prince, whose bilingual electoral advertisement ignored both the school and language questions.[96] In Alberta, Haultain and Oliver were again returned by acclamation, and the French Canadians at St Albert once more failed to field a resident candidate. Prince, opposed by Daniel Maloney (nominated by the Patrons of Industry), lost the election, chiefly because '... he was a professional man and a non-resident ... a strong cry in a purely farming constituency.'[97] The disappointed *Regina Standard* lauded Prince's courtesy, consideration, and geniality, and lamented: 'Who will now lead in the soul-stirring "Marsellaise" [*sic*] and mirth-provoking "Allouette" [*sic*]?'[98] Even though Leduc had told Grandin that Prince deserved the minority's encouragement and support for his work at Regina,[99] there is no evidence that the mission supported either candidate. The territorial election was, in fact, a rather dull affair. The impressions of an Ontario visitor were only slightly exaggerated: 'I have discovered one thing in the west, and that is that the row in Ontario and Quebec about racial and religious questions ... is pretty much confined to those provinces. In the Territories we have not heard a word about dual language or the separate schools ... The people seem to be too busy making a living to bother with such things.'[100]

The Catholic leaders said nothing publicly after the election. Privately, Lacombe wrote Grandin and criticized Leduc's performance at Regina.[101] Leduc himself was more pleased. The occasional and exclusive normal sessions for sisters in centres with convents were, he told Grandin, a significant achievement. So also was the fact that several assembly members had criticized the manner in which the school ordinance had been administered.[102] In keeping with his view that immediate steps be taken to secure further concessions, Leduc saw Haultain at Regina in October about the four non-voting members on council, but returned empty-handed.[103] Grandin, too, reminded Governor-General Lord Aberdeen of the minority's difficulties during a visit to St Albert in the same month.[104] At year's end, then, the minority had clearly not given up, though there was little room for optimism.

7

The school question becomes a permanent issue, 1895-6

In 1894 the North-West school question had had, at times, to share the national stage with the Manitoba school question; in 1895 the latter superseded it entirely. On 29 January the hopes of Manitoba's minority brightened momentarily as the judicial committee of the Privy Council ruled that the 1890 provincial legislation had indeed affected Catholic schools adversely and that an appeal to the governor-general-in-council was in order. Although pleased by the decision, Bishop Grandin complained to the new archbishop of St Boniface, the Quebec-born, thirty-nine-year-old Louis Philippe Adélard Langevin, that the territorial question was being ignored.[1] And in March, when Cardinal Ledochowski, prefect of the Sacred Congregation for the Propagation of the Faith, informed the Canadian hierarchy by letter that Rome fully supported its stand against neutral or godless schools in Manitoba,[2] Grandin, troubled by the lack of specific reference to the North-West, wrote to Louis N. Bégin, coadjutor to the archbishop of Quebec, Roman Catholic primate in Canada, outlining the territorial situation. He stressed, for the first time, the subject of provincial autonomy (then being revived in southern Alberta), which ten years later would involve the church and state in another major school crisis. A settlement in the Territories, he argued, would not only be less difficult to effect than in Manitoba, where the government was more independent, but it would be a useful precedent for Manitoba's case. Fully aware of the importance of provincial status, Grandin feared that, if Ottawa did not ensure a just territorial settlement before autonomy was granted, the minority's school rights would experience even greater difficulties in the future.[3]

However, the Manitoba situation deteriorated so rapidly that it all but wiped the territorial problem from the minds of Catholics in the rest of the country. Premier Greenway ignored the federal government's chastening remedial order (21 March), and when Parliament prorogued on 22 July, Sir Mackenzie Bowell, a former grand master in the Orange order and prime minister after Thompson's sudden death in December, was definitely committed to remedial legislation at the next session if Greenway remained adamant. During the parliamentary recess, when Bowell visited the west he was welcomed by the Catholics at St Albert and assured them that the government's policy would be 'adhered to and faithfully carried out let the consequences be what they may.' On a visit to the school he was greeted by 'a poetical recitation' given by six little girls, each dressed in white with a maple leaf on the shoulder surmounted by a gold letter spelling the name BOWELL. The girl bearing the letter 'E' recited the following stanza:

> I come, sir, EDUCATION is my name
>> My cause by you upheld enhances your fame.
> And I come though crushed, to lay at your feet
>> Gratitude's tribute. The duty is sweet.
> In this noble cause, so unjustly torn,
>> You upheld our rights throughout the storm.
> May your efforts be crowned and victory swell
>> The name and fame of Sir McKenzie Bowell.[4]

This was one of the few occasions on which the territorial school question received public attention, though Grandin was doing his best to keep it before the local authorities. When Governor Mackintosh and Premier Haultain toured the Territories in February, their visit to St Albert was strained. Haultain, Grandin thought, was ungracious and Mackintosh declared he had no authority to make promises on the volatile school question.[5] Mackintosh later wrote Grandin a warm personal letter from Regina, generous in praise of the clergy's industry and loyalty and solicitous of the minority's 'legitimate aspirations.'[6] Grandin's reply, equally effusive, instructed the governor on the dire social consequences of neutral schools, which could only prepare godless or indifferent people inclined towards socialism, anarchism, and the different utopias which are the real scourge of society. With many immigrants boasting a disbelief in both God and the devil, it was regrettable that statesmen of the time appeared to understand so little the importance of religious instruction.[7]

Grandin also continued to press Langevin. An Oblate as ultramontane as his predecessor, whose vicar he had been since July 1893, Langevin was as determined to reverse the secular tide in education without compromise. Deeply involved, however, in the controversy over Manitoba schools, he cautioned Grandin against overloading the government: a territorial settlement had to precede provincial autonomy, but little could be done until the Manitoba minority was on a solid footing. Grandin, in the meantime, could prepare his arms – a pamphlet relating the tyrannies of '*Sieur Goggin*' – to show how the territorial Catholics were practically in chains. The document would be published as soon as the Manitoba question was settled. Grandin hesitated. The work would be useful but Leduc, who was closest to the territorial school situation, suffered from inflammatory rheumatism and was reluctant to undertake it. Moreover, it would be difficult to obtain evidence for all the facts that should be included. Grandin's consent to the project, however, was only a matter of time. Concerned that the Territories might become the model for a settlement in Manitoba and aware that Senator Thomas Bernier and LaRivière both regarded the document important, even necessary (in view of still another North-West bill by McCarthy), he informed Langevin, late in June, that Leduc would make a supreme effort to produce the pamphlet.[8]

At Regina, for the third straight year the Council of Public Instruction issued no report. When Brett finally raised the matter in the assembly in 1896, Ross, a member of the executive committee, denied a report was needed because the council and committee were practically one and the committee reported to the assembly directly.[9] According to a brief report in the *Regina Leader*, the council met in Regina on 9 April 1895, with Forget and the Reverend J.C. Sinnett[10] representing the minority. The meeting was 'most harmonious' and agreed upon a 'secular' curriculum for 'all' schools. At another meeting on 9 July the August 1893 regulations governing teachers' certificates were modified slightly. First- and second-class certificates, issued in Canada or Britain since 1 January 1886, were acceptable, if the council deemed them satisfactory. This placed Quebec and Ontario certificates on the same footing for the first time. However, the regulation barring certificates issued by convents and religious teaching orders remained. A new series of supplementary readers was discussed, but when the Catholic representatives re-introduced the Metropolitan Readers, the executive committee rejected them 'unanimously' and the matter was dropped.[11]

The assembly passed no legislation in 1895 that affected Catholic educational interests and indeed the school question was hardly mentioned. More significant was the appearance of Leduc and Forget before the school committee on 19 September 'to declare publicly' that the existing ordinances and regulations of council 'never had, and shall never have the consent of the Catholic minority,' that the complaints of the previous year had not been redressed, and that annual protests would be lodged until the minority received justice.[12] Two days later a rather stormy exchange followed on the old problems of teacher certification and textbooks.[13] Leduc objected to Goggin's refusal to exempt the sisters from normal sessions 'under any pretext' and to Goggin's concession of a separate session in a convent only on the sisters' 'final and absolute refusal' to leave. Even then, only sisters who already held non-professional certificates issued at Regina were admitted.[14] Equally annoying were the temporary certificates granted to imported teachers. When Haultain referred to regulations excluding permanent certificates, Leduc admitted he referred to regulations passed in 1893, not those cited by the premier. Before July 1894, he declared, Manitoba and Ontario certificates issued after 1 January 1886 were exchanged at Regina for others 'of the same degree, and the same value.' Haultain refused to yield: 'We shall continue the temporary licences, and we shall not grant permanent certificates, except on the recommendation of our Inspectors.'[15]

From the available evidence it would appear that neither side was blameless. The government undoubtedly found it difficult to assess the credentials presented by some Catholic teachers. For example, what equivalence could a 'first class Model School Diploma' or a 'first class elementary English and French diploma' (both from Quebec) have in a region without diplomas, model schools, or 'English and French' certificates? What status could be given to teachers who brought an 'excellent professional certificate' from 'Dakota,' or who held a 'strong' certificate from the chairman of a nameless school board in Maine?[16] Such cases did not prove that the government was prejudiced against certificates 'guilty of bearing the stamp of anything Catholic and French,'[17] and the committee could hardly be blamed for dismissing Leduc's complaints. On the other hand, many of the difficulties might have been avoided had the authorities specified clearly when the certification regulations, adopted in August 1893, came into effect. The only date on those sent to Ottawa was '1894.'[18] Leduc, then, may well have been right that, before July 1894, all Manitoba and Ontario certificates were exchanged at par at Regina.

Leduc also objected to the council's 'flat refusal' to bring back the Metropolitan Readers. Haultain termed the readers an *'unfortunate choice'* because they did not 'correspond' to the work in territorial schools, being 'destined rather for religious instruction than for anything else.'[19] Leduc left Regina convinced he had clear proof of the territorial government's ill-will, even its hatred, towards Catholic schools and above all the teaching sisters.[20]

He had also obtained enough material to add another chapter to the pamphlet he was preparing.

The pamphlet, as we have seen, was the suggestion of Archbishop Langevin, to whom it was also dedicated. In the preface were supporting letters from Langevin, Grandin, and Bishop Grouard of Athabaska-Mackenzie,[21] though its purpose, contents, and date of completion were apparently Leduc's responsibility. The aim – to show that the territorial minority rejected the school system imposed on it and that the Manitoba minority should never accept a similar system[22] – was well taken, for on 17 July 1895 Davin had told the Commons he had 'pretty high authority' to state that the Manitoba minority would be content with the territorial school system.[23] Accordingly, the pamphlet dealt critically with all the usual subjects: the 1892 Ordinance, the Council of Public Instruction, inspection, textbooks, curriculum, and teacher education. Leduc also gave his version of what transpired when he and Forget appeared before the school committees in 1894 and 1895.

The pamphlet's release posed a serious problem for the minority. Completed in the fall of 1895, before the Manitoba issue was settled, it spared neither the territorial nor federal governments. Grandin himself termed it an acrimonious work, containing well-deserved epithets to be sure, which could only have a bad effect upon all anti-Catholics who could be won over to the Catholic cause. Langevin's opinion was similar,[24] and his decision not to release the pamphlet until after the federal election in June 1896, and its subsequent appearance in October, greatly undermined its impact. The fall of the Conservative government on the remedial bill made the school question unpalatable and the pamphlet anticlimactic; it was drowned, in fact, in the sorrow and embarrassment of political defeat. Grandin, in retrospect, thought it had little effect: no one had and, he believed, no one could reply to it, but it had not brought any great improvements that he could see.[25] Not having sanctioned the work, the archbishops who wrote Grandin were divided as to its merits. Only James V. Cleary (Kingston) and Duhamel were prepared to publicize it. Edouard C. Fabre (Montreal) counselled against lay circulation, and Bégin would limit circulation to the small number of public men who were intelligent, discreet and sincerely devoted to the Catholic cause. Cornelius O'Brien (Halifax) was most critical. It was 'too long' and 'sarcastic, continually insinuating wrong motives to the Council of Public Instruction and the Superintendent.' Moreover, '... no English speaking Protestant, and few English speaking Catholics will believe that the Freemasons, *as a body*, are at the bottom of the trouble.'[26]

Long before the pamphlet's release, Langevin took advantage of the consecration of Edmonton's General Hospital in mid-December 1895 to placate Grandin and aid the Manitoba cause by declaring that territorial Catholics 'were bound in conscience to fight to obtain here what they in Manitoba wanted, and were bound to have.' Only with their own books, normal schools, inspectors, and voting power on council would territorial Catholics have 'the same constitutional rights' as Catholics in Ontario. The address of the St Joachim trustees (read by Beck) showed that '... the laity were with the hierarchy on this question.'[27]

The Conservative *Calgary Herald*, undoubtedly embarrassed by the archbishop's open support of the Conservative government, represented the hierarchy as 'apparently set on creating a "school question" in the Territories': 'WAR IS DECLARED BY THE HIERARCHY ON OUR SCHOOL SYSTEM.'[28] Among the Catholic laity there was 'no dissatisfaction' with the existing school system and 'on general principles' it was 'well to let sleeping dogs lie.'[29] Langevin followed with several letters to the *Herald* under Father Fouquet's signature,[30] in which he defended the unity of view among clergy and laity and insisted that the hierarchy and clergy were not sowing discontent. Unmoved, the *Herald* warned the hierarchy not to arouse 'a powerful, nay, a preponderating class in this western community who, if they had their way would wipe out every separate school with one legislative stroke.'[31]

On 29 December the Reverend G.W. Dean, a Methodist minister in Edmonton, expressed surprise at the minority's 'bitterness.' He warned that Greenway might judge the territorial law to be as 'unpalatable' as Manitoba's and make compromise even more difficult.[32] The *Herald*, eager for a compromise that would save the government, was impressed by Dean and carried the *Winnipeg Tribune*'s editorial on his sermon.[33] From St Boniface Langevin wrote Grandin he was pleased with the results. Grandin encouraged him not to regret his remarks: the minority would always be blamed when it was necessary to condemn evil.[34] At Regina the government said little. Langevin's remarks, Neff told the *Manitoba Free Press*, had created 'much surprise,' considering that the minority 'already had as much as they could expect from the government in the way of schools.'[35]

II

Archbishop Langevin's revival of the North-West school question was a brief skirmish and of small consequence compared to the nation-wide attention the Manitoba issue now commanded. But the significance of developments in Manitoba for the Territories cannot be exaggerated. Once Parliament disciplined Manitoba the territorial minority would be in a good position to appeal for remedial legislation to dispose of the 1892 Ordinance. The latter, although not *ultra vires*, certainly did affect the minority's 'Right or Privilege ... in relation to Education' and, even though section 93(3) of the BNA Act referred specifically to provinces, an appeal from the Territories might prove successful. Manitoba's defeat would vindicate the act and perhaps even finally establish the federal government as the ultimate guardian of minority rights in education.

Of the many obstacles to the Manitoba remedial legislation, Laurier's opposition was probably the most serious. Father Lacombe therefore appealed to him in private on 20 January 1896: if the government fell, he warned, '... the Episcopacy and the clergy, united as one man, will rise to support those who may have fallen to defend us.'[36] Lacombe had four interviews with Laurier,[37] who warned him that Liberal support of the government's inadequate remedial bill could lead to virtual war. Within fifteen days of the bill's introduction, according to Laurier, the reaction would be so terrible as to set the country aflame. Already Lacombe himself had made Laurier appear as a knave of the church and Bishop Cameron of Nova Scotia had called him a hypocrite inspired by hell.[38]

On 11 February six weeks after Parliament opened, the government finally introduced its remedial bill. It granted separate schools supervised by an all-Catholic board of education, but, unlike the earlier remedial order, it denied the same schools public aid, even though it did exempt their supporters from double taxation. Unlike the order also, the bill gave Catholics the option of supporting Catholic or non-Catholic schools. A week later, Israel Tarte and the French-Canadian Liberals in the Commons, rankled by Lacombe's intervention, sent Archbishop Bégin a collective letter with generous extracts from Archbishop Taschereau's circular (18 July 1872), declaring that Catholics who disapproved of a law were free to choose the means to change it. Did the church, the members asked, approve Lacombe's letter and did the clergy really intend to oppose the Liberals at the forthcoming election?[39] Within two days, Lacombe's letter was released to the press, through ecclesiastical channels, according to one account, and through Liberal channels (Tarte and John W. Dafoe of the *Manitoba Free Press*), according to another.[40] Lacombe himself blamed Laurier and termed the act 'uncourteous and ungentlemanly.'[41] The source of the leak will probably never be known, but both sides had good reason to publicize the letter: the church because Laurier alone seemed to stand between the remedial bill and victory, and the Liberals because they disliked and feared church involvement in politics, especially in Quebec, and wished to place it in the worst possible light in the rest of the country.

From St Albert, Grandin, greatly concerned that continued support of the Conservatives might entail support of Haultain, asked Langevin to inform the government that he could never approve of him, an obstinate bigot and wretch who was the main cause of the minority's school difficulties.[42] He did not look forward to the election: if the sad consequences of universal suffrage were only understood, the minority might be delivered of them once and for all.[43] Nevertheless, he wrote Bowell an encouraging letter and was assured that the Manitoba minority had 'the absolute right ... to justice at our hands.'[44] Neither Grandin nor Langevin was initially upset by Lacombe's letter to Laurier. Lacombe, Grandin thought, was doing his best. If he should compromise himself, it was much better that he, rather than they, should do so.[45] Langevin agreed and hoped that God would aid them to win over the Liberal French Canadians.[46] Only when Lacombe's letter became the centre of newspaper controversy did Grandin become concerned that the blow might boomerang.[47]

In the debate on second reading of the remedial bill, which began on 3 March, the territorial members, apart from Davin, said little; all favoured the bill. Macdowall said he was pledged to support separate schools, and he and McDonald believed that public opinion in the Territories would sustain them. Davis made no effort to defend his stand, but Davin's defence on 19 March was clever. He had come prepared to oppose the bill, but with both parties favouring remedial legislation and differing only as to means (Laurier would consider remedial legislation should a commission of inquiry establish its need), a defeat for the government would hardly be a victory for provincial autonomy. He therefore decided to support the government and was pleased to learn from Mills that Wallace was mistaken in claiming that the remedial bill could affect either the territorial or British Columbia school systems.[48]

The federal government, late in March, made one last bid to negotiate a settlement with Greenway, and Grandin and Leduc were in St Boniface during the abortive Winnipeg conference.[49] Langevin left for the east on 7 April and from Ottawa informed Grandin that a combined Liberal and Conservative opposition had overwhelmed the bill. The former, in particular, dismayed him. By aiding the minority's tormentors, the Liberals behaved as religious and national apostates.[50] After interviews with the governor-general and Laurier and a letter to Sir Charles Tupper (soon to be prime minister), which described the remedial bill as 'a substantial workable and final settlement of the school question according to the constitution,'[51] Langevin returned to St Boniface on 18 May, just in time to participate in an electoral campaign in which, for the first and only time in Canada's history, a school bill which was obstructed and failed to pass before the mandatory dissolution of the seventh Parliament on 23 April, was the main issue.

III

After almost a decade of federal representation the Territories had still to return their first Liberal member. On 23 June 1896, they sent three: Frank Oliver from Alberta, Wilfrid Laurier from Saskatchewan (replaced by Thomas O. Davis after Laurier's resignation forced a December by-election), and the Reverend James M. Douglas from East Assiniboia, a retired Presbyterian minister from Moosomin sponsored by the Patrons of Industry. The lone Conservative, Davin, was re-elected in West Assiniboia by the casting vote of the returning officer. The Manitoba school question (and thus by implication the territorial school question) dominated the election and the Catholic church took an active part in the campaign.

In Alberta, Oliver began his campaign auspiciously in mid-April with a meeting at Morinville, chaired, inexplicably in view of the church's dislike of the Liberals, by the Reverend J.B. Morin in the parish residence of the Reverend A. Harnois.[52] With D.W. Davis now a customs officer in the Yukon,[53] the Conservatives ran Thomas B. Cochrane, a mediocre rancher and businessman in the Macleod district. 'Personally a believer in the principle of National schools,' Cochrane supported the remedial bill on constitutional grounds. The provincial government having failed in its responsibility, it was necessary to support Tupper's efforts 'to uphold the constitution in the manner directed by the judgment of the highest court in the realm.'[54] A third candidate, Calgary's Independent Conservative S.J. Clarke, 'a strong advocate of Non-Sectarian Schools,' opposed the remedial bill because it interfered with provincial rights.[55] Oliver preferred 'conciliation' to 'coercion,' no matter who proposed it. The remedial bill was inadequate because it denied public aid to Catholic schools and raised 'a bone of contention for all time.'[56] When Arthur L. Sifton, stumping for Oliver, advanced the same line, the *Calgary Herald* made the most of the unconventional stand: 'Mr Oliver and Mr Sifton declare the Remedial Bill inadequate and say it would give the minority no justice. Archbishop Langevin ... says the bill is efficacious and would be acceptable to the minority. The question is: who is the best authority, Messrs Oliver and Sifton, who would be insulted by any suggestion that they were in a position to speak for the Catholics, or Archbishop Langevin, who is the spiritual leader and highest representative of the agrieved [sic] minority.'[57]

To score this point the Conservative *Herald* had momentarily to side with Archbishop Langevin, clearly an unfamiliar role. And in fact the unsolicited alliance between the Conservative party and Catholic hierarchy played havoc with the *Herald*'s reporting throughout the campaign – and indeed with many of the views in the campaign. To discredit the Liberals it quoted Laurier generously to show he would go 'even further' in the direction of separate schools than 'the strongest Conservative advocate of remedial legislation.'[58] But to bolster Conservative hopes in southern Alberta, in danger in part because of the remedial bill, it reported that northern Alberta (where most of the Catholic schools were located) was 'safe' for the Conservatives.[59] This, however, did not preclude its criticizing Morinville for allowing Oliver to hold a big political meeting on the Sabbath (21 June). Mindful of the large Protestant vote in the south, it gave Morinville front-page coverage as 'the only place in Alberta where such a flagrant breach of Sunday observance could be made with impunity'; and on the back page under the caption, 'Hypocrisy,' it added: 'The spectacle of church members helping to put a notorious Athiest [*sic*] into Parliament – a man who scoffs at Christianity and who, in his fits of frantic profanity, has been known to pull off his coat and call on the Almighty to come down and fight him, is not calculated to inspire respect for modern Christianity.'[60]

The above, written late in the campaign, shows the extent to which personal vilification had replaced the discussion of basic issues. For this, two Liberals, Antonio Prince and W.B. Barwis of Calgary, were mainly to blame. Early in June they gave wide publicity in French-Canadian centres to a conversation between Cochrane and one John Quirk, a Sheep Creek rancher, in which Cochrane commented favourably on his chances in southern and central Alberta but believed that ' "those d—d Catholics in the north could not be depended on." '[61] This was certainly not true respecting the clergy, who watched electoral developments very closely, as in 1891. On 22 May, the eve of Cochrane's visit to St Albert, Grandin indicated he would show H.W. McKenney, the local Conservative leader, the collective pastoral letter drawn up by Archbishop Bégin, instructing Catholic electors to exact a formal promise from candidates in favour of remedial legislation.[62] Cochrane saw Grandin and gave him the following assurance in writing: 'I wish to inform you that should I be returned as member for Alberta in the Dominion House, that I will uphold the Remedial legislation for Manitoba and my sole wish is to uphold the constitution in every way.'[63] On 8 June Lacombe, Leduc, and Morin and 'ministers of other denominations'[64] graced the political platform when the minister of the interior, Hugh J. Macdonald, visited Edmonton on Cochrane's behalf. The Quirk incident was aired for the first time and documents were produced 'proving the whole thing a complete fabrication.'[65] Father Leduc came away seriously disillusioned. Cochrane was a poor speaker and his explanation of the Quirk incident was pitiful. Worse still Macdonald supported national schools completely and was convinced no remedial bill would trouble Parliament again. There was little to choose between the Conservatives and Liberals – both at bottom would give the minority nothing but Laurier's politics. But when three of St Albert's principal Conservatives asked Leduc to jettison Cochrane, he demurred. Cochrane might not be able to say a word in Parliament but he could always vote, and he had promised in writing to vote in favour of a remedial bill.[66]

During the final week the clergy intensified their efforts. Father Leduc, Father Henri Grandin (the bishop's nephew), and Father M.P. Merer, a member of St Albert's school board, attended a political meeting at St Albert, and Leduc and Bishop Grandin followed with another sermon urging the church's official position: support of candidates who favoured the remedial bill. On 22 June, the eve before the election, Leduc questioned Oliver publicly and definitely established his opposition to separate schools. All to no avail. Next day Grandin sadly recorded Oliver's victory and the support which the Catholics, above all the French Canadians and the Métis, frequently very drunk, had given him.[67] The victory was no landslide. Oliver polled 3647 votes for a majority of 784. North and south of Red Deer he received 65 and 57 per cent of the vote and carried 93 and 50 per cent of the polls respectively. He took four of the five French Catholic centres, including St Albert (121–106), and received about 57 per cent of the French Catholic vote. The Conservative vote in southern Alberta dropped from about 75 per cent in 1891[68] to 43 per cent, but the school question was not the main factor. 'Matters much more closely related to the everyday life of the pioneers, the tariff on agricultural implements, land policy, freight rates, and developmental projects by the federal government, attracted the most attention, and the strongest stirrings of agrarian unrest yet felt in the North-West were an important factor in the result.'[69] One can, of course, only speculate about the force of the school question as an issue in Protestant districts, had Cochrane's pledge to Bishop Grandin become public.

In Assiniboia McDonald and Davin defended their support of the remedial bill against the Reverend J.M. Douglas and J.K. McInnis, editor of the *Regina Standard*, both unequivocally opposed to separate schools and remedial legislation.[70] McDonald supported the bill because it would have been 'ungenerous and wrong to infringe' the conscientious convictions of Catholics, who constituted 41 per cent of the total Canadian population.

Then, too, there was 'the compact' with Manitoba when it entered Confederation and the fact that Laurier's 'greatest' objection to the bill was that it did not 'coerce' Manitoba into giving financial aid to a minority which had not requested it.[71] The explanations were insufficient to stifle Conservative dissent,[72] and the breach in party ranks was reflected in the split between the two most important Conservative newspapers in East Assiniboia, the pro-McDonald *Moosomin Spectator* and the anti-McDonald *Qu'Appelle Vidette*.[73] The extent of clerical participation is not apparent, but Father Hugonard did share Hugh J. Macdonald's political platform at Indian Head on 11 June, where the Oblates' Industrial School Band from Qu'Appelle escorted Macdonald into the hall.[74] Douglas carried East Assiniboia, polling 3539 votes to McDonald's 2499.[75]

The campaign in West Assiniboia was more bitter. With McInnis attacking Davin in the *Standard* and Walter Scott, another Liberal, assailing him in the *Leader*, and with the Conservative *Moose Jaw Times* uncommitted until 29 May, Davin, who had sold the *Leader* to Scott in March on the assurance of continued political support, forced him to relinquish the editorial post in mid-May for 'An Interregnum' lasting approximately five weeks.[76] Even so Davin was hard-pressed to defend his Commons vote of 20 March in favour of second reading, for it did appear that he had followed 'An Incomprehensible Course' on 15 April in speaking against the bill he had earlier approved. Although he admitted that second reading 'established the principle of the Bill,' he maintained that '... one may vote for the second reading of the bill on various grounds and without approving of a single clause, the principle ... being set out in the preamble.' His vote had been influenced by Laurier's own endorsement of the principle of remedial legislation, by the government's last-minute delegation to Manitoba and the feeling in the house that second reading 'would help forward' negotiations at Winnipeg, by Sir Donald Smith's assurance that second reading was not a commitment on third reading, and by the government's certain demise if McDonald and he had defected. The real issue was 'whether ... power should remain in the hands of the Conservative party or pass to another.' Although lacking a mandate on the school question, he had one on the government he should support and voted accordingly. Having since learned his constituents' views, his future position in Parliament would be very different.[77]

From Prince Albert, T.O. Davis wrote Laurier that the Liberals in Saskatchewan faced 'the entire power of organized officialdom and patronage ... backed with the utmost bitterness by both the R.C. & Episcopal churches.'[78] The strongly Conservative *Saskatchewan Times* directed a steady stream of abuse against Laurier and, had William Craig, the Independent Conservative opposed to remedial legislation, not split the party vote, Thomas McKay would probably have won, for Laurier's margin was only 44 and Craig's vote 213.[79] Laurier's ethnic and religious background confounded the loyalties of French-speaking Catholics like E. Bourgeois, the Duck Lake teacher. In 'fervent' platform appeals on behalf of the Manitoba Catholics Bourgeois urged his listeners to support Laurier and the Liberal party,[80] even though most Liberal candidates strongly opposed separate schools and remedial legislation.

The Liberals carried the election 114 to 87, their margin in Quebec being twenty-eight seats, in Ontario, only one. Conservative papers in the west generally took the defeat philosophically.[81] 'It may be bad for the party,' declared the *Calgary Herald* on 24 June, 'but looked at from the broader point of view of the country's nationality the fact that the hierarchy has been proved incapable of driving the great mass of Catholics like sheep to the poll, and that the average Catholic citizen has made up his mind that like his Protestant countrymen he will exercise his independent powers of reason regardless of clerical dictation, is something upon which, regardless of party interests, the country may be congratulated.' Grandin was stunned by the results. The clergy and laity, he wrote Langevin, had gone in opposite directions on the school question and that could be embarrassing.[82] A distraught metropolitan indicated he would soon leave for Rome.[83] To Tupper, Langevin confessed he could 'hardly realize this calamity.' 'Our friends have fought nobly. Honor is safe. Let us hope for better days; we must adore the divine decree.' Tupper replied *pro forma*: '... we did our best and fell in a good cause'; the Liberals would not hold power very long.[84]

The disastrous election over, the minority set to mending its political fences. First, Grandin wrote to Laurier. He offered no congratulations because his policy, he said, was to speak only the truth. The remedial bill had had its weaknesses but it could always have been improved. Nevertheless, God had called Laurier to govern and he hoped Laurier would be 'Son homme.' He asked that J.K. Barrett, editor of the *Northwest Review*, who had taken an active part in the campaign, be allowed to retain his post as inspector of weights and measures in Winnipeg. Laurier, magnanimous, was only too pleased to forget the incident; his own conduct, he added, was inspired in all things by what his conscience told him as a Catholic and citizen.[85] With Grandin in eastern Canada, Leduc sent Laurier an advance copy of *Hostility Unmasked* and asked him to settle the thorny territorial school question, which bristled with difficulties created by the most evil forces.[86] Lacombe was the last of the diocesan triumvirate to approach the new prime minister. Early in October he congratulated Laurier on his great victory, reminded him of his (Lacombe's) statement last January that he was not a party man, and asked him to support a projected Métis colony in north-eastern Alberta.[87]

As the clergy's prestige had been seriously impaired by political defeat, the Catholic laity in Edmonton framed a petition to the governor-general-in-council in August, declaring their 'entire agreement' with the clergy's stand on the education of their children. Catholics in Edmonton who had supported Oliver did so because they believed Laurier would deal more favourably with the Manitoba issue than did the remedial bill.[88] At Regina Forget and Reginald Rimmer, both prominent Liberals, did not welcome the petition. It could be troublesome, Forget wrote Laurier, if Beck, a prominent Conservative, was behind it. To Leduc, Forget complained that the petition ran counter to Laurier's policy of conciliation and compromise and stressed that only the Conservatives would undoubtedly sign it in large numbers.[89] Forget was right. The Liberals boycotted the petition and even a number of Catholic Conservatives refused to sign it.[90] Rimmer, more outspoken than Forget, wrote Leduc of the dilemma confronting Liberal Catholics during the recent election: 'Had Mr. Laurier's position on this question been such as was so frequently represented to us, the Liberal Catholics would still have found themselves in the difficult position of having to choose between exercising the virtue of obedience to their Superiors and at the same time sustaining a Government whose political corruption was a bye word amongst English speaking people.' He hoped Laurier's settlement of the school question would not be impeded by a 'too urgent insistence upon every right which Catholics formerly possessed.'[91]

In the North-West the territorial school question remained quiescent. There was a brief flurry in February 1896 when insufficient time to examine the 1895 School Ordinance led Governor Mackintosh to withhold his assent, but appropriate explanations followed[92] and the innuendoes subsided. At Ottawa the question had remained in almost total eclipse. On 14 January McCarthy re-introduced his familiar bill and it, too, disappeared after first reading.[93] More significant was the move by P.A. Choquette of Montmagny, Quebec. On 27 February he asked the government for Sir John Thompson's reply to the letter from Grandin and Pascal, dated 5 March 1892. When A.R. Dickey, minister of justice, denied any knowledge of the correspondence,[94] Choquette wrote Grandin for Thompson's reply, enclosing a copy of the remedial bill and inviting him to discuss it in terms of his own territorial experiences, thereby making it possible for debate on the territorial school question to resume.[95] Grandin was undoubtedly tempted to reply, but with Choquette a member of the Liberal opposition and the hierarchy pledged not to embarrass the government, the letter remained unanswered. Shortly thereafter, Grandin faced another challenge. On 12 June Goggin held a teachers' institute in Edmonton[96] and next day, practically unannounced, he and Mackintosh visited the school at St Albert, where Goggin offered to hold another session. The indirect invitation sufficed and on 14 June a class (termed benign enough by Grandin) followed. When Goggin suggested other classes attended by sisters from Edmonton, the embarrassed sisters insisted upon first consulting their bishop and the idea bore no fruit.[97]

IV

Some two months before the territorial assembly met, Langevin, Grandin, and Pascal petitioned Mackintosh for an opportunity to discuss the school question 'in a spirit of conciliation.' Leduc was authorized to explain their views more fully.[98] When the members assembled on 29 September Boucher and Maloney pressed for amendments to bring school legislation more in line with Catholic educational interests. Although the debates were extensive and at times bitter, the new school ordinance contained only one change that affected Catholic interests: business corporations could assign a portion of their taxes to support separate schools (s. 125). The change was not debated, and it is not known whether it was a concession extracted from the government or an act of good will on its part.

Early in the session Maloney complained that ten or eleven schools in his district were without teachers because the qualifications for rural teachers were too high. Teachers with Ontario certificates should be allowed to teach for three years (as in Manitoba), not one year, before having to attend normal school sessions.[99] Boucher and Maloney followed with a resolution condemning the school bill's provisions regarding the council, the inspection of schools, and the certification of teachers as 'contrary to the spirit of Section 14 of the *North-West Territories Act*' and an infringement of the rights of the minority 'conferred thereby.'[100] This was in line with the minority's memorandum to the assembly in 1894 which aimed to make more specific the general guarantee to separate schools. Boucher criticized the inspection of schools, but Maloney, intent on a Catholic normal school, insisted that teachers' qualifications were the main problem. Haultain replied that only five of Maloney's schools had been closed, not necessarily for want of teachers. The Department of Public Instruction did not enforce certification regulations 'strictly' in districts that were 'peculiarly situated.' The government also had no objection to a Catholic inspector, but one's religion was not a factor in appointments: 'On one occasion, on account of peculiar circumstances, it was thought advisable that a Roman Catholic should be appointed, but one with necessary qualifications could not be found.'[101] The motion was defeated twenty-two to two, with only the mover and seconder supporting it.[102]

The debate continued in committee of the whole, with Maloney advocating a vote for all members of council and Haultain insisting upon the principle of executive responsibility. When Maloney returned to the qualifications of teachers, Haultain declared that teachers' examinations had not affected the supply: 'Some localities seemed to demand special qualifications or non-qualifications that could not be recognized in law. One of these was to belong to a certain church.' Rules would be relaxed when circumstances warranted, but the problem was to exclude unqualified persons who 'traded upon the necessities of the people' and demanded renewal permits from year to year. 'It would be almost better to have no school than to waste public money in that way.' Official records and inspectors' reports disclosed that one of the four closed schools was established 'quite recently,' another was vacant because the teacher had married, another wanted a Catholic teacher, and still another had no school house. When Mowat asked that the reports be printed, Haultain advised him to direct the council accordingly. Haultain also approved Insinger's suggestion that announcements of the first school meetings be issued in different languages: 'Even rules and regulations might be given in different languages'; that would be 'a mere ... accommodation to older people speaking a foreign language, and would in the end strengthen English by abolishing mere duality of languages.'[103]

The school question therefore had received considerable attention by the time Father Leduc reached Regina on 5 October. For the first time, he ran into immediate opposition from Forget, who could not see what the minority had against the innocent readers. Catholic readers, though desirable, were not essential, and the minority did need to be more conciliatory. Religious instruction might be given outside the school. Neutral schools, after all, were not condemned by any commandment of God. Next day Leduc gave Haultain and Goggin copies of *Hostility Unmasked* (just released officially) and a serious but amicable discussion of the readers followed, especially on the naturalism or materialism which Leduc insisted they expressed. He also addressed copies to several assembly members and asked Mackintosh to arrange a meeting with the executive committee.[104]

The meeting did not take place until 16 October. Meanwhile John L. Reid (Prince Albert West), to meet the wishes of 'a number' of separate school ratepayers in his district moved that Catholics be given the option of supporting minority or majority schools. After Clinkskill criticized Reid for

applying 'the axe to the very root of the separate school system' Haultain
fell back on his usual constitutional argument and Reid withdrew his
motion.[105] Two weeks later, however, he introduced a private bill,[106] placed
in his hands by the 'public school people' in his district to meet the wishes of
Catholics who preferred public schools. The bill, Haultain observed, was
what the law 'ought to be,' but to pass it was to legislate 'directly contrary'
to the 1875 constitution, opening 'an avenue to litigation in its worse form.'[107]
He moved the six months' hoist, which carried thirteen to eleven with five
abstentions.[108]

In the interval Maloney objected to the allocation of taxes on property
owned by a Protestant and occupied by a Catholic (or vice versa) to the
property owner's school district. 'What was to be done,' he asked, 'when
the religion of the owner is unknown, or the ownership was vested in a
corporate body?' Inexplicably, Haultain merely pointed to the obvious fact
that a separate school could be organized only where a public school already
existed and would be supported by 'taxation of the property of persons of
its faith.' He did not indicate whether Catholic schools could share in the
taxes of individuals of 'unknown' religion. Also he flatly declared that 'corporations should be assessed for the support of the public school.'[109] Yet
the 1896 School Ordinance was far more liberal: A company in a separate
school district could voluntarily allocate part of its assessment to the separate
school, as long as the part allocated bore the same ratio to the total assessment of the company as the value of the stock of the company held by
separate school supporters bore to the total value of the company stock
(s. 125). There were, therefore, apparently some aspects of the school question which Haultain would not discuss and others which he either would or
could not control.

When Leduc and Forget met the executive committee (Haultain, Neff,
Ross, and Mitchell) three subjects were discussed: the meaning of separate
schools, teacher education, and *Hostility Unmasked*. To Leduc, separate
schools entailed nothing less than the essence of the judicial committee's
decision in 1895: Catholic textbooks, particularly in reading, history, and
literature; an active voice on council and in the appointment of examiners
and inspectors; and Catholic teachers capable of giving religious instruction.
(Leduc grossly misrepresented the Privy Council's decision. It had not dealt
in specifics. It had merely recognized that Manitoba's 1890 law affected
Catholic schools adversely and called upon others to decide what aspects
of the earlier school system should be restored.[110]) For the teaching sisters
Leduc recommended as a modus vivendi a normal department in at least
one convent, directed by the principal of the Catholic union school in the

area. Regarding his pamphlet, if, as Haultain observed, he had immortalized Goggin, it was '*a devil's immortality*,' and taking advantage of a jovial moment, he offered to immortalize them all if the government voted five hundred dollars![111]

On 21 October the assembly again discussed Catholic school inspection. Haultain assured Maloney that, 'other things being equal,' a French-speaking candidate was preferred, but the same held true for one who spoke German: '... if we can obtain a man who can speak all the languages spoken in the Territories, all these qualifications would be taken into consideration. (Hear, hear.)' Archibald B. Gillis (Whitewood), disturbed by this statement, pointed to the 'Swedes, Hungarians, Finlanders, Bohemians, French and Belgians' in his district and asked when the new inspector would be required to speak these languages: '... the people in his district should be taken into consideration as well as the people of other districts. (Laughter.)'[112] With waves of European immigrants about to enter the west, the argument that no group should receive special consideration soon became an integral part of the 'national schools' philosophy.

Before proroguing, the assembly took up Leduc's pamphlet. Brett introduced it because it was official and because of Father Leduc's position on the old Board of Education. Haultain personally opposed giving 'publicity and notoriety' to the work. He found Father Leduc 'an amiable gentleman in private life, but in controversy he knew him to be a truculent and pugnacious person.' The 'only' way he had 'ever' been able to deal with him was to give 'a point blank denial' to all he said. Accordingly, on behalf of Goggin and himself, he denied all the quoted conversations. The grievances in the rest of the pamphlet existed 'only in Father Leduc's imagination.' Haultain made the statement 'quite freely, willingly and emphatically that on every occasion that Father Leduc had been before the council or had made any statements, the rev. gentleman's "facts" had been found to differ from the real facts of the case. That had been the rule without exception. The pamphlet was not only extravagant but inaccurate.' Clinkskill declared that 'the statements of Father Leduc were untrue, and the language intemperate, and he was glad to be relieved of the sole responsibility of saying so.' No one defended the pamphlet and all who spoke condemned it freely.[113]

v

The 1896 assembly was the occasion of the last major debate on the school question at Regina. Shortly thereafter Archbishop Langevin defined the minority's minimal position, which changed little during the remaining nine years of territorial government. The first two goals – a 'certain' control of the schools and Catholic school districts 'everywhere' – were general. The minority also wished to train its own teachers, enjoy freedom of religious instruction, control its own school taxes and be free of double taxation, and be eligible for government grants to education. Granted this, it would accept government inspection and government control of finances and teacher certification to ensure that public funds were properly used and instruction was of a standard demanded in all schools.[114]

Langevin's position was not one a government could accept readily. It sought to share the control of public education with the state, but the line of demarcation was either vague or slanted in the church's favour. The state's subordinate role, however, followed naturally from the major premises in the archbishop's declaration, 'Droits et Devoirs en matière d'Education – Principes et Conclusions,' known also as the 'Credo.' The declaration was suggested by Langevin at a meeting of the archdiocesan hierarchy in April 1902 and is cited here as the best statement of his church-state philosophy and the key to his strong opposition to compromise after the electoral fiasco of 1896. The sixth section summarized Langevin's position:

6   La formation du *chrétien* étant la partie principale dans l'éducation, et les maîtres étant les représentants de l'Eglise pour tout ce qui touche à cette for-mation, il s'en suit que les maîtres dépendent plus de l'Eglise que des parents, et que c'est l'Eglise qui doit avoir le dernier mot dans le choix de ceux à qui doit être confiée l'éducation des enfants chrétiens. Ils ne peuvent être confiés qu'à des maîtres que l'Eglise approuve, et juge dignes de la représenter auprés de ces enfants, qui lui appartiennent aussi en vertu d'un droit surnaturel, auquel le droit des parents est subordonné. Il s'en suit également que le plan d'études, les livres, les doctrines, les programmes, les règlements de discipline, etc. doivent être soumis à l'approbation de l'Eglise, afin qu'elle puisse retrancher, modifier, adjou-ter, autant que cela est nécessaire pour assurer le fin principale de l'éducation, qui est la formation du *chrétien*.

The state could establish no monopoly over education, not even over special schools, although it could determine their content and require all candidates to pass examinations. The only compulsory instruction acceptable was religious instruction, which the church could compel parents to give or have given to their children. Since secular instruction was by its very nature, not obligatory, the state should be content to encourage and aid it.[115]

The concessions of state control of inspection, finance, and teacher certification were major ones for the church. But the Langevin statement also makes clear why the Laurier-Greenway agreement for Manitoba, announced on 19 November 1896, and negotiated largely by Clifford Sifton and Israel Tarte, could never satisfy the archbishop. Separate schools were not suppressed, but their maintenance entailed double taxation, with all Catholic ratepayers obliged to support the public schools and provincial grants not available to denominational schools. Although public school attendance was not compulsory, other concessions involving religious instruction, the employment of Catholic teachers, and bilingual education were made only after carefully defined conditions which favoured no religious denomination.[116]

It followed then that, in touring the west, Tarte's visit to St Albert would not be popular. Bishop Grandin dreaded the prospect,[117] and when Tarte arrived on 25 November, he and Leduc exchanged harsh words in the presence of a large delegation which included Oliver and Prince. Tarte and company left hurriedly and Leduc, already seriously ill, suffered a relapse that lasted several days.[118] While still in Edmonton Tarte had complained that his early upbringing in isolation from English-speaking people had bred prejudices that disappeared on contact with 'the English.'[119] Obviously, then, he would stir up controversy and could expect few favours at the mission.

At year's end Grandin and Langevin pressed the school question as diligently as ever. Even though Cardinal Ledochowski informed Langevin that Rome was aware of the minority's problem and had ample documents, Grandin was concerned about the priority assigned to Manitoba and sent the cardinal a full account of the territorial situation.[120] He also appealed to Laurier again. If granting the minority justice should defeat the government (which he could not believe), would not Laurier rather fall with honour than retain power by sacrificing it? Laurier's warm reply asked Grandin not to apologize for complaining, particularly as it was the previous administration that was being criticized. He promised to acquaint himself with the facts and render justice, if it were still possible to do so.[121] Grandin and Langevin, although not displeased, were not too hopeful. Grandin's letter, Langevin said, coming as it did from an honest man, was too gracious and civil for Laurier, who was a heartless knave, without faith and without honour.[122]

8
Futile negotiations, 1897-1903

The Laurier-Greenway agreement practically extinguished Catholic hopes for reversing the trend towards a single uniform school system in the Territories. Moreover, as had become clear with the report of the Council of Public Instruction issued in September 1897, the school system's programme represented the triumph of Ontario's Anglo Protestant way of life over Quebec's French Catholic way. Arthur R.M. Lower has contrasted Ontario's dynamic Calvinist-commercial civilization, 'with its devotion to acquisition and its haunting fear of animal "robustiousness," ' and Quebec's static Catholic-rural civilization, 'careless of well-being, not over-burdened with social responsibility, prodigal of life, welcoming many children, not grieving too intensely if many die and others live mis-shapen.' In the North-West, Ontario prevailed and commercialism gradually replaced agrarianism, bringing with it such mixed blessings as urbanism, individualism (sometimes rugged), and exploitative economies. Pushed into the background were such equally mixed benefits as short-life expectancy, communal segregation, and obedient attitudes. In time successful businessmen, 'the opportunists, the exploiters, the men with no past and little future,' replaced the struggling settlers, 'the custodians of society, the fathers of the race,' who gently coaxed a living out of the soil.[1]

The programme outlined in the Council of Public Instruction report was designed to prepare children in a business-like manner for the way of life anticipated by the 1892 School Ordinance. The extent to which Father Leduc grasped the full significance of that ordinance is difficult to say, but in some passages of *Hostility Unmasked*, with characteristic vigour, he gave no quarter to the social and moral philosophy reflected in the territorial programme. The basic orientation of the schools, Haultain wrote, was to provide knowledge 'helpful in the transaction of business, the duties of citizenship, the care of the body, and the formation of moral character.' There was no syllabus of religious instruction, its character and amount 'within a time-limit' being determined by the trustees, who 'may be presumed to represent the desires of the ratepayers.' In all standards above Standard II, textbooks were uniform, 'care being taken to authorise none written from a sectarian standpoint.' The inspector had 'nothing to do with religious instruction.'

Goggin, in a review of the history of teacher education in the Territories, condemned provisional certificates and, in strikingly modern terms, deplored employment practices influenced by patronage, low salaries, and religious beliefs. He also dealt extensively with moral education, giving the biographical study of history in Standard II (Canadian history) and Standard III (English history) as its basis. In both standards '... the lives of a small number of leading Canadians and Englishmen are described by the teacher and the children are led to consider their public acts and are guided in forming such judgments on the morality of these acts as they are capable of ...' Goggin's sections on temperance and manners and morals further underlined the moral basis of the school system. Abstinence was not emphasized: 'Love of the good is a higher motive to action than fear of the bad.' Politeness was encouraged, as were a number of external forms of conduct (each expressing 'a true sense of the proprieties of life'), including giving thanks for favours received, preference to girls, and deference to age and position. For a pupil to do his duty intelligently, he 'must know what his duty is, see the reasonableness of it and feel its obligatoriness.' The school provided this knowledge in 'substantially the same manner as the knowledge of grammar.' It was the duty of teachers to turn the pupils' attention to 'the moral quality' of their acts and to lead them into 'a clear understanding and constant practice of every virtue.' Among the means were the teacher's own influence and example, the narration of 'suitable tales to awaken right feeling,' the memorization of 'gems embodying noble sentiments, and maxims and proverbs containing rules of duty,' and direct instruction in a long list of topics, including cleanliness, kindness, truthfulness, courage, prudence, evil habits, and industry.[2]

Father Leduc was unimpressed:

It would seem forsooth, as if these framers of materialistic and godless laws could see nothing in man, but a perfected animal, the most intelligent, the noblest of all, unless, indeed, the education he is condemned to receive should make him the most cruel and most formidable of all animals ...

If the programme utterly neglects to impart the knowledge and love of

God to the pupils, we cannot charge it with neglecting their material welfare. Cleanliness, clothing, pure air, good water, bodily exercise, rest, wholesome food, praiseworthy and moderate habits, baths, accidents, poisons, disinfectants, circulation of the blood, care of the eyes, ears & all these are the subject-matter of ... many lessons ... All well and good; but why complain if Catholics, while carefully expounding these sanitary principles, take some care of the health, the strength, the purity of heart and soul? We, Catholics, disavow and reject, with all our might, schools in which the teaching is purely natural ... Are we in the wrong?

Teachers should take great care ... to inculcate on the minds of the scholars the necessity of practising all the civic and natural virtues; they must teach them to be polite, obliging, affable towards their equals, and kind to animals ... They should also say to their pupils: ... 'Be ever industrious, economical and prudent.'

Such is the decalogue of our Schools of the North-West, a godless decalogue, without punishment or reward other than those of human justice and the illusive satisfaction that follows upon the fulfilment of a duty.

This moral education ... paves the way to all kinds of errors; it allows one to be an atheist, a materialist, an infidele [sic], a rationalist, and even a pagan, so long as he assumes the cloak of honesty according to the world. Only let the Sepulchre be white-washed, clean and bright outwards; it matters little if within it be full of worms and all filthiness. To escape human justice and criticism, thanks to the practice of certain natural virtues, to make oneself agreable [sic], to get on in the world by industry, economy and prudence, this is the ideal of a perfect man according to our programme of moral education. Is it not humiliating? Is it not Contemptible?[3]

But the church was not yet ready to give in. After 1897 it entered upon a long period of negotiations with the state, in which it launched regular offensives on Regina and Ottawa for a French Catholic normal school, Catholic textbooks, and greater freedom of religious instruction. On occasion its efforts approached the heroic, particularly in the campaign for an inspector. The state refused to yield, however, and the church invariably came away empty-handed and disappointed.

II

In 1897 the school question was quiescent as the bishops awaited the report of the apostolic delegate, who had visited Canada in the spring in response to conflicting representations from Laurier and several Catholic bishops on the school question. The visit of Fathers Leduc and Lacombe to Ottawa in

March showed that it was not, however, forgotten. At dinner, Laurier told them that the church had to make concessions, as it did in France and in the United States; it could only lose from a war of race and religion. He saw nothing in the Manitoba curriculum offensive to Catholics. Leduc countered that true Catholics in France and America supported free schools, despite the double taxation. And, while the consequences of strife might be deplorable, they would be comparable to those which followed the church's failure to recognize Henry VIII's divorce. Could the church be blamed for that? The same argument would be applicable for the condemned principle of neutral or godless schools. Materialistic books were not acceptable and the minority only awaited a settlement in Manitoba to begin a fight on the subject in the North-West.[4] The meeting was no diplomatic success and, like others to follow, resulted in no definite agreements.

While the minority eagerly looked forward to the delegate's report, legislation at Ottawa made the territorial government even less amenable to Catholic pressures. In 1897 the new Liberal administration replaced the executive committee with an executive council and made responsible government in the Territories official. On Governor Mackintosh's invitation Haultain chose Ross, Mitchell, Magrath, and George H.V. Bulyea (South Qu'Appelle) to his first executive council. The new government naturally kept the contentious school question in the background. At a meeting held at Macleod in October Ross referred to the smooth working of the school system and gave Haultain credit for establishing it 'without any of the friction or heartburning seen in other countries'! Haultain, in his remarks, ignored the subject.[5] At the territorial session, in a brief encounter, Boucher criticized Goggin's salary and complained that several schools in his district had been closed during the year. Clinkskill and Haultain explained that the closures resulted from the cancellation of provisional certificates on the inspector's report. They had been extended from year to year but the holders 'had not qualified.'[6]

Early in January 1898 Rome's long-awaited encyclical on the school question finally reached Canada. The apostolic delegate, Raphael Merry del Val, archbishop of Nicosia, had arrived in Montreal in March of the previous year. His mission, he had said in a private circular, was one of peace, designed to restore unity among Canadian Catholics, assure the bishops' prestige, strengthen the faithful's obedience, and obtain from the government a solution acceptable to all. The circular imposed no silence on the hierarchy. It requested information on the constitutional, legal, and religious difficulties of the school question and promised that the view expressed would be confidential.[7] The silence of the circular on the North-West led Grandin to send Merry del Val a full account of the territorial situation, presenting the school question as a religious war where French was persecuted to annihilate the Catholic religion, inasmuch as French Canadians used their language to protect their faith by discouraging mixed marriages and the religious indifference and apostasy that accompanied them. Moreover, a heavy programme of studies had been imposed on the schools, when all that was needed were some lessons in home economics, manual training, and catechism, and enough of the elements of reading, writing, and arithmetic to write an intelligible letter and meet ordinary business needs.[8] When this letter received no more than an acknowledgment on 13 June, Grandin wrote again and complained that the silence, which he assumed the delegate had imposed on the hierarchy (the delegate had met the archbishops in Montreal on 8 April and recommended silence[9]), would encourage the conclusion that the pope approved the Manitoba settlement and condemned the conduct of the Canadian clergy.[10] Langevin, after learning that the delegate and a portion of the eastern hierarchy had fallen out at a meeting in Montreal on 18 May, had expressed sentiments similar to those of Grandin,[11] who now simply relayed them to the delegate.

The delegate, his visit almost over, merely sent Grandin another acknowledgment, and in a circular to the archbishops on 3 July counselled patience.[12] Langevin commended Grandin, who then sent Merry del Val a third letter outlining the consequences of subordinating the Territories to Manitoba. An early school settlement was important because Alberta would soon become a province and the legislators (termed the town-councillors) would like nothing better than to repeat the Manitoba experience. His newly appointed coadjutor, Bishop Emile Legal, would be pleased to discuss the situation with him.[13] An inquiry from Cardinal Ledochowski – apparently at the end of June – brought another long letter in which Grandin and Legal expressed disappointment at the delegate's failure to visit the North-West.[14] Ledochowski sent the letter to Merry del Val, who then wrote Grandin from Rome that he greatly regretted not having received a similar communication earlier. Territorial schools were not within the precise terms of his mission and he had not raised them in his contacts with the government. Had he realized the minority's predicament, however, he might have prevailed upon the government to help it a little. He was astonished that Langevin had not spoken to him of the North-West. The two issues should be separated and the differences pointed out to Laurier, quietly urging him to hasten a settlement.[15]

Uncertain about writing Laurier again, Grandin consulted Langevin, who was furious with the officious delegate. Having so seriously compromised the school question in Manitoba, Rome's sorry representative was a very poor judge of what was best for Grandin's schools. The delegate's childish confidence, Langevin added, again showed how much he had been taken in by Canada's political quacks. Instead of approaching Ottawa, Grandin should quietly introduce Catholic textbooks in history and reading without consulting other authorities. As bishops, he declared, they were defenders of the faith and the consecration oath did not oblige them to consult a superior authority at each stage.[16]

From these exchanges it would appear that neither Langevin nor the delegate had a high opinion of Grandin's political sagacity. Langevin did not deny the delegate's allegations; he ignored them and couched the whole in a scathing denunciation of the delegate and a lengthy episcopal dissertation, full of bravado, on textbook strategy. Langevin, of course, had good reason not to trouble the delegate about the North-West. His strategy from the outset had been to subordinate the latter to Manitoba. That Grandin required no further explanation is an indication of his complete submission to the political wisdom of his metropolitan. He had a self-confessed disinterest in politics and, as a result, was ill-equipped to deal with political situations. Langevin's indignant and evasive letter preyed upon their ecclesiastical relationship and showed how little attention the young and sophisticated, imperious Langevin thought he had to pay to his suffragan's political opinions.

Whether Langevin did ignore the North-West in his discussions with Merry del Val is impossible to say. No record of the discussions exists and Langevin's only letter to the delegate is concerned only with an abject apology for issuing a circular on the Laurier-Greenway agreement.[17] The delegate, too, treated Grandin cavalierly in declaring he was unfamiliar with the North-West situation and in suggesting that he first divide the two issues and then approach Laurier. Grandin had given him a full account of his difficulties and, even if the delegate had chosen to ignore them, it is doubtful that others in eastern Canada like Bishop Laflèche would have hesitated to point out the wider implications of the Manitoba school question. For the delegate to suggest that Grandin use the very strategy which Langevin had already rejected may indicate that the delegate was less innocent than his letter would suggest. He did have strong liberal leanings and an 'instant friendship and confidence' had developed between him and Laurier.[18] Laurier was certainly familiar with the North-West situation; but he also knew of Langevin's stubborn rejection of the Laurier-Greenway agreement. In the situation one school question was sufficient, and it would have been easy to advise the delegate to concentrate on Manitoba. Once the Manitoba situation ceased to be a public issue, he would use his 'sunny way'[19] in Manitoba and in the North-West to redress grievances quietly. But no matter how one views the situation, it seems clear that neither the delegate nor Langevin was too concerned about writing Grandin whatever they pleased. This was in sharp contrast to the uneasy feeling with which both Langevin and Grandin awaited the papal encyclical based on the delegate's report.

The encyclical was a balanced document. To soothe episcopal feelings, it declared the Laurier-Greenway agreement 'defective, imperfect, insufficient.' To heal the rupture between church and state and between Catholic Liberals and Conservatives (especially within clerical ranks), it counselled the minority to accept 'partial satisfaction' while continuing negotiations for better terms. Because there could be no foundation for morality outside a religious context and because there was 'only one true religion,' Catholics could 'neither accept nor recognize' a morality or religion drawn from non-Catholic doctrine. The encyclical therefore prohibited instruction of Catholic children in schools that ignored or repudiated the Catholic religion or that regarded all beliefs as equal, '... as if, in what regards God and divine things, it makes no difference whether one believes rightly or wrongly, and takes up with truth or error.' Teachers, books, and schools, in full accord with the profession of the Catholic faith, were also necessary.[20] Authoritatively expressed, the encyclical undoubtedly lifted sagging episcopal spirits and spurred Catholic leaders to greater efforts. Thus at a time when Ottawa finally made responsible government official in the Territories, Rome, too, re-invigorated the church by affirming long-standing educational principles. Neither church nor state would be in a mood to compromise in the immediate future.

Grandin's and Langevin's reactions were practically identical. At first reading the former was disappointed, but upon reflection he concluded all was for the best. The encyclical, Langevin wrote Bégin, greatly perplexed him: the pope, who had praised the episcopal attitude before the Laurier-Greenway agreement, now seemed to qualify his approval. Next day, however, he told Grandin that Rome had provided the true solution and that the Holy Spirit had obviously guided the pope.[21]

On 21 January Grandin read the encyclical from the pulpit at St Albert and two weeks later issued his own pastoral letter.[22] The church, he said, was non-political. Neither he nor the encyclical had condemned either political party, although politicians friendly to the church were naturally preferred. In religion, however, the same liberalism as in politics opened the door to many abuses. It compromised school instruction and led to mixed marriages and religious indifference. Grandin saw the school conflict as part of the larger conflict between God and Satan, with the pope, the bishops, the priests, and the valiant Christians, who stood for Catholic Christian education without compromise or temerity, on one side, and atheistic or irreligious governments, who denied the right to a Catholic education, ignored it, or trampled upon it, on the other. Indeed, Christian societies generally seemed to want to dispense with God, or at least feared to concede too much to Him. Nor were the faithful blameless; even Catholics who seemed to favour Catholic schools took pains to keep the priest away, yet one could hardly call a school Catholic if the priest, the representative of the highest authority, God, could not enter it at will. The laity had to establish more Catholic schools. If they did not know how, they should consult a priest, who would show them the way.

III

Even before the encyclical reached Canada, the church had embarked upon fresh negotiations at Regina. In the next few years it waged three main, long struggles for a French Catholic school inspector, a Catholic normal school, and Catholic textbooks. The series of skirmishes led nowhere – it was soon clear that the territorial government had the controlling hand and, further, that Laurier's government was prepared to act only if such action were not prejudicial to its own interests.

At a meeting of the hierarchy in mid-December (1897) Bishop Legal, Grandin's French-born, mild-tempered coadjutor, who for over ten years had been a missionary to the Blackfoot in southern Alberta, had been directed to approach the government.[23] Legal saw Haultain on 19 December. He reported to Langevin that, were Haultain unknown to him, he would be tempted to believe that the premier was prepared to meet all their requests.[24] To aid Haultain before the Council of Public Instruction, Legal sent him a summary of the minority's objectives,[25] but left it to Langevin to ask for 'a Catholic Inspector, subject to the approval of the Bishops concerned.'[26] Haultain, amiable as ever, assured Langevin that the Council of Public Instruction would deal 'in detail' with the minority's requests; the government meanwhile would give them the 'fullest consideration.'[27] With Legal and Langevin away in Europe, it was not until late summer that the church launched its first sustained campaign for a French Catholic school inspector, soon its most important goal.[28]

The first candidate was Charles Caron, a newly tonsured priest from Sherbrooke, Quebec, whom Langevin brought forward on 6 September. Three weeks later Langevin experienced the first of many set-backs, when Haultain informed him there was no vacancy. Caron's qualifications, however, seemed a more likely reason for not making the appointment. Although he had completed the classical course, taught for more than twenty years, was once a principal in Montreal, and knew English, he had no teaching certificate, and Langevin submitted no documents or details as to his education or previous experience. Moreover, there were passages in Langevin's letter to Haultain (7 September) which suggested that the archbishop considered the appointment a mere formality – a post to which the minority was entitled as a replacement for Gillies and one which the hierarchy should have an important hand in filling.[29]

On 26 September political developments unexpectedly intervened in the minority's favour. Malcolm C. Cameron, Mackintosh's successor as lieutenant-governor, died, and Forget, an earlier candidate,[30] was appointed on 13 October. Langevin, who had wired Laurier on the subject immediately,[31] was immensely pleased. He had already informed Forget that the first fruit of his appointment would be a French inspector. He demanded it in the name of both patriotism and religion.[32] Langevin took no further action, however, until 11 March, when he dined at the governor's residence with Haultain, Ross, Bulyea, and Goggin and learned that the government was prepared to replace the Anglican Canon Flett with a Catholic inspector who knew French, held a first-class professional certificate, and, if possible, a university degree.[33] Early in April, through the efforts of Lacombe, Father H. A. Constantineau, rector of Ottawa University, and Archbishop Paul Bruchesi of Montreal, he presented not one, but three, candidates, all from Quebec, complete with personal letters of application, appropriate testimonials, and other documents.[34]

Unfortunately each candidate lacked either adequate academic background, or professional training, or teaching experience. A. Bélanger, for example, like Caron, had no normal school certificate and his teaching experience was largely confined to high school,[35] a serious deficiency in the Territories, where less than two per cent of the school population attended high school.[36] Furthermore, Bélanger's written English was weak. Not surprisingly, Haultain rejected Bélanger's application, finding his credentials excellent but inadequate.[37] The next candidate, J.V. Desaulniers, did not have a university degree and, even though Lacombe managed to obtain one from the authorities at Laval University, Haultain, according to Frédéric Villeneuve, MLA for St Albert, thought the degree had the appearance of a service to the bishops and rejected Desaulniers' application in May.[38] G. Beaulieu, the third candidate, possessed a law degree and, like Bélanger, lacked experience in the elementary standards. His written English was even worse than Bélanger's. He was not, however, definitely rejected until January

1901,[39] because the clergy, having failed on three previous occasions and lacking a better qualified alternate, hesitated to bring the matter to a head.

With Beaulieu's rejection, it was clear that the government was not interested in the clergy's candidates. On 15 April 1899, the *North-West Territories Gazette* had announced the appointment as inspector of D.P. McColl, a resident English-speaking, non-Catholic principal from Regina, familiar with the territorial school system. When Legal insisted, a year later, that clerical pressure on Laurier had increased the territorial grant from which the church should also benefit, and Langevin threatened to bring the wrath of the entire Catholic hierarchy in Canada upon Haultain's head, Haultain's strongly worded reply brought church-state relations to the breaking point: 'We do not contempalte any immediate addition to our staff of Inspectors and although you have pointed out that we have obtained some financial assistance from Ottawa the question of our inability to indulge in further expenditure in any direction is one upon which we must exercise our own judgment.'[40]

While there is no evidence of the precise understanding which Laurier and Legal reached on the latter's visit to Ottawa in November 1899,[41] it is easy to conjecture that Laurier may have made some vague commitment which Legal interpreted as a promise to allocate funds for a French Catholic inspector. Legal himself was adamant on the point. He knew 'positively,' he wrote Haultain in April 1900, that '. . . the salary of a new Inspector has been offered by the authorities at Ottawa, and if the federal aid to the Government of the Territories has been increased, it is partly with that end in view.'[42] If Laurier did yield to Legal, he apparently said nothing to Haultain; on the other hand, Haultain, had he been so informed, was apparently not prepared to yield, and from Legal's own account the government was not bound to appoint a French Catholic school inspector.

Haultain, of course, was in an excellent position to delay. The federal government could not very well earmark funds for clerical ends. The scars of the last school controversy were still all too visible and the next federal election was only a few months away. If Haultain had really wanted to accommodate the church, he could easily have done so. The inspector's salary was not, after all, a major financial item. A life-long Conservative in federal politics, he may have wished to embarrass Laurier, who had good reason to want to improve his relations with the western clergy. But Haultain had all the advantage. If the clergy pressed too hard, he could always claim a shortage of funds, and any increase in federal subsidy could always be disposed of on any one of the numerous projects which the rapid growth of population required.

On 30 June 1900, A.M. Fenwick of Moose Jaw became the second non-Catholic teacher within slightly more than a year to join the inspectoral staff.[43] An exasperated archbishop, in a letter heavy with sarcasm, accused Haultain of 'a lack of that real good will and that spirit of fair play' which he had always supposed him to possess. At the same time, he continued to press Beaulieu's candidacy. Haultain, the problem of inadequate finances temporarily eased, made it clear that residence in the Territories was an important qualification for the vacancy which did exist. He advised the church authorities to use their 'undoubted' influence to induce qualified teachers to come west and 'earn their promotion in the same way as other people are obliged to do.'[44] Very angry, Langevin, in a last major effort, issued a memorandum to the directors of selected Catholic teacher-training institutions in eastern Canada which detailed the whole story of the search for an inspector and remarked pointedly: 'If it is required that the candidate to the inspectorship be *residing in the Territories* and acquainted with the *Normal* training given in Regina, why was not this condition specified at the very beginning!!'[45] By this time tempers were high on both sides. To the government, the clergy had become most obnoxious, constantly badgering the authorities and seemingly oblivious to all but the attainment of their own ends. To the clergy, the government had become obstructive for obstruction's sake, unwilling to grant what seemed so reasonable and seemingly determined to raise qualifications to keep their goal just out of reach.

The memorandum had its effect and by the end of the year (1901) the minority had another candidate, L.E.O. Payment of Ottawa, a law student at Laval with very impressive qualifications. Besides an honours B.A. from Ottawa University, he had attended a model school in Ontario and the normal school in Winnipeg under Goggin (1890), and had taught successfully in Ontario and Manitoba for over ten years, five at Ottawa University as professor of mathematics, history, geography, and drawing. His English was excellent and his supporting testimonials highly favourable. Laurier, whom he had seen on 23 December, was apparently so impressed he was prepared to forward his application to Regina.[46] On 29 January 1902, however, Grandin learned from Merry del Val's successor, Archbishop Diomède Falconio, that Laurier had changed his mind. Payment was pursuing legal, not pedagogical, studies and intended to join the bar as soon as possible.[47] Payment himself provided additional reasons for Laurier's action. Payment was anxious to resume his career as a literary and legal knight errant on behalf of Catholic educational interests in the west. He had told Laurier he would be an inspector only until the principle of Catholic education and separate schools was recognized. Politically, too, the Payments were no friends of Laurier. Payment's brother, as mayor of Ottawa, had detested Laurier and Payment had openly opposed Laurier's politics in Quebec City.[48]

Disgusted with Laurier, Langevin, as in 1899, resorted to personal contact at Regina. On 14 April he dined with Forget, Haultain, and Sifton and learned that the minority would definitely have to propose a candidate from its resident French-speaking teachers.[49] This ruled out M.J. O'Connor of Ottawa, who submitted his credentials to Langevin on 18 June.[50] Not until late in 1903, when L.L. Kramer, a Regina teacher, volunteered his services, was the minority in a position to re-open negotiations. The new prospect lacked a university degree and would hardly have impressed Regina. However, it was Kramer's inability to speak French which caused Langevin to terminate negotiations immediately,[51] thereby saving the minority still another embarrassment.

Kramer was the minority's last candidate during the territorial period. Failure to obtain the much-sought appointment was, of course, a bitter disappointment to the Catholic leaders. That the government increased, somewhat arbitrarily, the necessary qualifications did not help. Once the residency requirement was introduced the minority's cause was doomed. The larger Catholic schools were staffed by teaching sisters and the one-room elementary schools offered little incentive for ambitious French-Canadian male teachers to leave Quebec. There is also some evidence that in the only Catholic high schools in the Territories (Calgary and Edmonton) very few pupils attempted the high school studies preparatory to teaching in the elementary schools.[52] It would appear that Bishop Grandin's minimal definition of an adequate education[53] practically assured an inadequate supply of local teachers , thus ultimately defeating the campaign for a French Catholic inspector.

IV

On the normal school and textbook issues the minority was no more successful. Bishop Legal discussed both with Haultain in mid-December 1897, and in his written summary of Catholic objectives submitted early in January he criticized special normal sessions in convents not taught by teaching sisters, and asked that the readers and histories authorized in Ontario and Quebec be permitted in the Territories.[54] With the inspectoral issue the focal point of attention in 1898, neither subject received further attention until Legal's second meeting with the government a year later. From a report which reflected Legal's characteristic optimism, Langevin learned that Haultain and Ross were willing to accept a good series of English Catholic readers on an optional basis. Legal had no doubt that the series Langevin was preparing would be adequate. The government was also disposed to approve one or two sisters as normal school instructors with power to grant certificates. Sister Greene of Calgary would probably make the best normal school principal. Langevin replied that he would write to her immediately and also send Legal and Forget three readers in the new series. It was also important to have Buckley and Robertson's history revised, the former French readers re-adopted, and the illustrated Bible accepted.[55] Early in 1899 Legal asked Laurier to encourage the conciliatory attitude at Regina. In view of the minority's later complaints about the territorial government's ill will, Legal's comment on the degree of government commitment is important:

... ces Messieurs semblent disposés à approuver une série de *Readers* catholiques qui d'ailleurs serait reconnue recommandable au point du vue technique ... Ils consentiraient à l'établissement d'une Ecole Normale sous la direction d'une ou de plusieurs religieuses compétentes, remédiant ainsi à l'inconvénient d'exiger que nos religieuses fréquentent les cours publics d'école normale.

Pour les livres d'histoire, sans demander un autre auteur peut-être se contenterait-on de demander d'autoriser pour nos écoles, un supplément où les quelques passages objectionables au point de vue catholique seraient rectifiés dans le sens catholique.[56]

The government, it would appear, had made no definite commitments.

Impressed by Legal's letter, Laurier wrote Forget and learned that a private word to Haultain would be well received. Ross favoured the minority more than Haultain, but both, Forget believed, would give Langevin a normal school. However, the history books, after appropriate 'corrections,' would remain.[57] During Langevin's first visit to Government House in March 1899, he learned that to obtain a normal school proof was needed that the sisters in charge had held successful normal sessions elsewhere. This appeared to exclude Sister Greene, but, he informed Legal, she and Sister Madeleine Fennell should still send their certificates to Regina. If a sister with normal school experience could be obtained in England, both would assist her. To keep public costs down, however, the sisters would teach without salary, a proposition which, Langevin was told, Legal himself had already made. The government was also willing to remove offensive textbook passages, to accept teachers without certificates where certificated ones were not available, to approve books authorized in Manitoba, and to have French taught. Legal was not impressed. In December, he told Langevin, Haultain had not appeared to doubt Sister Greene's qualifications. Nor had the matter of teaching without salary or maintaining a normal school without state support been raised.[58]

Negotiations for a Catholic normal school continued to be unsuccessful in 1899, but it was the indifference of the minority's own teaching order, the Faithful Companions of Jesus, not the state, which frustrated episcopal plans.

On 24 March, following the conciliatory indications from the government, Bishop Grandin asked Sister Girod, the mother superior, to send an experienced nun from England to direct a Catholic normal school in the Territories. Even though no state aid could be expected, once a school was established ways would be found to maintain it. From Paris Sister Girod reported that the order had no sisters in England with normal school experience. Unconvinced, Grandin repeated his request on 14 May.[59] Two weeks later Langevin, his patience wearing thin, also wrote expressing dismay that Paris could send no one to save the territorial Catholics, if that were necessary. Sister Girod, however, held firm. The minority, she told Grandin, would have to pray that the Regina authorities judged the qualifications of Sisters Greene and Fennell sufficient.[60]

The authorities, however, would not commit themselves, probably because the sisters' qualifications were not uncommon, and gave them no special licence to hold normal sessions. Neither had an academic degree. (Of the five inspectors who assisted Goggin with normal sessions, only John Hewgill had no degree.) Neither had taught in a normal school.[61] In October Legal complained to Haultain about the delay: Some of the sisters were 'perfectly' qualified to conduct normal sessions and should be approved to do so under government supervision. He said nothing of the minority's failure to furnish an experienced normal school principal.[62]

Desperate for teachers, Sister Greene and Bishop Legal canvassed the possibility of preparing more girls for the third-class certificate, followed by a normal session in charge of the sisters.[63] With the territorial programme of studies eight standards since July 1895, the intention was to increase the enrolment in Standard VI, which entitled a student to a third-class non-professional certificate.[64] With more high school students the minority would strike at the root of the teacher shortage in the elementary schools, namely, the minute high school enrolment in Catholic schools. The limited local supply of potential Catholic teachers, coupled with the smallness of the numbers of teachers with first- and second-class professional certificates who came to the Territories from Quebec between 1901 and 1905 (one and 24 respectively compared with Ontario's 142 and 524[65]), more than justified the fears of the French Catholic clergy for the future of bilingual education in the Territories. The small high school enrolment was the reef on which the campaigns for a French Catholic school inspector and a normal school eventually ran aground.

In the midst of these negotiations the Council of Public Instruction, which had become the Department of Public Instruction in 1897, was replaced (1901) by a department of education, with Haultain in charge as the commissioner of education appointed by the lieutenant-governor-in-council. Provision was also made for a five-man educational council appointed by the same authority to advise the Department of Education, as had the former appointed members of the Council of Public Instruction. At least two of the council members had to be Catholics. The council would meet annually in July at a time and place designated by the commissioner, who could also call additional meetings as necessary. No 'general' school regulations could be adopted or amended without prior consultation with the council, which could also report to the lieutenant-governor-in-council on 'any' educational question in the Territories.[66] The ordinance was passed with little debate on 15 June.

With time for the appointment of an educational council short, no meeting was held in 1901. On 18 April 1902, Langevin wrote Haultain and J.A. Calder, the deputy commissioner of education, recommending Beck and the Reverend A.J. Van Heertum, parish priest at Regina, for the two Catholic positions.[67] The government, however, preferred Beck and the Reverend Gillies.[68] Although the results of its first two-day meeting, held shortly thereafter,[69] were meagre, Beck was pleased with the disposition of his colleagues on the council. Goggin was also present but kept himself a little in the background, as it was understood he was about to leave the superintendent's post.[70] On Catholic initiative it was resolved that each school be provided with an equal number of Catholic and Protestant reference books in history until a Catholic text was approved,[71] but there is no evidence that the government acted on the resolution.

The resolution showed that the textbook question, though usually overshadowed by other issues, was not wholly forgotten. In October 1899 Legal had complained to Haultain that the territorial minority was worse off in that respect than Catholics in Ontario or England.[72] Even though Langevin did not have the 'courage' to discuss textbooks with Sifton at their meeting in April 1902, he asked Haultain and Calder, shortly thereafter, to approve the first two books in the 'Catholic Canadian Readers of Ontario' series.[73] Calder indicated that the educational council would 'in all probability' discuss the question,[74] but no textbook changes followed the July meeting. In

1903, with the government concerned to authorize 'a new set of readers and history textbooks for public school purposes,'[75] H.L. Thompson, president of Copp, Clark Company, suggested that Langevin inform the Catholic representatives on council that Calder had 'no objections' to the Catholic Canadian Readers.[76] But despite these encouraging signs no further textbook changes were made during the territorial period.

In 1900 the continued shortage of Catholic teachers and thus ultimately of possible candidates for inspector led Langevin to consider ways to increase the supply. In March he proposed that the school law be amended to have all Manitoba and Quebec certificates accepted at par at Regina.[77] (Since 1895 only first- and second-class certificates had been on an equal footing.[78]) When Legal pointed out it was the regulations of the Council of Public Instruction, not the law, which had to be changed,[79] the idea was dropped. In November Langevin expected the Brothers of the Institute of Christian Education to establish two Catholic boys' schools in Alberta,[80] but that idea, too, came to nothing.

As the shortage of Catholic teachers grew worse, a third alternative – a Catholic normal school at Regina – grew more attractive. By 1902, with the Territories enjoying unparalleled prosperity and the population increasing rapidly, further delay in establishing a Catholic normal school would mean non-Catholic schooling for many more Catholic children. Particularly vulnerable were recent arrivals from the Austro-Hungarian empire, the most numerous being settlers from Galicia and Bukovina, today part of western Ukraine. Most of the Galician immigrants were Greek Catholics or Uniates.[81] Although the 1901 census does not give their number, the *Edmonton Bulletin,* in March 1902, reported the territorial Roman and Greek Catholics to be 30,089 and 7,039 respectively. Three years later Legal placed the Greek Catholic population at 15,200 in Alberta alone.[82]

The Ukrainian immigration posed serious educational problems for both the government and the Roman Catholic church. The government preferred to see immigrant children in schools where the language of instruction was English and the course of study Anglo Protestant in emphasis. French Catholic church leaders naturally favoured bilingual Catholic schools, devoid of Anglo-Saxon overtones. But church policy was complicated by the need to ensure that the solution of Greek Catholic problems did not interfere with the satisfaction of French Catholic grievances, and by the suspicious attitude, a projection of European prejudices, which Greek Catholic settlers had towards the Roman Catholic church. The first difficulty became apparent in 1900 when Villeneuve suggested that the minority's next petition to Ottawa enlist the support of the immigrants who also desired schools in their own language (for most immigrants language superseded religion as a school issue from the beginning). Grandin and Legal were apprehensive. To place these immigrants on an equal footing with French Canadians was not only to grant all a favour which by law belonged only to the French-speaking, but to justify, in part, the Protestant majority's reluctance to accept separate schools. Judge Rouleau definitely opposed the suggestion. The French should help others only after they themselves had obtained justice. Langevin agreed: French alone should be mentioned in petitions; other languages had no constitutional right.[83]

An equally serious obstacle to an alliance with the Ukrainian immigrants was the attitude of the Greek Catholic settlers towards their Roman co-religionists. Though wooed by Protestant missionaries[84] and by Russian Orthodox priests,[85] the Ukrainian settlers stubbornly refused the good offices of the French and Polish Roman Catholic clergy.[86] Bishop Legal was fore-warned of the problem by the Reverend N. Dmytriw, a priest from the United States who visited Alberta in 1897. Dmytriw, Legal recorded plain-tively, seemed insufficiently concerned to maintain close relations with Catholics of the Latin rite. He had even objected to the term 'Catholique Romain,' maintaining his people were Greek Catholics, not Roman Catholics of the Greek or Ruthenian rite.[87] Legal's amazement showed how little aware the French Catholic clergy were of the historic antipathy between the two rites, the basis of conflict in Canada for nearly two decades. Opposition to the traditional Ukrainian enemy, the Roman Catholic Poles, led Greek Catholics to believe all Roman Catholic clergy were out to latinize them, though Grandin strongly denied this.[88]

In the circumstances the Roman Catholics seemed prepared to have a 'loose' alliance and not to insist upon 'common' schools. Several unsuccessful appeals to Rome, Paris, and Vienna for funds to establish a Greek Catholic clergy and to finance churches and schools for the 'Galiciens' followed.[89] Grandin, in a letter to the Oblates' superior-general in Paris in 1899, noted the dangers and disclosed the church's helplessness before Protestants, some-times aided by Galicians (termed apostates to their faith and nationality), who ensnared the Galicians through government-supported schools.[90] The concern was exaggerated – the product of an overly anxious missionary bishop. The first Protestants were successful only where Ukrainian settlement impinged upon areas with public schools. In the early years of Ukrainian settlement few public school districts existed because the settlers could not understand English and were too unfamiliar with democratic processes to organize and manage their own schools. By 1902 Langevin thought the overall situation critical enough to warrant the establishment of two Catholic normal schools, one in Manitoba and the other in the Territories. The normal schools would supply teachers for Galician schools also until it was possible to provide religious institutions and leadership acceptable to the Galicians.

The government at Regina, as concerned as the church about the education of immigrant children, found itself almost equally powerless to take the initiative. Educational expenditures, though increased, lagged behind enrolment and per-pupil expenditure dropped from $8.33 in 1897 to $5.67 in 1902.[91] The government, Haultain said later, found that 'the immigrant was a distinct asset to the Dominion and, at that time [1897–1905], a distinct liability to the Territories, with their increased need for local improvements.'[92] Galician education was first discussed at the 1900 session, when Haultain informed John W. Shera (Victoria) that the government was considering a school commissioner for the Galician settlements.[93] He saw no reason, he told Dr T.A. Patrick of Yorkton, why Galicians and Doukhobors 'should not come under the school system the same as other settlers.'[94] Early in 1901 Ross, the territorial treasurer, summed up the government's position:

... it is in the interest of the State that these children be educated and brought under the influences of our public institutions at as early a date as possible. As soon as financial arrangements can be made it is proposed to deal with the question systematically by the appointment of Commissioners empowered to put the school law into force and effect in those districts where voluntary action to that end is not being taken. It is estimated that this will involve an additional expenditure of some $10,000.00.[95]

The subject was thoroughly aired at the 1901 session. Any group intending to build its own school system, Haultain declared, would receive no government grants.[96] When Patrick, in response to petitions from German settlers in Saskatchewan and Assiniboia,[97] asked that a primary course in German be approved, the earlier arguments against bilingual education were revived. The North-West, Haultain protested, was an English-speaking country. Moreover, the practical difficulty of teachers' qualifications would require that regulations be relaxed. With immigrant children generally in school a short time, it was not asking 'too much' to have all instruction in English. All trustees should be empowered to employ competent persons to teach special languages – not German alone – 'after ordinary school hours' and under 'certain safeguards' to ensure no decrease in the amount of English education. Patrick and Villeneuve accepted the alternative, but Villeneuve challenged Haultain's view that 'in principle this was a British speaking country.' There were two official languages in Canada, English and French. Like Patrick, he believed the opportunity to educate in the mother tongue should exist, there being 'no danger' that parents would not desire their children to learn English.[98] Haultain's suggestion was adopted during the session,[99] and government policy on the education of immigrant children was clear by the time Archbishop Langevin launched his normal school project. The government would confine the attenuated system of bilingual education to the French settlements and tolerate no unauthorized modifications in the routine of publicly supported schools. Such a policy left little room for the idea of a multilingual normal school at Regina or Calgary.

To Archbishop Langevin, however, such a school was indispensable if the church was to influence the education of immigrant children. Recruits from the ranks of immigrant youth and from the Province of Quebec[100] would be the best means to protect the faith and to give French the place it ought to have. By furnishing the example of bilingualism in a multilingual setting, it would forestall assimilation to Anglo Protestantism, which only strengthened the majority and weakened the French Canadians in their struggle for a bilingual and bicultural nation. In short, the pro-Galician movement would strengthen the French position.[101] But much depended on Langevin's ability to convince the North-West that the Galicians were deeply attached to their religious faith and language and would voluntarily send their children to bilingual Catholic schools.

Much also hinged on his ability to persuade the Faithful Companions of Jesus to assume control of the elementary Catholic school at Regina, preliminary to their engaging in normal school work. Early in 1902 Langevin outlined his plans to Grandin and asked him to sign a collective letter to Sister Girod.[102] On 5 January he addressed the Catholic Club in Winnipeg and applied the French Catholic thesis of the inseparable connection between language and religion to the Galicians. Was there a single man in the country, he asked, who dared to assert that Canadian immigrants would have to give up their mother tongue to become good citizens?[103] The campaign, then, was under way: the Reverend Vasyl Zholdak, special representative in Canada since the fall of 1901 of Count Andrew Sheptitsky, Greek Catholic metropolitan in Lemberg (Lviv),[104] was advised to advance the above thesis in the Winnipeg newspapers[105] (advice that he ignored); the western governments were briefed publicly on Langevin's policy for the education of Catholic immigrant children; and a collective letter from the western hierarchy was on its way to Paris.

On 16 January, after 'an influential deputation' had asked the Manitoba government to make 'special' provisions for the education of Galician children, Langevin held a public meeting in Winnipeg and stressed the importance of schools in which the Galician language and the Catholic religion were taught. The *Edmonton Bulletin*, an early critic of immigration from southeastern Europe,[106] thought Langevin had gone far enough, particularly as the Galicians themselves (not all of whom were Catholics) had still to be heard from. The *Bulletin* did not know what views the Galicians held towards religious teaching in the schools, but '... from all that has gone forward in their settlements here so far it is not by any means likely that they would agree with Archbishop Langevin any more than they would with each other as to the nature of that teaching were it insisted upon by higher authority.'[107] The *Bulletin*'s reference was undoubtedly to the famous dispute, then at its peak, between the Greek Catholic and Russian Orthodox factions over control of the church at Star.[108] There is no evidence that the first Ukrainians in the Territories took any notice of the controversy over religious education in Canadian schools.

The apostolic delegate, too, opposed Langevin's idea of two polyglot normal schools. While all Catholics required Catholic teachers, English and French being the only languages generally recognized in Canada, it was necessary to recruit the teachers in Ontario and Quebec.[109] The matter was finally settled by Sister Girod, who again refused to join in the archbishop's plans.[110] Despite appeals to Metropolitan Sheptitsky, Sister Greene, Sister Girod, and a host of Catholic leaders in Quebec and elsewhere,[111] Langevin's normal school campaign was frustrated by Sister Girod's adamant refusal to establish a convent at Regina.[112] Langevin, angered by the strange behaviour of 'les *Infidèles* Compagnes de Jésus,'[113] resolved not to visit their establishments.

In the end another church-state confrontation was narrowly averted by circumstances beyond the control of either church or state. If the government's financial resources had permitted a more vigorous educational policy among the immigrants, or if Sister Girod had been more sympathetic to the hierarchy's appeals, a crisis on the normal school question would have been difficult to avoid.

Without a Catholic normal school, Langevin was obliged to petition the government for teaching permits, which were frequently denied. The point at issue was an old one: the qualifications of teaching sisters. To Langevin bilingual teaching sisters deserved temporary permits; to Haultain the permits were exceptional privileges issued under reasonable restrictions which had to be met. Of these, attendance at normal school sessions was indispensable.[114] This, Langevin thought, humiliated the sisters and incidentally exposed them to Protestant ideas.[115] The convents, he insisted, needed to take advantage of the provision which allowed normal sessions when six candidates were available, but unfortunately, Legal reported, the minority did not have the required number of high school graduates to warrant such classes.[116] In September 1903, at a meeting in St Boniface, the hierarchy decided to approach eastern Canada for personnel to teach high school and normal school classes.[117] The advent of the crisis over provincial autonomy, however, overwhelmed this and all other plans.

9
Provincial autonomy and the school question, 1895-1905

Since 1890 southern Alberta (in particular, Calgary) had been the centre of agitation for provincial autonomy in the North-West. Both candidates in the 1891 federal election had favoured the move, but Haultain did not accept autonomy as a realistic goal until seven years later. It was an important issue in the 1898 territorial election, but no one urged the question which Thompson, Mills, and others had said would be raised in future autonomy discussions: the status of separate schools under provincial control. In 1900 Haultain's resolution requesting the governor-general-in-council to inquire into the terms and conditions of provincial autonomy passed unanimously, but in reviewing the terms Haultain made no mention of education.[1]

In May 1901, with the federal government willing to discuss autonomy,[2] Villeneuve raised in the assembly the question of territorial representation at future conferences. Only the government, Haultain replied casually, could represent the government of the Territories. When Dr D.H. McDonald (Qu'Appelle North) concluded from this statement that the government would consult no one, Haultain went on to declare that the government would only discuss, not settle, the terms. The question, Villeneuve then observed, was a delicate one. The French Canadians had special rights granted by law and the constitution and should be represented at any negotiations at Ottawa. A.S. Smith (Moosomin) objected vigorously to one 'class' being represented more than another: Canada had had enough of appeals to 'the prejudices of the people.' 'We never did,' Villeneuve replied curtly, but Haultain as usual had the last word. The French had special rights, but special representation was not one of them: 'The interests are Territorial interests; the questions are questions which do not affect any special race or creed. Our rights are not our rights as Englishmen, Scotchmen or Irishmen, or as Doukhobors or Galicians or anything of that kind but as citizens of a common country.'[3]

A conference was subsequently held on 25 October 1901, in the prime minister's office, with Haultain and A.L. Sifton representing the Territories before a cabinet committee consisting of Laurier, C. Sifton, Tarte, W.S. Fielding, R.W. Scott, and Sir Richard Cartwright. Laurier asked Haultain to submit the territorial case in writing and Haultain prepared his famous draft bill, described by Lingard as 'perhaps the most important document dealing with the autonomy movement.'[4] The bill[5] (dated 7 December) made no explicit reference to education. Section 2, however, specified that the BNA Act would apply to the new province visualized by Haultain, as if the latter 'had been one of the Provinces originally united by the said Act,' excepting such sections as applied only to Ontario and Quebec, and those parts which by 'reasonable intendment' could be held 'to affect only one or more' province(s).

Was it reasonable, then, to suppose that section 93(1) would apply to the new province? Would the government possess full powers over education, or would it need to legislate so as not to 'prejudicially affect any Right or Privilege with respect to Denominational Schools which any Class of Persons have by Law in the Province at the Union?'[6] Haultain's clause did not answer the question. 'With regard to the question of education generally,' he wrote Laurier some years later:

... you are no doubt aware that the position taken by us was that the Provinces should be left to deal with the subject exclusively subject to the provisions of the British North America Act, thus putting them on the same footing in this regard as all the other Provinces in the Dominion except Ontario and Quebec.

The question is one of Provincial rights. It is not a question of the rights of a religious minority which must be properly and may be safely left to the Provincial Legislatures to deal with subject to the general constitutional provisions in that regard.[7]

The only federal protection for the minority's rights favoured by Haultain was the right of remedial legislation granted the federal government by section 93(4). He had always contended that the Territories were part of the union since 1870,[8] thus nullifying in his view section 93(1), for there were no rights or privileges with regard to denominational schools that any class of persons had *by law* in the Territories at the union. But it appears that Haultain also envisaged no change in the status quo of separate schools once the Territories became a province: 'If I were made dictator tomorrow,' he told a *Toronto Globe* reporter on 25 February 1905, 'I would not change it.'[9] His draft bill, however, was not explicit on this point, thus contributing to a great deal of the later controversy.

One should not suppose that the bill in general omitted details. Indeed, Haultain included lengthy explanatory memos after each section, memos which left little doubt as to his intentions on other subjects. That after section 2, however, was strangely brief: 'This is the provision adopted on the incorporation of each of the Provinces since the Union.'[10] Haultain must have suspected that Catholic leaders would try to secure a school clause that increased their educational influence and ensured against a repetition of the Manitoba experience. He could have concluded that they would have at least the *ear* of the government at Ottawa. It was also clear that the federal Conservatives, who had lost power in 1896 on an earlier school question, would be pleased to return to office on another. If, as he claimed later, Haultain truly wanted the new provinces 'to work out' their own futures free of dissension,[11] it is odd that he did not include a more explicit clause in section 2 and a more extensive explanatory memo. Haultain may have sought to avoid controversy by saying little and thus providing little to quibble over, but this seems unrealistic in view of past history. In the end he only encouraged the dissension he wished to prevent.

Haultain hoped for provincial status by 1 January 1903. In March 1902 Clifford Sifton informed him that autonomy would be delayed because the rapid growth of population materially altered conditions, and because there was no general consensus on the number of provinces.[12] Although Sifton did not mention it, there was also no general agreement on another, even more prickly, issue: Should Manitoba's boundaries be extended westward and/or northward, and if so, would the school system of Manitoba or the Territories prevail in the enlarged province? Parliament discussed the subject of autonomy at great length in 1902. Apart from Walter Scott (Davin's successsful opponent in 1900), the territorial representatives were lukewarm towards immediate autonomy,[13] and the opposition alone raised the school question. On 21 March Senator Perley attributed the government's delay to a reluctance to do anything before the next federal election 'on account of some difficulty that may arise in connection with the school question.' Senator Richard W. Scott, the Roman Catholic veteran on the school question who had been in the Senate when the territorial separate school clause was passed in 1875, only replied that he had not heard it mentioned 'in that connection.'[14]

When Manitoba's Nathaniel Boyd advanced Perley's line in the Commons, Walter Scott praised the territorial school system and stressed its establishment 'without any of the turmoil which was created before the Manitoba system could be brought to its present satisfactory state.' Manitoba's Clifford Sifton, the Protestant veteran on the school question, denied that any 'political game' could be played with the issue, as it was settled in the Territories. Both Catholics and Protestants felt they had 'a satisfactory compromise,' and the house 'may possibly' look forward to disposing of the matter 'without any acrimonious discussion.' Robert Borden, the opposition leader, was glad to hear of the satisfactory settlement: '... I trust that it is so.' Boyd expressed a similar hope: '... whatever will satisfy them will satisfy me.'[15]

In what was to be the final general election in the Territories (May 1902) only Haultain's opponent at Macleod opposed provincial autonomy.[16] All but one of the incumbents who sought re-election (all supporters of Haultain's autonomy resolution in 1900) were returned. According to Lingard, Haultain regarded the results as 'practically a unanimous mandate' for the immediate granting of autonomy 'along the lines of his draft bill.'[17] The school question was not an electoral issue. Preoccupied with the tremendous development of the country, most people probably felt as did Laurier in a letter to his biographer, J.S. Willison, editor of the *Toronto News*, at the beginning of 1903: 'Happily, there is before me now no burning question, no irritating problem. The only thing to do is to push forward as fast as possible the development of the country and to keep in motion the forward movement which is now in progress.'[18] Ironically, it was the same Willison who would shortly help to make the territorial school question a 'burning issue' and an 'irritating problem.'

In the exhaustive debate over autonomy in 1903 the school question was ignored. However, Oliver, Davis, and Scott made it clear that they and the entire North-West supported the terms in Haultain's draft bill.[19] Douglas, an Independent Liberal, said nothing at all about Haultain's bill, and Lougheed and Perley in the Senate did likewise.

There were, however, rumblings below the calm political surface. Late in 1901 the former territorial governor, Joseph Royal, in an interview in *Le Pionnier* (Montreal), had declared that, if the autonomy question ever came before Parliament, the minority's friends would have to keep 'their eyes open.'[20] In 1902 when Borden toured the Territories, he asserted ominously that he favoured giving the fullest control of local affairs to the people.[21] Subsequent references to the subject were more frequent, and reports by eastern newspapers were carried regularly in the Territories. In

July D.J. Goggin, now president of the Dominion Educational Association, told the Conservative *Toronto News* that it was 'hinted that certain powerful political influences, operating outside the Territories, have made it clear ... at Ottawa that a guarantee of separate schools and dual language must be an integral part of any autonomy measure.' And in August James Clinkskill, who had retired from the assembly in 1898, declared in the same *News* that the separate school system pleased the Catholic laity but that the hierarchy wanted an autonomy clause which would give it 'absolute control' of the schools.[22]

In the general calm, the attitude of the Catholic laity towards autonomy is difficult to assess. Support for pro-autonomy candidates was general in the May 1902 election, and not until late in September 1903 was there any evidence of concern. From Montreal, Villeneuve asked Laurier to appoint a commission to study the many problems involved, especially for the French people in the west. Laurier rejected the idea because it was clear that the powers to be given the Territories were those usually given to provinces.[23] And when many months later, on 1 February 1905, Villeneuve approached Louis P. Brodeur, minister of internal revenue, on behalf of several friends in the Territories, he said the Catholic position was good but that two improvements could be made: the school ordinance should be more explicit on the teaching of French; and to help French Canadians obtain qualified French-speaking teachers, those imported for the rural schools should have shorter normal school sessions without examinations.[24] Laurier personally favoured both changes, but, he told Villeneuve, the desire for provincial autonomy was now so strong that the new provinces would not be satisfied with having their powers limited as suggested. Catholics would damage their legitimate claims by opposing the established principle of provincial autonomy.[25] A few days later the St Jean Baptiste Society in Edmonton forwarded four resolutions to Laurier, asking that the self-evident rights of the French Canadians in the North-West be respected by guaranteeing in the autonomy bill the official use of French and its place in the school curriculum. Laurier informed Antonio Prince that a settlement of the language question in the manner requested was absolutely impossible and asked him not to raise it as the school question was now (1905) sufficiently embarrassing.[26] The new province(s) were not to be bilingual.

The autonomy question had been discussed periodically by Catholic church leaders in the Territories since 1895, but the group was ambivalent. Grandin remarked to Langevin in 1896 that he had feared autonomy ever since developments in Manitoba had shown that the federal government would not protect the minority in the provinces. Father Leduc favoured it, however, in the belief that a new government would in time turn the minority's 'écoles libres' into what their title signified.²⁷ Extensive discussions by the hierarchy of the probable constitution of the new province(s) took place in 1902 and 1903. Letters to Laurier and Haultain were proposed, but with no one assigned to write them, apparently none were sent.²⁸ Langevin asked LaRivière to discuss the possible westward expansion of Manitoba's boundaries with the new apostolic delegate, Donatus Sbaretti, archbishop of Ephesus. Assiniboia, he said, should retain its separate school rights while Manitoba's confessional schools should be restored.²⁹

With autonomy a lively issue in the Commons in 1903, Sbaretti asked Legal, bishop of St Albert after Grandin's death in June 1902, for a complete report on the territorial school situation.³⁰ Legal gave, as the school system's advantages, the formation of Catholic public and separate school districts, the right to Catholic school taxes, trustees, and teachers, and government aid to Catholic schools. To the usual objectives still to be atttained he added: an end to the suppression of the word 'Catholic' in the title of Catholic public school districts and a share of the school taxes paid by industrial or commercial companies that were 'anonymous.'³¹

II

As the agitation for autonomy gained momentum in 1904 there could be little doubt that Sir Wilfrid Laurier would have a difficult time. On the one hand, his own party expected him to champion provincial rights. The Liberal nominating convention at Strathcona in January expressed 'utmost confidence' that the government would deal 'justly and fairly' with the people in the Territories, as the Liberals had always supported the principle of local self-government.³² On the other hand, most French Catholics looked to Laurier to maintain separate schools.³³ And in a German Catholic newspaper, L.L. Kramer called on Catholics to 'stand together for the day is perhaps not too very far distant when we here in the North-West will also be obliged to stand shoulder to shoulder in order to guard against being robbed of our rights and privileges.'³⁴ Diverse expectations were brewing a major crisis for Laurier and the Liberal party.

The date on which the first discussion of the autonomy question between the apostolic delegate and the federal government began is not certain. On 1 March, after an earlier, cordial meeting with Senator Scott, Sbaretti reminded Laurier of his promise (he did not say when it had been made) to insert a clause in the autonomy bill 'guaranteeing the Catholics the system of Separate Schools,' and asked that Laurier communicate 'the declarations made and the assurances given' by Scott to Sbaretti in a signed document.[35] Laurier obliged with an explicit statement of his position. It was very clear that minority schools in the Territories should receive the same protection as in Ontario and Quebec. The provincial legislature should be unable to abolish them or affect them prejudicially, as provided in section 93. Territorial separate schools were introduced by 'positive enactment of the law' in 1875, and since that time Catholic settlers had established hundreds of schools. They had 'the same right to the guarantee of their schools under the constitution' as had the inhabitants of the older provinces where the same system existed at Confederation.[36]

Laurier's position in 1904 was in line with his remarks ten years earlier.[37] To protect separate schools the Territories were to be treated as if they were already provinces which were now entering Confederation as Ontario and Quebec had in 1867. The position had its difficulties. For if one accepted Haultain's thesis that the Territories entered the union in *1870*, it followed that separate schools were introduced by the federal government *after* the Territories had joined the union and the application of section 93(1) was, then, at least debatable because there were no legal separate school rights or privileges in 1870. If one took the Liberal view that the Territories entered the union in 1905 (complete with separate schools), the fact remained that territories, not provinces, were joining the union, a contingency not precisely within the scope of section 93. The situation was not comparable to that which existed when Ontario and Quebec – provinces with *self-imposed* separate school systems – formed the union in 1867. The prime minister, however, stubbornly refused to recognize that fact.

Despite Laurier's clear commitment to protect the minority's educational interests, the apostolic delegate asked him to assure the Canadian hierarchy and Rome that his government 'pledges itself to insert a clause in the Constitution Acts of the Provinces, to secure the system of Separate Schools ... as they are in Ontario and Quebec ...'[38] (Sbaretti's goal, he had himself confessed to Charles Fitzpatrick, minister of justice, earlier, was to obtain two strictly official documents, one signed by Fitzpatrick and Henri Bourassa, and the other by Laurier himself, guaranteeing separate schools in the new province(s).[39]) Laurier found the delegate's request 'of a very unusual character.' It did not seem to be 'in accordance with our system of government.' Moreover, it was unnecessary, as he had already given 'a clear & categorical' commitment.[40] The delegate did not insist; his request was prompted by 'a person highly located in the Church,' who had expressed some doubt about the clarity of Laurier's earlier letter.[41]

With legislation imminent Sbaretti asked Legal to suggest a wording for a precise clause to protect the separate schools.[42] To Legal, section 93 had been precise enough until events in Manitoba had mutilated it. To exact too much, he warned, might compromise the basic essential – tax support.[43] Nevertheless, the document he sent contained a comprehensive school clause.[44] Unlike Laurier, Legal recognized that the Territories were only territories and that the province(s) had still to be formed. Like Laurier, but unlike Haultain, he therefore wanted a clause to place the separate school system beyond the reach of the new provincial legislature(s). The 'essentials' of a separate school system – taxation, representation on an educational council, inspection, textbooks, and normal schooling – were to be guaranteed. The change that went unnoticed in 1886 was to be repealed: separate and 'undenominational' school districts should have 'the same or different limits.' One-third of the members on the educational council and on the inspectoral staff were to represent the minority, 'whether Protestant or Roman Catholic,' and section 93(4) was to apply.[45] Sbaretti recognized, as did Legal himself, that it would be very difficult to have all the points incorporated into a bill.[46]

Simultaneously, the territorial government continued to negotiate with the federal government. In May Premier Haultain informed Laurier that the new Redistribution Act was no substitute for provincial autonomy. The population of the Territories ('about 450,000') was large enough to warrant eighteen members, not the ten the act granted.[47] In Toronto Haultain expressed confidence he could give the Territories a satisfactory law 'if the Dominion Government would give him the power to enact it and keep their hands off the funds.'[48] On 1 June he asked Laurier to resume negotiations on the basis of his earlier draft bill. At the top of his eight-point summary of acceptable terms was 'the application of the British North America Act as far as possible to the area dealt with.' The fourth point was equally vague: 'The preservation of vested interests.'[49]

The prime minister sent no immediate reply. He had already told Cardinal Merry del Val that autonomy would result in new agitation. It was significant, he thought, that Haultain's draft bill made no mention of separate schools. While the boundary question might lead Manitoba to recognize the minority's rights, he was not as hopeful as the delegate who had not witnessed the agitation that had convulsed the nation in the 1890s. He would heed the cardinal's wish to negotiate the school question himself, but he wanted no embarrassing interference from the clergy at home, least of all at election time.[50]

On 30 September, with an election imminent, Laurier promised Haultain that, should the government be returned, immediate negotiations would follow to settle 'the various questions' involved in granting autonomy at the next session of Parliament. Haultain, about to take to the Conservative hustings, merely acknowledged the letter.[51] With provocative newspaper references to the school question on the increase, Senator Scott asked Sbaretti to ensure that Catholics would not react to them: '... if the subject becomes a live question during the election campaign it will result disastrously.' It would not do for most members to come to Ottawa 'pledged against the recognition of the rights of the minority.'[52] Sbaretti, attending the annual meeting of the Catholic archbishops at Three Rivers, agreed to enforce silence.[53] He had, however, to contend with Archbishop Langevin, who not only took 'an active interest' to aid the Conservatives in Manitoba, but urged, at Three Rivers, the very course Laurier wished to avoid: a formal intervention under the hierarchy's direction to secure the minority's acquired rights.[54]

In the Territories the election went off without incident; the school question was not an issue. The Liberals tried to keep the autonomy question under wraps, but with Haultain making it a major issue in his tour of the Territories, even the school question had an airing at Regina. On 12 October Haultain challenged Clifford Sifton to state the government's policy on separate schools. When Sifton refused, the debate withered. 'If it is important to know the views of the Government,' Walter Scott's *Regina Leader* lectured Haultain, '... it is equally important to know where Mr Borden stands.'[55] On 7 November the Liberals carried seven of the ten territorial seats and the nation reflected the territorial verdict (139–75).

III

The election over, Langevin and Sbaretti entered upon a determined but careful campaign to secure the minority's educational interests. Sbaretti saw Laurier on 11 November and was promised a copy of the school clause as soon as it was ready.[56] None, however, was forthcoming in 1904 and Sbaretti was obliged to request it on three separate occasions.[57] Langevin took the initiative in another direction. On 26 November he wrote his suffragans and suggested that the Canadian hierarchy send the governor-general-in-council a petition requesting the maintenance of separate schools in the Territories and their restoration in Manitoba.[58] Langevin also asked Beck to prepare 'a *memo*, or a pamphlet, or an open letter on ... the *vested rights* of Catholics and of others to *separate school* districts (I think this is all what [*sic*] remains now)' in the North-West.[59] Next he wrote the delegate and stressed the significance of securing Rome's support. An official declaration by the pope or the delegate, denying that the school question was settled, would persuade the people to follow their bishops. Without it, an episcopal petition was out of the question, and without a petition the minority could expect little. Premier Roblin of Manitoba, he had learned, would amend the school law if Manitoba's boundaries were extended, at Assiniboia's expense, if necessary. Roblin himself had informed him that Laurier had the power now to pass a school bill for the whole of western Canada.[60] A similar letter to Cardinal G.M. Gotti, prefect of propaganda in Rome, followed, with a copy to Cardinal Merry del Val.[61] On 28 December Langevin again wrote the delegate about the importance of a petition, preceded by a word from Rome.[62]

On 22 December Father Leduc, in charge at St Albert during Bishop Legal's European absence, again appealed to Laurier's ethnic and religious background, as he had done eight years earlier.[63] Laurier could atone for his one big mistake by introducing the separate school question into the cabinet's autonomy discussions and by informing Roblin that the condition of Manitoba's expansion westward was the granting of full justice to the Catholic minority in that province.[64]

A week later Beck, the minority's legal adviser in Edmonton, informed Langevin that a public statement would be 'a diplomatic mistake, at least at the present time.' Newspaper controversy would only 'intimidate' the government. On the constitutional question he dismissed section 2 in Haultain's draft bill. He supported the view that the Territories entered the union in 1870 when 'no "class of persons" in the Territories had "by law ... any right or privilege with respect to denominational schools." ' Section 93(1) therefore would give the minority 'no protection whatever.' Even if the date of the union were 1905, section 93(1) 'would probably not apply' as the Territories were not a province. He therefore proposed a clause which guaranteed the minority the rights it already had. There were, he thought, really no other substantial rights that could be claimed under the law as it then stood. Without 'appropriate and effective remedies' to meet 'a wave of fanaticism' in the new province should it come, he advised the minority to go as 'safely' as it could towards 'a uniform system,' giving no one the opportunity to say that Catholic teachers or pupils were below Protestant standards.[65]

IV

Final negotiations between the federal and territorial governments continued through to 21 February 1905. The Territories were represented by the Conservative Haultain, whose record of public service made him a leading candidate for the post of provincial premier, and by the Liberal Bulyea, minister of public works, who soon became the first lieutenant-governor of the new Province of Alberta.[66] The federal government was represented by Laurier, Fitzpatrick, Senator Scott, and – the lone Protestant – Sir William Mulock, postmaster general. Laurier also held discussions with the seven territorial Liberals in the Commons and Haultain and Bulyea 'occasionally' met J.H. Ross and T.O. Davis, the two territorial Liberals in the Senate.[67] According to Walter Scott, Laurier and Fitzpatrick talked 'pretty reasonably,' but in reviewing the proposed autonomy terms for George Brown, Regina's MLA, Scott said nothing about a school clause.[68]

The school clause had, in fact, received little attention. 'We have no school question on our hands and do not expect any,' Bulyea declared on reaching Ottawa,[69] and negotiations were conducted as if that were so. Haultain, in an open letter to Laurier, declared later that, beyond 'a casual reference' to it on 17 February, education had not been discussed until noon on 21 February, the day Laurier introduced the autonomy legislation in the Commons.[70] 'What may have been casual to Mr Haultain,' Laurier told the Commons on 15 March, 'may have been thorough to somebody else.' From discussions on the twenty-first, Laurier continued, two views emerged: 'Mr Haultain took the ground that section 93 ... applied mechanically to those new provinces. The ground we took was that section 93 ... should be made to apply in the legislation we offered to the House, subject only to such modifications as the circumstances of the new provinces would warrant.' Fitzpatrick's explanations on the same day were similar.[71] The government, then, was satisfied that education had been discussed sufficiently, but it is also clear that important differences had not been resolved.

The clause in question had been drafted by Fitzpatrick in consultation with Laurier and Sbaretti, and on 10 January Fitzpatrick finally gave it to Sbaretti.[72] The latter, in a '*sub secreto*' communication, then sent it to Langevin with two suggested amendments. The government's clause was essentially a restatement of section 11 in the 1875 NWT Act. The delegate, however, thought that two of Legal's recommendations should be included: the repeal of the 1886 restriction on separate school organization and the designation to the minority of a 'proportionate' share of the school revenues from the sale of public lands.[73]

Langevin thought the government's clause was not explicit enough to counter a hostile government, and held that it was also important to guarantee all funds and legislative grants voted for schools, not just a share of the school-lands fund.[74] Beck suggested a more careful definition of the term 'proportionate,' a provision for separate schools to obtain a share of corporation taxes, and a guarantee that high schools (should they be centralized) would not suffer the fate of normal schools.[75] Accordingly, Sbaretti asked Laurier for an explicit application of section 93 to the province(s). Catholics should also have the right to establish and maintain schools 'as they think fit,' with power to share in all 'public funds, resources or powers – whether Dominion, Provincial, municipal or other.'[76] Laurier referred Sbaretti's suggestions to Fitzpatrick: 'In all these matters, it is far preferable to leave the drafting to experienced jurists, and, in that class, he has no superior.' The words, ' "subject to the provisions of the B.N.A. Act," ' were not necessary because the bill would automatically apply that act to 'the Province.' The point was not of 'much consequence,' but the delegate's second point carried 'a very serious import' and Fitzpatrick would be asked to discuss it with Sbaretti.[77]

On 21 January the delegate introduced a new issue. Having learned from the newspapers of the Manitoba Legislature's resolution to have Ottawa extend its boundaries, he suggested that Laurier use the resolution as 'a lever to bring Manitoba to ameliorate' the Catholic position there. The government should experience 'no great difficulty' in 'forbidding' the extension of Manitoba's school law to any territory that might be added, or in reserving to the minority 'for all time to come' the right to establish separate schools therein. The stand would accord not only with the general principle of separate schools which existed throughout the Dominion and was 'spreading throughout the Empire,' but also with the policy of the Liberal party, which had established separate schools in Ontario and the North-West. In Manitoba, Parliament's will (as expressed in 1870) had been 'thwarted' by the Privy Council in England, and the time had now come to settle all questions 'authoritatively.'[78]

Laurier replied he had no intention of taking up Manitoba's resolution in 1905. He wanted a short session and the autonomy legislation gave the government enough to do. The boundary between Manitoba and the Territories, he had definitely concluded, should not be interfered with.[79] At a meeting with Sbaretti on 1 February Laurier agreed that all school funds should be guaranteed to the minority. The delegate also wished to have the phrase, ' "for the continuation of separate schools," ' added to the school clause, but as Laurier opposed it and Fitzpatrick was disposed to insert section 93 'in extenso' into the bill, he suggested that section 93(1) be changed to read as follows: 'Nothing in any such law shall prejudicially affect the existence of, and any right or privilege with respect to denominational schools which any class of persons have in the Province at the time of the passing of this Act.' He was anxious to remove any doubt as to whether the words in the section meant 'the time of the Union as Territories or as a Province.'[80]

On 7 February Fitzpatrick sent Sbaretti a revised clause which gave no explicit guarantee to either the public funds or the separate schools. Sbaretti wrote Laurier immediately and pressed for his earlier amendment – '*for the continuation (or existence) of Separate Schools*' – and for the minority to '*make the necessary assessments and collection of rates thereof,*' with rate-payers 'liable only to assessments of such rates as they impose themselves.'[81] Three days later Laurier handed Sbaretti another revised clause which con-tained neither amendment.[82] Sbaretti proposed immediate changes, but Laurier would not commit himself. Next day he informed Sbaretti that the government's law officers believed the slight changes did not really improve the sense of the clause and would only complicate a sentence that had been prepared with great care. He hoped the existing draft would be satisfactory.[83] Sbaretti did not insist: he wrote Laurier that he was glad they had succeeded in agreeing upon a clause, through which, he had no doubt, the rights of the minority would 'always [be] safeguarded.'[84] But the next day he sent the clause to Legal and asked whether he should insist upon the following: ' "and may make the necessary assessments and collection of rates therefor" ' and ' "whether a public school has been established therein or not" '[85] (a phrase which Fitzpatrick had included on 7 February and omitted on 10 February). As Legal apparently considered only the second change important and neither essential,[86] Sbaretti explained to Laurier that an explicit guarantee to separate schools would ease the problem of organizing Catholic separate schools where Protestants eventually became the majority in Catholic public school districts (as has happened in St Albert in recent years[87]). It would also show that the rights of the minority were not dependent upon the dispo-sition of the majority and make the inconsistency between the liberal NWT Act and the restrictive school ordinance clearer, leading 'no doubt' to the amendment of the ordinance. However, he left the matter to the prime minister's discretion.[88] Laurier appreciated this and wrote to Sbaretti that unlike the other parts of the proposed clause, which stood 'on the firm ground of precedents and existing laws,' the addition contained 'new' words which opened the way for 'a somewhat dangerous attack.' He intended to omit it: 'I now see my way perfectly before me.'[89]

The apostolic delegate was pleased and said so 'very confidentially' to Langevin: 'I have every reason to believe that the rights of Catholics in the North West Territories to separate schools will be guaranteed in the consti-tutions of the new Provinces.' Success depended upon 'avoiding everything' that would call 'general attention' to the subject and 'especially any public act that would excite Protestant animosity.'[90] Langevin promised extreme prudence to prevent fanaticism.[91] On 20 February Sbaretti sent the final revision of the school clause to St Boniface. It spoke of 'an equitable share or proportion' of public moneys for both public and separate schools, but contained no formula for their apportionment. It specified that section 93 would apply to the new provinces and defined the term 'Union' to mean the day on which the autonomy legislation came into force, the territory involved being treated as if it were 'already a province.' Without explanation, the first of Sbaretti's additions was also included: the minority could assess and collect rates for the support of separate schools. 'If Parliament passes the clause as it stands,' Sbaretti admitted, 'we shall have more in the Constitutional Acts of these Provinces than in any of the Constitutional Acts of the other Provinces of the Dominion.'[92] Haultain and other territorial representatives, it should be clear, had not participated in these negotiations and did not see the clause until it was introduced in the Commons on 21 February. The secrecy only helped to fan Protestant suspicions once the clause became a public issue.

Bishop Legal, too, had not participated in the negotiations. He returned from Europe early in February[93] and, accompanied by Leduc, saw the delegate on 9 February.[94] Both were undoubtedly cautioned to maintain 'absolute silence.'[95] On 11 February, however, Legal was interviewed by a *Toronto Star* reporter in Montreal and was quoted as follows: 'From our standpoint, there cannot be any compromise on this question. Our schools are not only places where children are taught, but where they receive their religious training, and it should ever be so. This is the only advice we have given to all our people, and it is this we have urged them to obtain.'[96] Surprised, Sbaretti wrote Legal that, even if he had given the interview, Sbaretti felt 'sure' Legal had not given it in the manner reported, 'for its tone is such as might excite Protestant animosity.' He thought it best to give no more interviews on the subject.[97] Legal, however, had already given a second, milder interview in the same city: 'In the Territories we have seperate [*sic*] schools and we get along splendidly. Different denominations never have trouble. Seperate schools are the only ones [?] to be called national. The population is catholic and protestant and neither can dictate to the other. A neutral system would be a protestant school system. Commissioners, teachers and books would be protestant. The catholic population in the Territories is one in four, but we cannot see that any improvements can be made. If any change is made we will fight till we get seperate schools, but there will be no change.'[98] At the same time from St Boniface Langevin sounded a more jarring note when he gave the Winnipeg correspondent of the *Toronto Globe* to understand that the territorial school system was as unacceptable as Manitoba's.[99] Legal's guarded satisfaction contrasted sharply with Langevin's open dissatisfaction – the first indication that the two prelates could move in opposite directions on the school question. The ingredients for a political and religious explosion were therefore present. Only a lighted match was needed and this the minister of the interior, Clifford Sifton, provided when he submitted his resignation on 27 February.

Sifton, away in Indiana for his health, had been conspicuously absent during the negotiations. Before leaving Ottawa he had left his comments in the margins of Haultain's draft bill, but, like the bill itself, they contained no reference to any school clause. Opposite section 2, Sifton (according to Fitzpatrick) wrote: 'Make memo of present provisions in law relating to the Northwest Territories as to public schools and provisions in other constitutional Acts.'[100] Sifton kept in touch with Laurier during the negotiations. On 22 January his letter noted his pleasure that everything was going well and that rapid progress was being made. 'You do not say any thing about the school question. I assume that you have not as yet discerned any serious difficulty in dealing with it.'[101] In reply Laurier's reference to the issue was brief: 'There also remains the school question which I am slowly working out. I am satisfied with the progress which we have made on it, though everybody dreads it.'[102] This was the *only* reference to the subject in the Laurier-Sifton correspondence.

Rumours, however, were current, and a full ten days before the event the Conservative press in Alberta carried bold headlines over brief news dispatches from Toronto: 'Clifford Sifton May Retire Over the School Question,' 'Sifton May Withdraw/Not in Sympathy with Cabinet on School Question.'[103] The source of the information was not given. Undoubtedly the invention of hopeful Conservative politicians, the headlines were highly prophetic, for Sifton returned to Ottawa on 23 February, met with Laurier on the next day,[104] and resigned on the twenty-seventh in opposition to the government's school clause.

v

... The government should in the political organization of those provinces remove all causes of friction, of national and religious discontent ... The winds which blow from the northwest are violent and sometimes they bring storms which more than once have shaken the foundations of confederation. Experience is a lesson and a source of wisdom for statesmen.[105]

With these words Senator L.O. David, Laurier's old friend, had opened debate in the Upper House on the throne speech on 17 January, with Laurier in attendance. In the months preceding his own autonomy speech Laurier had done as Senator David advised – he had preoccupied himself with Canada's constitutional 'experience' in defining government policy on the school question. Not surprisingly therefore, his discussion of education in the Commons on 21 February[106] was steeped in history. 'If we look back to the history of our own country, if we find what is the origin of the separate schools, perhaps history may be the pillar of cloud by day and the pillar of fire by night to show us the way and give us the light.' The rest of Laurier's speech was largely an historical defence of the thesis he had first presented to the delegate a year earlier. 'Is it reasonable to suppose,' he asked, 'if the Confederation Act recognizes that other provinces were to come into con-federation similarly situated to Ontario and Quebec, that the same privileges should not be given to the minority [in the Territories] as were given to the minority in Ontario and Quebec?' An extensive account followed of the circumstances under which the provinces of Ontario and Quebec came to *accept* a system of separate schools and the North-West Territories came to *possess* a system of separate schools, a distinction which Laurier himself did not recognize. He quoted section 93(1) to show that the federal govern-ment had an obligation to protect minority rights in education, but said nothing of the possibility that a separate school system having its origin in federal legislation might require a less doctrinaire application of that section.

Laurier also quoted Senator George Brown extensively and was particu-larly impressed by his short statement in 1875: 'The moment ... this Act passed and the Northwest became part of the union, they [the Territories] came under the Union Act, and under the provisions with regard to separate schools.' Laurier did not notice that the date of union in the above was 1875, not 1905, the date of union in subsection one of the government's school clause. Consequently, Brown could be a difficult authority. Moreover, even if one accepted Brown's date and granted that the North-West came under the provisions of section 93(1), the fact still remained that separate schools in the Territories did not precede the union in 1875, but were introduced concurrently with the passage of that act. The Territories were then by no means 'similarly situated' to the provinces of Ontario and Quebec in respect of the BNA Act and the government could be accused of invoking section 93 for other than constitutional reasons. The prime minister eulogized separate schools and blamed the 'social condition of civil society' in the United States on the absence of schools in which 'Christian morals and Christian dogmas' were taught. In Canada, unlike the United States, there was 'a total absence of lynchings and an almost total absence of divorces and murders.' Such moralizing encouraged speculation at the time about other considerations that might have affected Laurier's reading of Canada's constitutional history.

The government's clause naturally reflected the delegate's influence.[107] In addition to the implicit indirect application of section 93 through the usual general application of the BNA Act to each new province, the delegate had managed to obtain an explicit reference to section 93 in the school clause. The clause also contained a provision that must have surprised even the delegate himself. Provincial school legislation not only had to respect the provisions of section 93, it had also to be 'in continuance of the principles heretofore sanctioned under the Northwest Territories Act.' While it would appear that the full implications of this phrase, drawn by Fitzpatrick, were not clear to Sbaretti, Laurier, or even to Fitzpatrick, there is no evidence that Laurier or Fitzpatrick wished to nullify any of the territorial school legislation that had modified the status of Catholic schools after 1884. It is true that the delegate tried to enhance as well as preserve the minority's educational position, but Laurier refused to include 'new' words in the clause that could expose the government to charges of favouritism. There is no evidence that either saw what Sifton later read into the statement, namely, that a court of law 'might' preserve 'everything that is set out in section 14 [sic] of the Act of 1875,' thus jeopardizing the school legislation since 1892.[108] The delegate undoubtedly would have welcomed a return to the earlier dual school system, but Laurier and Fitzpatrick had both made clear their intention not to tamper with existing school legislation in the Territories.[109] While Sifton accepted the denials at their face value, he did think that Fitzpatrick's instructions to the draftsman were either 'wholly misunderstood' or the draftsman possessed 'a most remarkable faculty for covering things which were not covered by his instructions.'[110]

There can be little doubt that Laurier only wished to secure the educational status quo. He redrafted section 93(1) because he wished to treat the Territories as provinces, thus guaranteeing the minority what it already possessed. It is true that subsection three of the government's clause gave the minority a share of the school-lands fund for the first time, but it is also true that financial aid to separate schools had never been a contentious issue in the Territories. Moreover, Sifton's compromise clause gave the minority practically as much later. Subsection two of the government's clause, although admittedly ambiguous, as Skelton points out,[111] did not automatically signify a return to the school legislation of 1884, or any other year. There is no evidence that Laurier, Fitzpatrick, or Sbaretti understood its meaning in that way. The subsection was a by-product of Laurier's failure to recognize that the admission of the Territories posed a unique problem, not covered by any previous act of Confederation. The majority-minority relationship that had gradually evolved in the Territories had no parallel in the rest of the Dominion. Because the school clause had been a sensitive issue for several years, any pointed reference to the original NWT Act could readily be interpreted as a threat to the existing school system. By subordinating the history of territorial school legislation to the history of the school clause in the federal constitution, Laurier's autonomy speech only intensified fears once Sifton developed the full implications of Laurier's remarks. But Laurier was neither guilty of 'unpardonable bungling,' as Walter Scott declared, nor was his act 'a carefully thought out bit of strategy,' as John W. Dafoe, Sifton's biographer, maintained (leaning heavily on Sifton).[112] Laurier was sincerely convinced that emphasis on the history of the school question in eastern Canada was the best means of securing the educational status quo in the two new provinces without arousing controversy or friction.

For the moment Borden, the opposition leader, took a liberal view and supported the prime minister's appeal to take 'the higher ground of Canadian duty and Canadian patriotism'[113] on the school question: 'It is above all things desirable that these questions and considerations, touching sometimes upon differences of races and dealing with matters of dogma and creed, should not be introduced into the political arena more than is absolutely necessary.'[114] Sifton's resignation less than a week later, however, sent all members scurrying for the political trenches and erased what chance there was to exclude race and religion from the autonomy battlefield.

10
The school question
a national issue again

Initial reactions to Laurier's speech and to the government's school clause were generally as favourable as Robert Borden's. Most in the west interpreted the clause to mean the continuation of the existing school system.[1] The emotionalism of the Toronto press which soon engulfed eastern Canada was absent in the west in spite of the *Edmonton Journal*'s headline (23 February): 'Laurier's Guarantee of Separate Schools a Political Crime.' Laurier himself thought his explanation of the historic side of the question would be 'appreciated by the country.' '... The only thing that we have provided for is the continuance of the [educational] system which has existed in the Provinces for the last thirty years and which, as I understand, has given satisfaction.'[2] He did not say, however, which of the systems current during that thirty-year period he had in mind! Not surprisingly, the clause soon became a political football. 'The Liberals,' Peter Talbot, Strathcona's member of Parliament, wrote A.C. Rutherford, soon to become Alberta's first premier, 'say it means nothing more than what we have in the NWT now. The Cons. say it gives the R.C. much more than they have now. It is certainly causing some feeling.'[3] And once Sifton's objections became public, it was 1896 all over again.

Clifford Sifton made his position clear on 25 February in a private letter to J.W. Dafoe, editor of the *Manitoba Free Press*, Sifton's newspaper. He and Scott and, he understood, all the North-West members were agreed that '... the present system of separate schools ... should be perpetuated.' But Fitzpatrick's clause 'seems to go further and it seems to be vague.' He would not accuse Fitzpatrick of 'intentionally deceiving anyone,'[4] but the latter's well-known desire to meet the views of the church did not increase his confidence. Two points particularly troubled Sifton. First, the power of the central authority to regulate separate schools, textbooks, and teachers, 'admitted by everyone to be essential,' was uncertain. Secondly, the subsection on the school-lands fund was 'altogether new' to him. He had never discussed it and he was 'disposed to be very much opposed' to it in its present form. Laurier, in a long interview that day, had concentrated on the difficulties he had had and did not solicit Sifton's views: 'Sir Wilfrid's procedure in matters of this kind is always to assume that everyone agrees with him until they insist upon quarrelling. He finds this much the easiest way of getting on.'[5]

Next day Sifton described the school-lands subsection to Laurier as 'a most colossal endowment of sectarian education from public property.' The rest of the clause was ambiguous, but he was quite satisfied it did not safeguard the right of the legislature to control all schools. It was a 'very great sacrifice' of his personal views to support the 'permanent establishment of separate schools,' even in their modified territorial form. He would only do so now 'to assist in arriving at a compromise which will prevent the splitting of parties upon religious lines.' But he would retire from the government 'as a matter of course' if Laurier proceeded with the clause as it now stood. Even if it were modified, he could still be accused of altering his well-known views by remaining in office.[6]

That evening Laurier saw Sifton again and, apparently unimpressed by Sifton's intentions, refused to modify the clause, intimating *he* would resign immediately if Sifton did so. Sifton doubted Laurier would hold to 'this determination,' but his own course seemed 'absolutely clear,'[7] and on the twenty-seventh he resigned. Laurier accepted the resignation with much regret. Since their differences were 'more of words than of substance,' he had hoped for a 'comparatively easy solution.' On 1 March Laurier informed the House of Sifton's decision. Sifton explained that he had discussed the various subjects with Laurier before leaving for Indiana, but he did not think the autonomy legislation would be introduced before his return. He could not endorse or support the principle of the school clause as drawn.[8]

The political peace was broken and the school question was once more a national issue. The Opposition, through William F. Maclean, founder and editor of the *Toronto World*, quickly reminded the government that 'those who take to provincial rights and school questions will die by provincial rights and school questions. The handwriting is on the wall.'[9] When W.S. Fielding, minister of finance, also threatened to resign, Sifton intervened ('one resignation will probably accomplish the desired result'[10]) and Fielding remained. The search for a compromise that would not involve 'too much sacrifice' began immediately.[11]

Sifton's resignation brought as little public reaction in western Canada as had the negotiations leading up to the government's school clause. Protestant Ontario's indignation over the continuation of separate schools was in sharp contrast to the general calm which prevailed in the area directly affected by the new legislation. Among the Catholics Beck and George Roy, president of the Edmonton Liberal Association, declared they were satisfied with the existing school system. Beck was 'decisively' opposed to leaving the protection of minority rights to provincial legislatures. 'It is not necessary to suspect the majority. The majority of the majority could deprive us of our schools.'[12] From Prince Albert the recently retired chief justice of the territorial Supreme Court, Thomas H. McGuire, a Liberal Catholic who had commended Laurier's school policy before Sifton's resignation,[13] undoubtedly voiced the view of most Liberal Catholic laymen when he advised Laurier privately after the event to place party welfare above the guarantee to separate schools: '... I do not think that, outside of the Clergy, and apart from the humiliation of having to knuckle under to the brute force of a fanatic majority, there are many Catholics here who would care so very much if the Separate schools were wiped out ... It is not the same as if the exercise of our religion were at stake.'[14]

Among the non-Catholics public reaction, although more widespread and vocal, was also moderate. The emphasis on provincial control of education was the dominant theme, but, except for the Conservative press, calm prevailed even at the height of the agitation in eastern Canada. Before his speech of 21 February Laurier received only four petitions from non-Catholics in the Territories, two each from Alberta and Assiniboia.[15] Once Fitzpatrick's clause became public prominent territorial Conservatives, like R.B. Bennett,[16] opposed it strongly. In Winnipeg Senator Lougheed preferred no provincial institutions to having one's hands tied for all time.[17] And in eastern Canada Premier Haultain criticized Laurier's reading of Canadian history: 'There is a vast difference between Upper and Lower Canada going voluntarily into confederation with certain conditions attached, and our being created into a province with those conditions attached.'[18]

The overall attitude, however, remained apathetic. From Calgary John Ewan of the *Toronto Globe* reported that the school question was discussed 'so little ... that even among highly intelligent men some erroneous ideas prevail.'[19] After Sifton's resignation Ewan wrote Laurier from Edmonton that '... the school question really excites but a languid interest here. I can quite believe that if one hunted up all the fiery Methodist or Presbyterian clergy that strong expression of opinion might be obtained, but the average Western man is not much worked up about it.'[20]

Sifton's resignation emboldened Conservative leaders and began a massive flow of petitions to Parliament. The Territories, however, sent only forty-five, none Catholic. Manitoba sent more (forty-six) and New Brunswick sent almost as many (thirty-nine). Altogether there were 643 petitions (448 from Ontario) opposed to separate schools (dual language was often included) and ninety-two in their favour (eighty-seven from Quebec and five from Ontario).[21] Baptists, Methodists, and Presbyterians in convention, trades and labour councils, Liberal associations, and citizens holding public meetings in the Territories (mainly in Assiniboia) sent Laurier approximately twenty resolutions between 1 March and 22 June. While some specifically disliked the continuation of separate schools, all opposed limiting provincial power over education, a distinction which the east in its preoccupation with separate schools seldom made. The lone Catholic resolution came from the Métis at Fish Creek, Saskatchewan. On 8 April twelve signatories, including two Oblate priests, submitted that Confederation would be best served if the federal government gave Catholics in the new provinces the rights enjoyed by Protestants in Quebec.[22]

The Catholic hierarchy itself was silent. Archbishop Langevin had written Laurier an appreciative letter on 23 February, but fortunately (as Langevin indicated in a marginal note in 1907) the letter was never sent 'car Sir Wilfrid a, ensuite, capitulé.'[23] From Lebret, Father Hugonard congratulated Laurier on his logical, firm, and eloquent speech which would impress all who were not prejudiced.[24] Bishop Legal said nothing about the clause or the resignation. On or about 28 February, however, he gave another interview in Calgary and denied there was any compact between church and state:

Neither myself nor Father Leduc saw any of the ministers. I have just passed through Ottawa but I did not go to see Sir Wilfrid Laurier nor [sic] any member of the cabinet.

We are satisfied with the system of separate schools which we have. I do not say it is the best possible system for us. A system can be modified from time to time by ordinances and other measures so that you can never say that a system is the best possible. But we are getting along peacefully, and we only hope that we will be allowed to retain what we have. Our Protestant brethren seem also to have taken the view that it was better to live on in peace.[25]

Silence then descended upon the western church until 15 March, when *Les Cloches*, Langevin's religious journal, openly criticized anyone who would approve the state of affairs in the Territories. Territorial separate schools were neutral schools, not the confessional schools of Quebec, which the government's clause ('un grand acte de justice') sanctioned. It was becoming increasingly apparent that Legal and Langevin held different views of the territorial school system's acceptability, a fact which to Langevin's great surprise would soon play havoc with his plans for a vigorous prosecution of the minority's cause.

The difference between the two prelates was neither philosophical nor doctrinal but a matter of political strategy. The difference emerged naturally, for neither in temperament nor in circumstances did they have much in common. The Canadian-born Langevin, with roots that went back some nine generations, exuded confidence and disliked compromise. Aristocratic in bearing, he was 'a born fighter,' accused by some of 'too much vehemence' and too little concern 'for the need of diplomacy' in the pursuit of church goals for which, he felt, his courageous predecessor, Archbishop Taché, had given his life. Zealous, tenacious, and candid, Langevin 'despised subterfuge,'[26] the result undoubtedly of many frustrating years in coping with evasive politicians. By contrast, the French-born Legal was a political pragmatist, less naive than his apolitical predecessor, Bishop Grandin, but like the latter, far more comfortable as a missionary priest than a protagonist in the hurly-burly of frontier politics. As a result he sought and took advice readily and, like Judge McGuire, adjusted easily to changing realities which did not affect fundamentals. Of course, the fact that, unlike those in Manitoba, Catholics in the North-West had not experienced double taxation for educational purposes made it easy for Legal to be more tolerant of existing circumstances and less militant in his political relations. Catholics in the North-West were less pinched financially and Legal was not pressed to ease burdens as was Langevin, whose own truculence was undoubtedly designed to inspire his people, some of whom after fifteen years were beginning to question his wisdom in demanding seemingly interminable financial sacrifices.[27] Enveloped by a different set of circumstances, Legal momentarily reversed his tactics, if not his ground, for official church policy had long condemned the view that the territorial school system was adequate for Manitoba, and Legal did not now challenge that view. His brief stopover in Ottawa, however, had had its effect. Assorted fears, particularly the dread of double taxation, ensured that in a crisis he would take his cues from Ottawa, not St Boniface, to secure the well-being of Catholic schooling in the former Territories.

Sifton's resignation plunged the apostolic delegate into a new round of negotiations. On 3 March Sifton gave Laurier a revised draft clause, which the cabinet discussed next day.[28] On the fifth Laurier and Senator Scott presented Sifton's clause to Sbaretti, who rejected it two days later because it did not 'sufficiently' secure the minority's rights, particularly the share in the school-lands fund. Sbaretti did not want the government to fall, but since the former clause had satisfied all, he suggested that Laurier should try carrying it, 'even with great difficulty.'[29] That was precisely the move Sifton feared: 'There is just a bare possibility that the Catholic party might be able to convince Sir Wilfrid that he could carry it [Fitzpatrick's clause] over our heads – I doubt it but it might. In that case the danger would be irreparable.'[30]

On 9 March after further reflection Sbaretti wrote Laurier that Sifton's clause appeared 'less satisfactory' than ever. It made no mention of the 1875 Act, 'which safeguards the rights of the majority as well as the minority,' and therefore it did not 'seem' to cover the case of Catholic *public* schools. (With the demise of Fitzpatrick's clause the 1875 phrase, 'a majority ... may establish such schools therein as they think fit,' had disappeared, thus depriving Catholic public schools of legal protection.) It also failed to ensure continued state support to Catholic schools or flexibility in the established schedule of support to meet changes in the country's wealth and population. Its worst feature, however, was the failure to guarantee separate schools a share in the school-lands fund. With the government distributing the fund in the most expedient manner, all Catholic schools could be excluded. The 'more reasonable and dignified' course for Laurier was to adhere to the original clause and hope that his 'influence, ability and strength' would carry the day.[31] Laurier, with the political situation volatile and Sifton's strength in the cabinet unknown, said nothing; Fitzpatrick too remained silent. On the eleventh Laurier heard from the delegate again: under this new ('practically useless') clause, a hostile legislature could abolish the district system by establishing, 'let us suppose, provincial or municipal schools,' thereby endangering the separate schools, as hypothetically their existence depended upon the creation of school districts. The right to separate schools must be guaranteed 'beyond any doubt.'[32] (The delegate was anticipating Alberta's 1936 school legislation, which began the movement to replace the small rural school districts with large school divisions and centralized schools, very few of which were Catholic.)

The delegate's objections accomplished little; the new clause, Sifton wrote Dafoe on the same day, was 'practically' agreed upon. The final draft followed Dafoe's telegram to Sifton on the tenth, suggesting a 'general provision applying the B.N.A. clause' without any 'special enactment of the remedial provision.'[33] As a result, section 93(1) was included and so modified as to guarantee only the educational system as it existed in 1905. The new clause confined separate school rights and privileges specifically to 'the terms of chapters 29 and 30 of the ordinances of the Northwest Territories, passed in the year 1901.'[34] It was of the 'utmost' importance, Sifton told Dafoe, to have Methodist, Presbyterian, and Baptist clergy in Winnipeg 'express themselves for publication' once Ottawa released the new clause. The point to stress in confidential interviews was that the Catholic church's special position was 'absolutely eliminated' under the new clause unless it could get the people in the new provinces to give it 'something more' in the future, which, he thought, placed the matter of limited support for Catholic education upon 'very safe ground.' (The reaction of Winnipeg's Protestant clergy, inexplicably confined to the Presbyterians, was not only minimal but delayed until mid-summer.[35]) The conflict was 'hottest' over the school-lands fund. The Catholics did not expect much more in the way of separate schools, but they had hoped to obtain 'a vested interest in the proceeds of the School Lands which would be an inducement to the Catholic people to organize as many separate schools as possible.'[36] Sifton's clause ignored the fund and provided in general terms that in the distribution of 'any moneys,' there would be 'no discrimination against schools of any class described in the said chapter 29.'

Liberal member, Peter Talbot, found the new clause 'fairly satisfactory.' The matter, he admitted to Rutherford, had 'shaken the Liberal party to its very foundations. But I suppose that was necessary to prove to Quebec that that Province was not the whole of Canada.'[37] The apostolic delegate liked the final clause even less than Sifton's original draft, particularly the financial provisions: '... you well know that the Government cannot distribute any money for any other purpose than that for which it is apportioned by legislative authority, but the School Trust Fund is already appropriated for the support of public schools and there is nothing in this new clause to prevent the Provincial Legislature from refusing to appropriate for separate schools.' The earlier clause (5 March) was 'less objectionable'; Laurier should at least return to it. He did not want the government to force upon Catholics the necessity of open opposition to a clause which was detrimental to their 'present' rights.[38]

Sbaretti made no other written appeals before 22 March, the day on which Sifton's clause came before Parliament. From Ottawa, where Lacombe and Beck were advising Sbaretti, a worried Lacombe informed Legal on the fifteenth that the delegate appeared ready to cede something to the fury of the Protestants. Beck wired Legal to come east, but Legal replied that he had 'perfect faith' in Beck and did not think his own presence of vital importance. To guide Beck, he added that Catholics must have the right to establish separate schools, to be taxed only for their own schools, and 'to share, in due proportion, in the other government grants of whatever source these might come.'[39] On the nineteenth Lacombe wrote Legal again. Laurier and Senator Scott were being overwhelmed by the systematic opposition of the dirty bigots; Scott had never seen similar Protestant fanaticism.[40] From St Boniface meanwhile an intransigent archbishop encouraged Fitzpatrick to stay with the original clause, which upheld the constitution by giving the minority not only separate, but confessional, schools.[41] All to no avail. On 25 March Sbaretti informed Langevin he would accept Sifton's clause. Although he did not approve of it, he would rather tolerate it than lose everything.[42] Laurier, according to Beck, had offered to resign if Sbaretti preferred that to Sifton's clause. But with Beck of the opinion that 'nothing could be hoped for from the Conservatives as a party,' Sbaretti had accepted the clause, hoping for improvements during its passage in the House.[43] Rome attached much importance to Laurier's stand. From Joseph Lemius, general procurator of the Oblates in Rome, Langevin learned that belief in Laurier's good faith was as strong as ever.[44] Langevin's plans to have the pope reprimand Laurier had thus failed completely.

But if Rome was pleased, Haultain was not and he said so in an open letter to Laurier, dated 11 March and published in the *Toronto Globe* two days later.[45] A 'final' statement on the subject, it sought to absolve Haultain of all blame for the political crisis facing the nation. Although Parliament's power to create new provinces was subject to the provisions of the BNA Act, the only jurisdiction Parliament had in education, Haultain insisted, was remedial, as provided in section 93(4):

The proposed attempt to legislate in advance of this subject is beyond the power of Parliament and is an unwarrantable and unconstitutional anticipation of the remedial jurisdiction. It has, further, the effect of petrifying the positive law of the Province with regard to a subject coming within its exclusive jurisdiction ... It is an attempt to create a Province retroactively. It declares territorial School Laws passed under the restrictions imposed by the North-West Territories Act to be Provincial School Laws. It clothes laws imposed by the Federal Parliament with all the attributes of laws voluntarily made by a free Province. It ignores territorial limitations and conditions. It denies facts and abolishes time.

Since 1872 each Dominion Lands Act had made it 'perfectly plain' that the expenditure of the school-lands fund was 'entirely' at the discretion of the provinces. It was with regret that he termed the government's legislation an attempt to dictate to the two new provinces, but he felt he had to place 'on record the fact that we are not responsible for the situation.'

Laurier's private reply[46] rejected Haultain's view that all existing federal legislation in the Territories had to be ignored. It was 'just and reasonable in conscience' to take account of 'obligations undertaken and engagements of the good faith of the Federal Parliament legitimately made.' Even Haultain's own draft bill (s. 2) applied the BNA Act and did not leave the provinces absolutely free to legislate. Here Laurier touched the heart of the matter. Both governments wished to apply the act with appropriate modifications for territorial circumstances. Haultain, however, interpreted the circumstances differently and disliked Laurier's modifications. At the same time he offered none of his own, presumably expecting the courts to judge the reasonableness of those passed by the provincial legislatures, a situation which the minority, with a long history of fruitless litigation, wished to avoid.

Further, Laurier could not see how the government's disposition of the school-lands fund could be 'a direct interference' by Parliament with the rights of a province 'which does not yet exist, and when it does will do so with such rights as Parliament ... permits to the Province.' (That was just Haultain's point: Parliament had no discretionary power at all over provincial rights in education.) Moreover, to confine the funds to public schools required a definition of that term, something which Haultain had not provided. To Laurier, public schools in their 'natural and literal sense' meant all public schools, while Haultain apparently understood them to exclude some. Several questions which soon became the focal point of bitter debate in Parliament followed:

Is a practice uniformly acted upon for thirty years and for years deliberately concurred in by yourself, and the intended permanence of which was proclaimed from its very inception, to count for nothing? Are not the interests which have grown up founded on such practice entitled to the recognition of vested interests? Does any one at the present day propose to withdraw any such rights from any class of persons and is it not perfectly reasonable that when providing for the establishment of a Province Parliament should provide security for the permanence of such established interests as it has itself created?

II

The debate on second reading[47] which opened on 22 March lasted some six weeks and was prolonged and embittered by revelations concerning Sbaretti's influence in Canadian politics. Of the ten territorial representatives in the Commons the three Conservative members, Maitland S. McCarthy (Calgary), John Herron (Alberta), and Richard S. Lake (Qu'Appelle) spoke first and, following Borden, attacked the government for not consulting the west's representatives sufficiently during the negotiations. The North-West was not as satisfied as the Liberals claimed, but it could not be properly heard without a minister of the interior in the cabinet. The Liberals from the Territories, on the other hand, minimized the place of separate schools in the existing school system. Failure to realize that territorial separate schools did not constitute a separate school system, Oliver said, was responsible for most of the agitation in eastern Canada. The historical origins of the school system were detailed, with emphasis on its increased efficiency after 1892. Separate schools were 'so near' public schools that John G. Turriff (East Assiniboia) did not think it 'worth while' to protest. Oliver, as forthright as ever, wondered whether all the petitions, newspaper headlines, mass demonstrations, indignation meetings, and parliamentary opposition were to be taken seriously. After all, he argued,

... there never was a word of protest from the Ministerial Association of Winnipeg, from the Orange Grand Lodge of eastern or western Ontario, from the preceptory of the Black Knights of Ireland in Strathcona, nor from any of those other petitioners, during that whole 30 years during which it was in the power of this parliament to do away with this national outrage of separate schools in the Northwest ... If this attack is honest, if it is against the separate schools and not against the French premier, it is in order for the leader of the opposition ... and the gentlemen behind him to introduce a Bill into this parliament as they yet may do to abolish separate schools in the Northwest by repealing the section of the Northwest Act. I am against separate schools but I want some company in my opposition and I do not seem to be able to find it.

John H. Lamont (Saskatchewan) also cut to the core of the matter when he said:

We say that the present law is the best. Hon. gentlemen opposite admit that. We say that the law has worked to the satisfaction of Protestants and Catholics, Liberals and Conservatives alike. They admit that that is true, but they want to force the minority to accept the right to give their children education in the schools as a concession from the Protestant majority in the new provinces and not to claim it as a matter of right from this parliament. They say, and they have said over and over again – cannot you trust the majority? But I want to point out ... that is a question that must be asked ... the Roman Catholic minority, and the Roman Catholic minority not only on this side of the House, but also on the other side of the House, have answered that question with no uncertain sound.

All territorial members supported public or national schools and provincial rights. All opposed federal coercion, but none opposed separate schools as openly as Oliver. To Talbot, the school clause made the meaning and intent of section 93 explicit, ensuring thereby the continued existence of *national* schools. The courts on appeal might decide the minority was entitled 'to the rights which they had by the provisions' of the 1875 Act and the dual system would return. Dr Edward L. Cash (Mackenzie) termed the separate school guarantee 'a commendable exception to the theoretical doctrine of provincial rights' because it gave the minority minimal concessions in return for 'peace, harmony and unity.' In any case, it was no worse than the Conservative tax exemption to the Canadian Pacific Railway in 1881: '... no one desires to see parliament repudiate its obligations, and hon. gentlemen opposite have not raised a single howl about this interference with provincial rights.'[48]

The Liberals made much of the point that Haultain's draft bill intended to preserve the educational status quo. What else could the federal government do, Oliver asked, when even the territorial government thought 'existing conditions should be continued?' Haultain, Scott insisted, was as much to blame as the government for keeping the school question under wraps. He had discussed autonomy for years without mentioning education until the recent general election. How, moreover, could Haultain blame the government for treating the Territories as provinces when he, too, had treated them as a province in his own draft bill. Scott, ignoring Haultain's well-known insistence upon 1870 as the date of union, quoted the pertinent section ('... the provisions of the British North America Act ... shall be applicable to the province of Saskatchewan ... as if the province of Saskatchewan had been one of the provinces originally united by the said Act') and observed indignantly:

As if Saskatchewan had been a province and not a territory! Create a province retroactively! Treat territorial school laws as provincial school laws! Ignore territorial limitations and conditions! Deny facts and abolish time! Declare what was not to have been and perpetuate as existing what never was nor is! Ridiculous when proposed by this government! But high statesmanship when proposed by Mr Haultain!

The Liberal positions in 1905 and 1896, the clever Scott explained, were not incompatible because the Liberals in both instances were only upholding 'established rights' or the educational status quo.

The Liberal spokesmen had their effect, particularly in the Territories. Early in April separate reports from Bulyea in Regina and Senator Davis in Prince Albert assured Laurier of continued support.[49] From Lebret, Father

Hugonard congratulated Scott on his 'logical, impartial and impassionate' speech: 'After your defense of the bill, we feel no more uneasiness about it and your words had a beneficial effect through the country to promote peace and abate ill feeling.'[50]

For the Conservatives McCarthy, a lawyer, treated the constitutional question with penetrating subtlety. He was much impressed by Sifton's statement in the House on 24 March that the territorial assembly, in 1892, 'did go beyond the powers that were bestowed upon it' by section 11 of the 1875 Act.[51] He was also impressed by Sifton's reference to Thompson's opinion (10 January 1890) that (to quote Sifton again) '... one of the ordinances passed shortly before 1892, but somewhat similar in its effect ... contracts or diminishes the rights of minorities to an extent not contemplated by the Act of 1875,' but the latter 'must nevertheless be held to remain in force notwithstanding the passage of the ordinance.'[52] If the 1875 Act had been violated, then Sifton's clause might ensure the legality of chapters 29 and 30 and meet the criticism that the territorial school ordinances which 'pared down the Act of 1875 were ultra vires,' but McCarthy asked, was this sufficient to secure regulations (passed under *ultra vires* ordinances) that introduced such presumably *ultra vires* practices as uniform inspections, textbooks, and normal sessions? His *tour de force* followed: If the territorial school system rested on *ultra vires* legislation, and if the alternative was 'all the evils' associated with a dual school system described by Sifton in referring to school systems in the west before 1890, why, then, not 'protect the rights of the majority' if the intention was to secure the status quo? The need obviously was not for guarantees to anyone but 'absolute freedom' for the people in the new provinces: 'If the present system proves to be satisfactory, it can be preserved; if the time comes when it does not prove satisfactory, the people of the west desire to have reserved the right to repeal it ... They are not coming into this confederation with a separate school system that they have chosen for themselves; but I believe that if this administration had trusted the people of the west any rights possessed by minorities there would have been respected.' The argument moved easily into a defence of the Conservatives as the protectors of provincial rights. The historic reputation of the Liberals in that respect notwithstanding, there was 'not a very great distinction between overriding an Act in existence to-day, and picking out of our ordinance a certain portion and saying that suits us, and we will adopt it so that you cannot repeal it for all time to come.' He reminded Oliver and Turriff, moreover, that in 1889 and 1890 they had endorsed the principle of unrestricted local autonomy by supporting the territorial assembly's appeal to Parliament to repeal the 1875 separate school clause. The separate school guarantee would not attract immigration. The literature of the Department of the Interior stated that territorial schools were 'non-sectarian and national.' Moreover, the great mass of the immigrants came from the United States, where there were no separate schools.

John Herron, in Alberta since 1881, denied that the minority had any vested rights. The French Catholics were not the first to open up the south country; nor, as was frequently alleged, were they the only ones to civilize the west. R.S. Lake, the other territorial Conservative, maintained that the terms of Haultain's draft bill had been before the people and their elected representatives and had been endorsed by all. Everyone in the Territories approved the school system and no one, least of all the Conservative party, wished to change it, even though the separate schools did create a 'hardship' for the 'many' territorial Catholics who preferred public schools. As a layman he was bewildered by the many legal opinions on the meaning of Sifton's clause, but he was inclined to agree with McCarthy that it meant 'just about the same thing' as the government's original clause.

On 5 April, at the height of debate, the Liberals were suddenly stunned by newspaper reports that Sbaretti had tried to use the boundary question as a lever to have Manitoba's school legislation modified.[53] Robert Rogers, Manitoba's minister of public works, divulged details of a meeting on 23 February between Sbaretti, Colin Campbell (Manitoba's attorney-general), and himself. The Manitobans, in Ottawa to press the boundary question, had had an inconclusive session with the federal government on 17 February and four days later heard Laurier rule out any immediate boundary changes. Against this background the delegate's letter to Campbell on 20 February, suggesting (according to Sbaretti's public statement on 5 April) that certain changes in Manitoba's school law would be (to quote Sbaretti) 'politically expedient and tend to facilitate the accomplishment of his object,' was badly timed. Manitoba's frustrated delegates may well have concluded that there were other reasons for the government's failure to meet their requests. Both Sbaretti and Laurier had tried unsuccessfully to re-open negotiations on the Manitoba school question in 1903,[54] and this was probably common knowledge among Manitoba's government members. It was easy to conclude that negotiations on the question had taken place between Sbaretti and Laurier (as indeed they had), and that Sbaretti, on the twentieth, was acting with the government's knowledge and approval (which he was not). Any doubts Rogers may have had about making the disclosure would have disappeared in the knowledge that Laurier was a Liberal, and since Greenway's defeat in 1900 the government in Manitoba had been Conservative; that the Liberals had frequently accused the Conservatives of being in league with the

Catholic church; and that the Liberal government, after a few critical moments, was riding out the school crisis and the Conservative chances for victory were fading quickly. A great opportunity to embarrass the Ottawa Liberals was at hand and Rogers seized it, even though, according to the delegate,[55] he was not even at the meeting!

The Conservatives, assuming that a delegate who would meddle in Manitoba would not hesitate to do likewise in the Territories, seized the opportunity to attack Sbaretti's role in drafting Fitzpatrick's clause. The debate, now widened to include a rehearsal of all the time-honoured arguments over the relation of church and state, became acrimonious, even vicious. Sensational newspaper headlines fanned the agitation in Ontario to a fever pitch. Before the 'big fuss'[56] died down much privileged correspondence was read into Hansard, including the letter from forty Liberal Catholic members of Parliament ('the forty immortals,' the embattled Maclean called them) to Pope Leo XIII, early in 1897, demonstrating the need for an apostolic delegate, and extracts from letters by Laurier and Charles Russell, son of the influential English Catholic, Lord Russell, to Cardinal Rampolla, in 1897, requesting a delegate. Laurier insisted that the Liberal Catholics had not appealed to Rome as a government but 'simply' as Catholics with 'trouble over matters of ecclesiastical policy.' The appeal, Fitzpatrick added, was designed to obtain a representative who could establish 'peace' and 'political liberty' in Quebec after the 1896 election. But the Conservatives, led by Borden, Maclean, Colonel Hughes, and Dr George Sproule, the latter two stout Orangemen from Ontario, pursued their prey relentlessly. The delegate's mission, Maclean declared, was 'practically' political:

... that ablegate from Rome has been here as an appanage of the Grit machine in this country ... he was to be the Papal policeman with a big stick to keep the bishops and clergy of this country in order ... I know it for a fact – at least I have seen it stated and I do not think it will be denied – that at the recent election [1904] and at other times Liberal candidates in all parts of the country, or some of them, when they had a grievance against any of the clergy of the church of Rome, immediately telephoned to the big policeman at Ottawa to take his big stick and wire back disciplining the Roman Catholic clergyman who dared to hold an opinion of his own in regard to politics.

As the debate lengthened, the government's stubborn refusal to divulge details only increased Conservative indignation. Borden tweaked Laurier that he did not see fit to discuss the delegate's role, even though he was 'always' ready in 1895 and 1896 to ask for ministerial explanations and if necessary to adjourn the House to have them supplied. Maclean was more direct. Whatever the church-state relationship, it was clear that Fitzpatrick's clause was introduced by three government members who 'happen to be of one religion' and who did not consult their colleagues before introducing it. Both Mulock and William Patterson, minister of customs, 'who are supposed to represent Ontario opinion,' were not present 'as far as we know' when it was drawn up, and by some 'process of stealth' it was 'got past' Sifton and Fielding, 'who were supposed to represent the Protestant faith in the government.'

... by stealth it was taken past the members of the west, by stealth it was taken past the representatives of the government in the Northwest Territories, and by stealth it was taken past the caucus of hon. gentlemen opposite ... There is evidence now in this country that the right hon. gentleman [Laurier] is paying his political debts at the expense of the civil and educational rights of the people of this country.

'You need not lie about it,' Mulock interjected, but Maclean took no notice.

Long before this point had been reached, political, ethnic, and religious lines were hopelessly entangled. After two Protestant lectures from Sproule and George E. Foster on the principle of 'the complete separation of church and state,' Fitzpatrick asked for the difference in principle between the Conservatives' consulting of John Ewart of Winnipeg in 1896 and the existing situation, 'assuming it to be true that the delegate was consulted.'[57] Andrew B. Ingram of East Elgin, Ontario, replied that the prime minister, after consulting his cabinet, could approach the Catholic bishops but, as the delegate was not a citizen, to consult him was, Protestants believed, to go 'beyond the proper line.' The remarks were made at two in the morning (7 April).

For two days the delegate's office was the focal point of parliamentary debate. Concerned that representations might be made to have Sbaretti recalled,[58] Senator Scott urged Rome (through Merry del Val) not to heed the 'four or five' bishops, who, it was 'rumoured,' had assumed an 'unfriendly' attitude towards the delegate. To recall Sbaretti would so 'prejudice' the government as to weaken it 'materially,' leading to its possible defeat and destroying 'the last chance' for protective legislation in the new provinces.[59] Coming from an important member of the government, the letter undoubtedly had its effect. The delegate was not recalled and the badly battered Liberal ship of state weathered still another political storm.

The debate on second reading finally ended on 3 May. On division

Borden's amendment to give the provincial legislature 'full powers of provincial self government including power to exclusively make laws in relation to education'[60] failed 140 to 59, and Laurier's motion for second reading then carried by an identical vote. The territorial members divided their votes along party lines.[61] Thirteen Conservatives voted with the Liberals, ten from Quebec. The only Liberal to bolt was L.G. McCarthy (North Simcoe), D'Alton McCarthy's nephew. There was a majority of twenty for the bill outside Quebec and an overall non-Catholic majority of fourteen.

III

Needless to say, the government's new clause had not pleased Archbishop Langevin. On hearing of Sbaretti's acceptance of it, he complained to Bruchesi that the minority was again being sacrificed. And, of course, the prime minister was once more out of favour: some people considered him more important than the Holy Church.[62] A public declaration by the church was required to counter developments at Ottawa and to show the country that the western hierarchy was united, a goal pursued relentlessly by Langevin while the debate in the Commons raged on and on.

The issue of episcopal unity had become most important, for Legal's Calgary statement had appeared in several Quebec newspapers and so impressed the Liberal *Le Canada* (Montreal) that it carried it 'every day' to win support for Sifton's clause.[63] The publicity had had its effect and even militant Catholics had begun to wonder whether the statement could be true. Langevin denied that Legal or any other intelligent, informed, and conscientious Catholic could be satisfied with the territorial school system. Legal, he wrote a priest in Quebec, had not said all that had been attributed to him.[64]

An appeal to Legal himself had followed.[65] The difficult 1901 law, although better than nothing, was inadequate. Should the western hierarchy remain silent, their enemies would conclude that they tacitly approved the government's legislation. Legal was undoubtedly aware that at that very moment certain papers were crying aloud that Mgr so-and-so supported the new clause; he was satisfied. Friends in Quebec had made inquiries. If an episcopal declaration obtained no more than they already had, they would only have to agitate later, and objections now would help. A desperate letter to Sbaretti, suggesting a declaration from the entire Canadian hierarchy, followed the next day. He would, he admitted, prefer to lose everything a hundred times over than to have the hierarchy declare itself satisfied.[66]

The archbishop wrote with confidence at this stage. He had just outlined a four-point programme for territorial schools to Father Bruno Doerfler, editor of *St Peter's Bote,* a German Catholic newspaper in Winnipeg, and Doerfler had already conveyed in an editorial just the kind of 'guarded' approval for Sifton's clause Langevin had suggested. Doerfler also intended, he told Langevin, to encourage Protestant minorities from Europe to co-operate with Catholics on the understanding they would later enjoy the same separate school rights as Catholics. The German Protestants, 'who as a rule are still deeply imbued with faith (erroneous as it is),' were particularly anxious for separate schools, and if they and the Catholics could join forces, '... the fight would no longer be considered one between *Catholics* and *Protestants,* but between *Christian* and *Non-Christian schools.*' Such a policy was being followed in Minnesota with great success.[67] Langevin was definitely impressed. German Catholics and even German Protestants, he observed, could indeed prove useful in future battles with the intolerant Protestant majority.[68]

The present, however, had overwhelmed the future, as both Sbaretti and Legal refused to fall in with Langevin's plans. The delegate would not oppose Sifton's clause openly. Defective as it was, he wrote Langevin again, the clause was the best that could be obtained from the Liberals and more than the Conservatives would grant. Even Fitzpatrick's clause did not give Catholics any right to their own teachers and inspectors. Sifton's clause could not be approved and he had not approved it, but it did sanction the principle of separate schools and the minority did obtain a proportionate share of the public funds. Although these advantages were not guaranteed 'absolutely,' once the provinces came into being 'a judicious action, backed by the strong Catholic vote,' could supplement them.[69] Legal's position was the same. Detailed objections now would only endanger the principle they wished to protect.[70] Leduc and Beck agreed.[71] As a result, when Legal refused to follow Langevin, he knew he had the weight of minority opinion behind him. With Catholic school districts, taxes, trustees, and teachers to provide the 'essential' Catholic atmosphere in the school, the teachers could easily moderate the effect of non-Catholic textbooks. This detail and others like the normal school and the half-hour of religious instruction could be worked out later. If Langevin thought he had to issue a declaration, he should do so in his own name. Legal would only protest if the minority were refused the minima outlined above.[72] On 14 April, in a long circular to his clergy, Legal singled out the so-called neutral textbooks as the main deficiency. But the government and minority both desired effective schools and there was no need to try to escape government control.[73]

With Rogers' disclosures agitating Ottawa Sbaretti again urged Langevin 'to keep silence and not complicate matters.'[74] On 8 April Langevin sent Legal his own clerical circular, dated 9 March, and complained bitterly of Legal's decision. It had led him, he admitted, to yearn for Legal's predecessor, Grandin.[75] The circular, written in the main after Sifton's clause was introduced, reflected the archbishop's 'unspeakable sorrow' over the turn events had taken. Catholics could not tolerate this 'spoliation' of their rights, so 'shamefully violated, in spite of the constitution.' 'Catholics who express their satisfaction at such a state of things betray not only unpardonable ignorance of Catholic educational principles but lack of understanding of the painful position in which we are placed since 1892, ostracized, as we truly are, in the Territories.' 'Opportunists' who ask the clergy 'to be silent for the sake of peace or because it is impossible now to recover our rights' should be told that 'there can be no peace except with justice. There can be no prescription against right. No question of principle is truly settled except when it is settled according to justice and equity. Our cause is that of justice and peace, because it is the cause of conscience and truth, and truth, like God, never dies.'[76]

While Langevin was not alone (on 4 April Bishop M.T. Labrecque of Chicoutimi consoled him[77] and on 9 April Bishop F. Cloutier of Three Rivers declared from the pulpit that Sifton's clause was 'not acceptable to Catholics'[78]), his position was not enviable. He congratulated Cloutier, through whom he thought Laflèche still lived, and wished he could say the same for Grandin.[79] Legal, he feared, had become an opportunist.[80] To make matters worse it was rumoured that the delegate himself believed Catholicism would gain ground if French Canadians began speaking English by degrees, co-operating eventually in the establishment of a single language in Canada.[81] If only Rome were more responsive. But, he wrote Labrecque, the request for aid made last December was being ignored on the pretext that the letter had not been received.[82] He feared that opportunists like Merry del Val would prevent the desired results. Since the cardinal's visit to Canada in 1897, the hierarchy had become the victim of diplomacy, a very polite word for blackguardism or human wisdom, which St Paul had equated with death.[83] The archbishop was clearly in no mood to be trifled with.

One important alternative, perhaps the only one, remained: an outright appeal to the hierarchy of Quebec. Among Quebec's most influential prelates was Montreal's Paul Bruchesi, Laurier's close friend. If Bruchesi could persuade Laurier to modify the clause, the situation might still be saved. Accordingly, when Bruchesi asked Langevin for his opinion of Sifton's clause, Langevin expressed strong dissatisfaction on his own *and* on Legal's behalf. The delegate, too, he added, had not accepted Sifton's clause; he only allowed it to pass, saying nothing. Bruchesi's interest had emboldened Langevin. On the same day he wrote the strongly Conservative Reverend C.A. Marois, vicar-general of Quebec, that he had finally decided to urge an episcopal declaration early in May, on the occasion of the consecration in Montreal of Bishop Racicot, Bruchesi's coadjutor and Langevin's uncle.[84] Then, at the editor's request Langevin gave *La Vérité*, a Conservative newspaper in Quebec City with a long ultramontane tradition, permission to print the sections on the school question contained in his recent circular.[85]

Before leaving for Montreal Langevin held an abortive meeting with Legal at St Boniface on 27–28 April,[86] and on the twenty-ninth he sent him a sympathetic letter from Marois and a critical article by Henri Bourassa on the territorial situation. Legal, however, would sign no declaration that lacked the delegate's approval. Bourassa, he replied, understood the situation imperfectly; it was not as bad as he had described it. Where there were no Catholic schools, Catholics were either too few or there was no one to organize them. In any case, the fault did not lie with the system. He disapproved of Bourassa's agitation because he feared that his zeal might compromise the passage of the school bill[87] – a sentence that could have been directed at Langevin himself. In Montreal Langevin gave the Conservative *La Patrie* to understand that no Catholic loyal to the pope and no citizen interested in justice could declare himself satisfied. The minority would claim its rights and the western episcopate was unanimous on that point.[88] Disturbed by the publicity, Sbaretti reminded Langevin that on 3 May the bishops at Montreal had ruled out any public protests. Langevin's statement only embarrassed the efforts being made to improve the clause. 'As I have in my hands the negotiations and the responsibility as well, I beg Your Grace to write me before taking any public action in the matter.'[89] Next day Sbaretti commended Legal and told him that the bishops who attended the May meeting endorsed his stand.[90]

On 17 May, from Saint Sauveur, Quebec, a very disgruntled metropolitan lectured Legal on his episcopal duties. The harm done by *Le Canada*'s publicity was truly catastrophic. All who had studied the territorial school system – Laurier, Fitzpatrick, Tarte, Monk, Bourassa – agreed that the minority had nominal Catholic schools (neutral in fact) and favoured amendments to ensure separate schools, wherever there were groups of Catholics. (Langevin had told *La Patrie* earlier that the 1901 Ordinance, strangely enough, had limited the right to separate schools to places where Catholics were a minority.[91] Like Bourassa,[92] he was concerned to expand the meaning of the term 'separate' to include Catholic public schools, of which there were thirty-four according to Sbaretti, and forty-nine according to Brodeur.[93]) At Montreal the hierarchy had decided not to declare itself satisfied, but merely to say that it would suffer a particular situation if it could not be improved. Archbishop Duhamel of Ottawa had even objected to the word tolerate. How then could the clause be desirable if it were not even tolerable? Bruchesi had shown Legal's telegram accepting Sifton's clause[94] to all present to support his advocacy of episcopal silence. However, Rome had condemned neutral schools, and bishops in the west, duty bound to secure their school rights, could not abdicate their responsibility to the delegate. The salvation of souls and hierarchical discipline required common action. Legal's recent circular treated fundamentals as questions of detail and it was rumoured he was ignorant of the difficulties Langevin and Pascal had encountered in maintaining French Catholic schools under the strict regulations of the Department of Public Instruction at Regina. If all was rosy where Legal was concerned, then Langevin congratulated him, but he should remember that four bishops were involved and they ought not to weaken themselves by presenting the Canadian public with the sad spectacle of a divided episcopate. Neither the 1875 law nor the documents signed by their predecessors had lost their power. Fitzpatrick himself had declared in the Commons that the ordinances which had violated their rights were not *intra vires*.[95] If all Catholic and right-thinking Protestant members in Parliament united, the minority could still recover its rights. Only common action and expectations were needed.[96]

Legal said nothing, but he eagerly accepted Langevin's invitation to attend another meeting at St Boniface on 27 May.[97] He did not capitulate, however. According to Langevin (writing eighteen months later), Legal, when pressed, maintained it was

'... mieux n'avoir plus cette section catholique; c'était une source de trouble. Les inspecteurs protestants valent mieux, parce que leur rapport, s'il est favorable à nos écoles, n'est pas suspect et a plus de poids. Nous sommes contents d'eux.' Et comme je disais qu'il fallait des livres catholiques, Sa Grandeur me répliqua que ceci n'était pas un droit de par la loi, mais un simple règlement scolaire! Or, nous avons été en possession de livres catholiques dans les Territoires de l'ouest durant dix-huit ans! De 1874 à 1892.

'Et les maîtres catholiques?' lui disais-je – 'Oui, il nous les faut, s'ils sont diplômes; sinon, il vaut mieux en prendre d'autres avec des diplômes!'

Et comme je ne paraissais rien gagner, même en disant que la Pape Léon XIII, dans l'Encyclique 'Affari vos,' exigeait que l'école fût contrôlée par l'Eglise, je m'écriai: 'Monseigneur, vous me désolez; en France, vous seriez un évêque gouvernemental! Oh, je vois que Monseigneur Grandin est bien mort!'[98]

Langevin admitted to Leduc that Legal had refused to correct *Le Canada*'s editor or to complain to Bruchesi for making ill use of his telegram. Legal approved the last half-hour of religious instruction and seemed to censure the attitude which Taché and Grandin ('l'ancien régime') had towards the unjust spoliations of 1892. Langevin was now more convinced than ever that his own attitude was the only one befitting a bishop, and could not allow opposition to a position approved by the bishops at Montreal without ties to the government at Ottawa.[99]

The break between St Albert and St Boniface was complete. During the next month the archbishop frequently complained of Rome's silence; condemned Laurier and diplomacy; praised Fitzpatrick; criticized Sbaretti and Bruchesi, who with two other French bishops and those from Ontario had opposed a declaration at Montreal; attacked the lack of unity in high places to provide the much needed opposition; and, with Legal undoubtedly in mind, declared that it took no courage to support a delegate attacked by our *'ministres cowboys.'*[100] Legal's attitude, Langevin told Pascal, astonished everybody, even the Liberals, who were amazed that a western bishop could be content with so little. It was, to say the least, heart-rending.[101]

The subject of Legal's statement was not raised in the Commons until 18 May, when Armand Lavergne, Bourassa's *nationaliste* colleague from Montmagny, Quebec, got Laurier to deny it had any official status.[102] Five weeks later when Laurier himself invoked the statement in support of Sifton's clause, Bourassa objected that it had preceded the clause by 'about' a month. What both ignored, however, was that Legal had expressed satisfaction with the existing territorial school system, not a particular school clause. The only other reference to the statement was by a Quebec member who pointed out that Langevin and the two remaining suffragans did not share Legal's opinion, and that Legal's predecessor had 'strongly condemned' the school legislation of 1892–3.[103]

IV

Despite Langevin's poor opinion of Sbaretti, the delegate did not abandon the minority's cause. On 2 May, with the end of debate on second reading in sight, Sbaretti urged Laurier to secure the district system of school organization, the minority's share of the school-lands fund, and the last half-hour of religious instruction in the public schools to protect Catholics in large communities ('destined to be very numerous, as Catholics usually group themselves ... apart from other elements of the population'). To save embarrassment the government might have a private member move the changes. Laurier termed the minority's position 'absolutely secure' and warned that the delegate's confident tone suggested he had 'no adequate conception of the intent forces which oppose this legislation, and of the efforts ... necessary to overcome them.' Sbaretti thought he understood the government's difficulties very well; he had, however, suggested amendments to persuade the bishops at Montreal not to oppose Sifton's clause, and Laurier should do something to meet the hierarchy's expectations.[104]

After two interviews[105] and an extended lull, Sbaretti took up the questions with considerable insistence and persistence on 20 June. The permanence of the district system had to be guaranteed. It was so important that he hoped Laurier would push it through, even if some of his followers objected. Laurier remained calm. There was 'absolutely no possible danger' the district system would be abolished. The basis of the school system was local taxation under the municipal system, which implied that school districts 'in one form or another, in one name or another ... must always exist.' The tenacious delegate then suggested an addition to subsection one of Sifton's clause: '... and Separate School Districts, with all the rights and privileges of Separate School Districts contemplated by said Chapter 29, may be established in any locality, although no public school district exists therein.' The change would enable the minority to form separate schools in case the district system disappeared. Laurier refused to budge. The mere attempt would raise 'another storm,' whose consequences would be 'more dangerous' than the last. Sbaretti, however, persisted: all the church wanted was *favourable consideration* for the proposition. Beck, too, now pressed Laurier, having become a convert to the view that a guarantee of the district system was of paramount importance. Laurier refused to bend in that direction; there was, however, very strong hope, he told Sbaretti, that an amendment respecting religious instruction, first mentioned to the delegate's secretary on 20 June, might be adopted.[106]

The government's clause, discussed at great length in committee on 8 June,[107] flared up again on 28 June. During the next two days four amendments were proposed and one was adopted. The first, offered by Borden, asked simply that the provisions of section 93 apply to the provinces 'in so far as the same are applicable under the terms thereof.' Fitzpatrick objected. The amendment would lead to litigation and it was the House, not the courts, which should settle the question of the minority's rights and privileges. If the House, Borden countered, had the power to change section 93, it had better continue the 'good work' and make 'absolutely plain for all time to come' the area of federal and provincial jurisdiction in the controversial sections 91 and 92.[108] On division the amendment was lost eighty-seven to thirty-seven.

The next amendment, proposed by Bourassa, secured the existing separate school system and a share of the school-lands fund,[109] but from Bourassa's remarks it is clear that much more was intended. What the minority wanted was not merely the nine 'paltry' separate schools then in existence or the half-hour of religious instruction, but government-controlled separate schools 'where they are a majority as well as where they are a minority.' If the Commons agreed to separation on such terms, he would not only accept the uniform system, which the prime minister had declared would be 'an act of infamous tyranny if committed by the province of Quebec,' but 'trust to the generosity of the people of the Northwest.'[110] Separation, Lavergne explained, was important because a report of 'the inspector of schools for Northern Alberta'[111] viewed the common schools as ' "the quickest and surest method of assimilating the foreign elements" ' in the population. For this purpose the best teachers (' "better for not using the language of the locality" ') had to be secured. As French, Lavergne added, was considered a foreign language in the North-West, a school system that 'more easily' assimilated the French Canadians was objectionable. Parliament should differentiate between the French Canadians, who had been in Canada for three hundred years, and 'the Galicians and Doukhobors or any other of the breeds imported lately.'[112] Bourassa and Lavergne, concerned to realize their concept of a bilingual and bicultural Canada,[113] wanted separate school status for all Catholic schools, but it is not clear how an amendment that accepted the territorial status quo would have attained that objective. On division the amendment was overwhelmed 126 to 7. Besides Bourassa and Lavergne (both Liberals), the other gallant souls (to use Langevin's description[114]) who supported the amendment were Monk, E. Léonard (Laval), J. Bergeron (Beauharnois), J.B. Morin (Dorchester), and E. Paquet (L'Islet), all Conservatives.

Bergeron then proposed to guarantee separate schools for the minority and 'full liberty for the majority of any school section' to have the kind of school it desired.[115] After lengthy discussion, in which Borden, Bourassa, Lavergne, and Bergeron defined, re-defined, and defended their respective positions, Bergeron's amendment was also defeated 125 to 6 (Paquet abstaining). Next, Sbaretti's concern for the safety of Catholic public schools finally bore fruit, when J.H. Lamont, a Liberal backbencher who became Saskatchewan's first attorney-general, moved to amend Sifton's clause to prevent the repeal of the territorial provision for permissive religious instruction. Introduced at midnight, the surprise amendment prompted little debate, and by two in the morning the House had passed it (99 to 27) and the school clause (90 to 28).[116] Lamont, a Presbyterian, said he wanted a provision that 'for all time to come' would give all school districts the right to religious instruction. He was satisfied that his contemporaries would not deny the right, but

... the 250,000 people who now constitute the estimated population of each of these two provinces will be but a small percentage of the millions who will find homes on our prairies, and it may be that future legislatures, elected by the immigrants from all quarters of the world, may not be of the opinion that the inculcation of religious and moral principles in the schools is necessary to the welfare of the state, and if not this amendment is desirable.[117]

Thus, to ensure that Catholic public schools would have the same guarantee to religious instruction as Catholic separate schools, the government made the permissive religious half-hour inviolable in *all* provincial schools. This meant that the distinctive character of Catholic public schools would be preserved and met one of the delegate's earlier objections.

On 30 June Frederick D. Monk, Borden's deputy in Quebec, introduced another volatile issue, the dual language question, which Laurier thought he had shelved in February by rejecting the resolutions of Edmonton's St Jean Baptiste Society. The legislation of 1877 (as amended in 1890), Monk thought, had to be entrenched in the new provincial constitutions. While the provisions of the North-West Territories Act which were not inconsistent with the new constitutions were being continued, it was equally important to make explicit that the French language, like the separate schools, was beyond the reach of the local legislatures. Bourassa agreed and pressed to set aside the 1890 changes as well. Monk did not object, but in the long and bitter debate that followed[118] only Bourassa touched on the question as it affected education:

If we make the French language one of the official languages of the provinces of Alberta and Saskatchewan it will be a further reason why French speaking fathers of families will, especially in separate schools, teach French to their children. In fact, one of the reasons that were given in 1893 against the ordinances of 1892 was that it was against the spirit of the constitution of these Territories to abolish the teaching of a language which was acknowledged as an official language by the constitution of that country.

Most of the leading members in the Commons, including Laurier, Borden, and Fitzpatrick, participated in the debate and many old wounds were re-opened. At midnight, however, the government easily overwhelmed Bourassa's subamendment (60–5) and Monk's amendment (69–6), and the attenuated bilingualism of the territorial period not only crossed the provincial threshold through the side, instead of the front door, but its legal status in the schools remained as imprecise as ever.

On 5 July, four and one-half months after introducing the autonomy bills, Laurier moved third reading, and another round of amendments followed. Borden, Bergeron, Bourassa, and Monk re-introduced theirs and all were defeated by large majorities. Colonel Hughes, who moved the first of two new amendments, proposed to apply the BNA Act and even to restrict the provinces in education after a ruling to that effect, presumably by the courts. The amendment was defeated 106 to 37, with the territorial vote divided along party lines as usual. The second new amendment, proposed by Léonard, sought to have the separate school clause in the 1875 Act brought in as a subsection to Sifton's clause. The move was defeated 124 to 6 (Paquet again abstaining).[119] Finally at one in the morning the bills were given third reading.

With the bills on their way to the Senate, Sbaretti wrote Senator Scott in a last attempt to nullify one of the first and, from the Catholic standpoint, one of the most damaging changes in territorial school law: the requirement that public school districts precede the organization of separate school districts.[120] Scott, who introduced the autonomy legislation in the Senate on 10 July, initiated no amendments, however, and apparently ignored the delegate's communication.

Of the four territorial senators only Ross did not participate in the debate.[121] On 13 July, with the thermometer at eighty degrees, Lougheed insisted the school question would become a 'burning' issue and remain 'a bone of contention' for many years in the new provinces because the school legislation of 1875 was only 'temporary,' pending the erection of the Territories into provinces. Like many others, Lougheed quoted generously from Thompson, Mills, and Laurier in 1894, apparently unmindful that each held a different view of Parliament's role when autonomy was granted. As usual, the meaning of the phrase 'province at the union' came in for attention, and during a heated exchange Quebec's Senator Beique defined the term 'union' broadly to mean 'the provinces or territories coming into confederation as a union.' Lougheed advised the minority, however, to interpret the constitution according to the 'strict' letter of the law, not its spirit; otherwise the 'different races, religions, and sentiments' of the Canadian people offered little hope that 'a conclusion could ever be arrived at.' The minority, nevertheless, could look to the 'moderation and toleration' of the same Canadian people to grant it the rights to which it was 'entitled.' The inability of church and state to agree upon the minority's rights did not deter him. Differences had to be decided by 'a judicial tribunal,' not by 'a party majority in a parliament assembled for the purpose of arriving at a conclusion decided upon beforehand.' His amendment to expunge Sifton's clause might have led to the courts, but it was defeated thirty-five to eight on 18 July, two days before the session ended.

Senator Davis, a farmer and businessman, disliked Lougheed's emphasis on the constitutional question. Lougheed, a lawyer, could argue either way: 'It all depends on whose ox is gored.' Davis found equally distasteful the contention that strife would continue. The west was satisfied and wanted none of the agitation being stirred up by Conservatives for political advantage. Parliament made a 'contract' in 1875, and it would be 'highway robbery' to tamper with the opportunities for religious instruction enjoyed by Protestants and Catholics alike for twenty years. Provincial rights were not an issue because the Territories, in 1905, were joining the union as territories. Even so, the BNA Act should specifically apply because, if Conservative policy were followed, the unprotected separate schools would disappear. By his own admission he put 'no stock' in legal arguments and his single sally into the area proved it.

Senator Perley, the Conservative elder statesman from the Territories who abstained on Lougheed's amendment, believed that the North-West possessed the best schools in Canada. All that was needed was a law guaranteeing religious instruction which was so plain that 'any Galician in the country who read the language' could understand it. He therefore proposed to guarantee that the minority or majority in any school district could have 'the doctrines of their religious faith taught during the last half-hour of any school day.' Teachers, textbooks, school inspections, and examinations, however, would remain under provincial control. As the amendment only granted what Lamont had already secured, it was rejected twice, once in committee and again on third reading. 'I presume,' Perley observed sarcastically, 'that my motion was rather too plain and pointed to meet the views of the ordinary politician, and this is the reason that it was defeated.' On 20 July the autonomy bills received royal assent and the scene of controversy shifted from Parliament Hill to the political hustings of the two new provinces.

v

While the end of parliamentary debate did not terminate discussion of the contentious school question in the North-West, subsequent events were distinctly anticlimactic. The first provincial elections in Alberta and Saskatchewan were held on 9 November and 13 December respectively,[122] but only in Saskatchewan towards the end of the campaign did the school question reach the frenetic heights of the by-elections at London and North Oxford, Ontario, in June. In the Edmonton by-election in April it was a minor issue and the uncontested campaign was of slight consequence when compared to Ontario's, where the success of government candidates ensured the political viability of Sifton's clause. Ontario, of course, had been aflame since early March, but the Liberal victories dampened the heather, and the prairie fires which followed were for the most part tame affairs by comparison. Liberal victories were, of course, important to indicate that the new provinces themselves favoured the autonomy terms and school settlement. But in the end other issues or personalities were often the deciding factors in individual constituencies.

There were several reasons for this. The most important was undoubtedly the country's unprecedented prosperity. 'Agricultural development was marked, immigration grew steadily in volume, and financial conditions continued buoyant, while, in popular *parlance*, good times were everywhere in evidence.' As one visitor to the west quipped in May: '... he did not think that they thought much about any bills except dollar bills.' The generous financial settlement of the autonomy bills only reinforced that view. Other telling factors were the few separate schools in actual operation – six in Alberta (one Protestant) and five in Saskatchewan (two Protestant); the satisfaction of the seven western Liberal members in the Commons and of Sifton himself with the compromise clause; the general confusion created by the press, particularly as it plunged deeper and deeper into the tangled web of the constitutional argument; and the touring tariff commission, after 7 September, which evoked much interest and numerous briefs from the west on 'bread and butter' issues.[123]

The well-organized Liberals too were quick to make the most of every advantage. The two new governments, entirely Protestant, were obliged to defend educational settlements generally believed to favour the Catholics. Not surprisingly, the Conservatives accused them of sacrificing principles to party interests and promoted the impression that Liberal power rested on immigrant support. The Liberals, however, were more united on the school question (especially in Alberta), had no record that could be attacked, and had the benefit of federal patronage and leadership. Moreover, their commitment to the educational status quo promised peace and continued 'Liberal' prosperity, which were repeatedly stressed in carrying the offensive to the 'Provincial Strife party.'[124]

The Conservatives, on the other hand, were plagued with difficulties. In Alberta they had no leader. Bennett's own vanity and the ambitions of others caused the Red Deer convention to accept him only as 'temporary leader.'[125] In Saskatchewan Haultain, as determined as ever to avoid party politics in the former Territories, formed the Provincial Rights party to the consternation of Conservative veterans like Senator Perley,[126] and pressed to have the school clauses tested in the courts without making any unequivocal declaration in favour of national schools until late in the campaign. As a result, despite his ability, experience, and reputation, he failed to capitalize on the anti-separate school feelings in the well-populated, fairly homogeneous, older Ontario- and British-born, predominantly Protestant area of settlement along the main line of the CPR, while the Liberals busily harvested votes among continental immigrants and Catholics (frequently identical) in other parts of the province.

There is little evidence that the Roman Catholic church was deeply involved in any of the electoral campaigns until the startling revelation late in November of Archbishop Langevin's activities in Saskatchewan. Forget wrote Fitzpatrick apprehensively in May that a Conservative victory in either province would mean litigation of the Manitoba variety,[127] a view which undoubtedly prevailed among Catholics generally. In the Edmonton by-election, apart from Oliver's visit to Bishop Legal on 15 April after a public reception at St Albert,[128] the Catholic clergy took no part in the campaign. At St Boniface Langevin's *Les Cloches* agreed with *Le Nationaliste* (Montreal) that, even if Oliver was a fanatic who wished to see western Canada completely English and had opposed Catholic schools, he was nevertheless 'un homme juste' who more than once had served as a spokesman of French Catholic interests in the assembly.[129] The results in Ontario pleased both Legal and Leduc. Bennett might, Leduc wrote Oliver, 'now take *his rifle and shoot at his heart content* [sic]. Fortunately for those he would kill he is always aiming too high.' Ontario, he hoped, would be 'more quiet' now; it was obvious that 'intolerance and fanaticism is far from being on our side.'[130] The results, Legal wrote Forget, would undoubtedly facilitate passage of the autonomy bills. On a personal note, the bishop welcomed the newspaper reports that Forget would become Alberta's first lieutenant-governor.[131] The reports, however, were premature. With Talbot and Rutherford opposed to Forget's transfer,[132] the latter remained in Saskatchewan and Bulyea was appointed in Alberta.

In the election in Alberta the Roman Catholic church supported the Liberal cause quietly. In reporting the delegates to the Liberal convention in Calgary, the *Edmonton Journal* included twelve French Canadians and singled out Father F. Therien of St Paul de Métis for special attention. Whether he was the bishop's representative was not clear, but he had 'to be reckoned with as a political force in the North.' When Father A. Jan informed the editor that Therien was in Calgary to attend 'the annual Retreat of the Oblate Fathers,' the *Journal* published the letter without comment, for it had no way of knowing that Therien was in fact Legal's political agent in southern Alberta.[133] After the election Legal reprimanded the mayor of Wetaskiwin, a Catholic, for opposing the separate school in Wetaskiwin during the reception for Rutherford.[134] Both Beck and Legal were, of course, very pleased that the Liberals, termed the partisans of the constitution, had triumphed.[135] Neither noted the fact that H.W. McKenney, the former Conservative and one of two Liberal candidates at St Albert, was the only Catholic elected to the new legislature.

The influence of the Catholic church and the school question on the Liberal landslide in Alberta was not marked. It is true that Bennett blamed his defeat on Catholic influence,[136] and in a close contest this might have been a factor. More plausible reasons were his prolonged absence on business in Ottawa and Victoria, his frequent forays into other constituencies, the 353 votes polled by the Labour candidate,[137] and his indefinite status as leader. The *Journal* thought the school question was used 'to good purpose' to secure 'the foreign vote,' the immigrants being led to believe that the Conservatives stood for 'the abolition of religion and religious training.' It did admit, however, that the capital question in the north and 'the cry' of the hated CPR 'monopoly' in the south were largely responsible for the Conservatives' poor showing.[138] (Bennett was the railway's solicitor and the Liberals exploited the connection to good advantage.[139])

Imperceptible in Alberta, the Catholics were equally inconspicuous in Saskatchewan until late in November. Thereafter, according to Scott, '... it was not a question of schools at all but a question of Roman Catholic domination.'[140] At the heart of the controversy was Archbishop Langevin who, though described by Beck as irreconcilable towards the Liberal legislation,[141] found Haultain and Bennett equally unacceptable.[142] Liberal candidates had to be supported of necessity, but in doing so there was to be no enthusiasm and no alliance.[143] The results from Alberta cheered him: 'I really think it is, for the moment, a victory for us. It consecrates the principle of *separate* if not denominational schools.'[144]

A month earlier, however, in a decisive step, he had written a confidential circular letter to his clergy and enclosed an unsigned memorandum entitled 'Simple Facts/The grievances of the Catholics of the Territories against Mr Haultain,' in which he urged Catholics to vote for 'the leaders who favor separate schools and for their followers.' Obliged to choose between the lesser of two evils, he urged his clergy to give the faithful a 'direction' in favour of Scott's candidates.[145]

Having learned of the circular, Haultain, on 14 November, in a non-confidential letter, asked Langevin for a copy of the grievances being read in the churches.[146] Langevin, in a private letter, refused the request: 'You know as well as I do what you have promised me and how you have fulfilled your promises [which] you have termed as mere parlor talks ... As for what you have said publicly, in Ontario, about our separate schools, and your utterances and deeds in the Territories on the same subject, you need not be reminded of them!' He hoped none of his clergy had made 'any public or private appeal to the passions of the people,' but Catholics needed no lessons in loyalty from any one in a country where they had done 'so much to maintain and strengthen the British rule.'[147] Haultain repeated his request on 20 November. He wished to know 'definitely' why Langevin had thrown his 'great influence' on the side of one party, when Scott had pledged to maintain the uniform school system created by Haultain. He suggested there was some other reason for Langevin's action, 'not consistent' with Scott's public declaration in favour of a school system objectionable to the archbishop. With Haultain unwilling to consider their correspondence confidential,[148] the archbishop terminated the exchange. On 22 November the *Regina Standard* headlined Langevin's memorandum: 'ROMAN CATHOLICS MUST SUPPORT WALTER SCOTT.' Haultain followed with a manifesto on the twenty-seventh, declaring the memorandum to be 'ample proof' of 'an understanding' between Scott and Langevin to modify the existing school system. He admitted the latter's uniformity had been attained by administrative, not legislative, means, and argued, as had McCarthy in the Commons in April, that the regulations, as well as the ordinances, needed protection: '... the only safety for our educational system lies in once and for all establishing it on an absolutely national basis, with equal rights to all, and special privileges to none.' This was, as the *Standard* noted, a 'flat-footed' commitment in favour of national schools; Langevin had now made the school question 'a real issue.'[149]

With the electoral situation again fluid, Scott embarked upon the fight of his political career. First, the *Leader* categorically denied that any understanding existed between Scott and the Catholics. Catholic support, where it existed, was the result of Haultain's abusive campaign oratory.[150] On 6 December Scott followed with two open letters in the *Leader*, one to the electors and the other to Haultain. In the first he pledged that 'every separate school shall be a national school exactly the same as the public school.' In the second he challenged Haultain to prove his 'infamous accusation' of an understanding at a public meeting in Regina on 11 December. Haultain accepted Scott's challenge, but in pressing the conspiracy charge cited Laurier and Sbaretti as principals. Both intended to establish separate schools to please Quebec. Repeating his commitment to national schools and a test case, he declared: 'When we are free the people of Saskatchewan will exercise the powers of freedom and give the Roman Catholics what Mr Scott says they want, public instead of separate schools.' He would not say when asked, however, whether he would abolish the half-hour for religious instruction or the five separate schools in Saskatchewan.[151] Scott, in a letter to Senator Ross, admitted that the memorandum left the Liberals helpless: '... we could say nothing. The compact charge gave me opportunity to say something, and I think that I said it good and hard.'[152]

Langevin's memorandum was as embarrassing to some Conservative Catholics as it was to Scott. In a letter to Langevin, a prominent Oxbow resident accused him of committing 'a grievous error' in asking Catholics to turn down the party for which 'we have so long been taught to vote,' in favour of another that had caused Langevin and the church 'so much trouble in the past.' The minority had compromised itself with both parties. Haultain, who would have treated the minority 'fairly,' could no longer do so. Scott, too, would be 'scared' to favour the minority in view of public opinion.[153] Langevin, who understood the minority's precarious position only too well, said nothing. There was, he confided to a priest in Montreal, little to choose between Haultain, the champion of Masonic Orangeism, and Scott, a strange person who had practically cut Laurier's throat by objecting to his giving the minority confessional schools.[154] Still, Haultain's personal defeat in South Qu'Appelle was important for the separate school principle, and Langevin advised the German Catholics, whom he believed Haultain feared, to vote against him.[155]

With an upswing in Haultain's fortunes among non-Catholics a dangerous possibility, Langevin gave the Liberal *Manitoba Free Press* a public interview and expressed surprise to see his name appended to a document that was neither a pastoral letter nor 'any command' to the Catholic voters, but 'simply' a recital of grievances against Haultain's administration. As a British subject, he could not understand why he should be refused a privilege enjoyed by 'every other clergyman or Orange lodge' in the country. He dismissed the charge of a compact between Scott and himself: 'In politics I know nothing outside of the Imperial pledges, which are founded on principles guaranteeing the individual liberty of every British subject the world over. My friend, Mr Haultain, when he dreamed of such a compact, was certainly under the influence of a nightmare.'[156] Four days after the election Langevin, in Regina, denied he had reason to favour Scott over Haultain. The only difference between the two was that Haultain had broken his promise to appoint a Catholic school inspector, while Scott had made no promise.[157] Haultain denied he had promised Langevin anything and, not being 'an expert in casuistry,' could not appreciate Langevin's 'fine distinction' between a pastoral letter and a memorandum. The latter was intended to defeat him and to a 'very large extent' he felt it had succeeded.[158]

The memorandum undoubtedly influenced the final verdict, but Scott thought it helped Haultain more than the Liberals: '... where it was used to full advantage we were simply mowed to pieces.'[159] The Liberals lost nine of the twenty-five seats, five or six because of the memorandum, according to Scott. Haultain's manifesto, he said, had been placed 'in thousands of Protestant homes': 'In some of the districts at the end the canvas was a straight "Are you going to vote for Haultain or for the Pope?" the same as in Oxford and London last June.'[160] The bitterness at the end amazed him: 'Three months ago I simply could not have believed that sheer lies or any kind of distortions about a system of schools which they had lived under during fourteen years, could so affect ordinarily sane and stable men.'[161] That political victory almost eluded the Liberals is clear from Bulyea's report to Laurier: 'I have very little hesitation in saying that had Haultain's manifesto been issued a week or ten days sooner, Scott could not have carried the province.'[162] Laurier termed Langevin an 'impetuous man' and expressed anxiety that Haultain and his supporters might revive 'the scare of clerical interference' in the future. The archbishop, he told Bulyea, was 'no friend of ours.'[163] Scott, in a letter to Turriff, was more optimistic. The school question, he observed correctly, would be 'an absolutely dead issue long before another general election.' In the meantime he intended to do nothing that could be construed as extending the minority's separate school privileges.[164]

VI

During the elections Bishop Legal's attitude towards the government's school clause remained a contentious issue within the church. In September Archbishop Bruchesi criticized the responsibility Legal had assumed and attributed the government's retreat to him.[165] Langevin relayed the opinion to Legal and admitted that his conduct continued to perplex him, particularly as he had just heard that Laurier was tempted to publish appreciative letters from Legal, Leduc, and Lacombe.[166] Legal refused to become Bruchesi's scapegoat. If, he told Langevin, Bruchesi now judged Legal's earlier telegram accepting Sifton's clause harmful, why had he released it in the first place, particularly as it was confidential and in Latin? He was still convinced an episcopal protest would have imperiled everything, but he did not have the 'courage' to blame anyone; all had worked hard to obtain the best settlement possible. He did not know whether Leduc or Lacombe had written Laurier, but he himself had not.[167]

Langevin, it would appear, found it hard to forgive his suffragan. He discussed Legal's stand at great length in a memorandum to Cardinal Gotti late in 1906 and returned to the subject in a long letter to Pope Pius X in May 1907.[168] Some two years later, events that had led to the episcopal falling out were outlined at great length to show that Langevin's stand was at all times consistent with the church's teachings and Rome's special direction in the encyclical, 'Affari vos.' It could hardly have been otherwise: 'Quel grand homme Mgr Langevin serait aux yeux des Protestants, des francs-maçons, des athées, des libéraux catholiques, s'il avait voulu abaisser les couleurs de l'Eglise devant le pavilion de la franc-maçonnerie et disé à celle-ci: Vous nous avez rendu justice. Nous sommes satisfaits.'[169]

The twin Liberal victories disposed of the school question in the two new provinces, free of tension between the bishop of St Albert and the governments at Ottawa and Edmonton. At Regina, Scott was determined to hold the line against the doughty archbiship of St Boniface. For the Catholic church in western Canada, however, the price of political and religious calm was episcopal disunity, a high and unprecedented price. The disunity inherent in the western school question, which had haunted every federal administration since Confederation, had finally split the western hierarchy itself. The breach should not, of course, be exaggerated, for Legal did play a prominent role in the consecration of the new cathedral at St Boniface in 1906.[170] But it is also true that for Archbishop Langevin, at least, the wounds inflicted by the North-West school question healed slowly.

And well they might. In 1905 the French Catholic minority in Canada lost another round in its struggle to establish a bilingual and bicultural nation from coast to coast. Had Fitzpatrick's clause passed, the basis for a return to the dual school system of an earlier period, indispensable to a viable bilingualism and biculturalism, would probably have been established. Whether Confederation could have withstood the resulting litigation is problematic. In the end, however, the issue was simply too explosive and the position of the French Catholic minority too weak for either political party to heed its importunities in the face of determined Anglo Protestant opposition. The minority was again reminded how fragile is the reed of political power in Canada where religious and/or ethnic issues are involved.

Appendix: clauses proposed for inclusion in autonomy bill

CLAUSE NO. 1
Proposed by Bishop Legal, 29 April 1904
Section – The local Legislature may exclusively make laws in relation to Education, subject however to the general principles laid down in the B.N.A. Act. (30–31, Vic. Cap. 3) respecting denominational or Separate schools, and to the following provisions.

1 / Nothing in any such law shall prejudicially affect any right or privilege with respect to denominational or separate schools, as hereinafter defined in all the clauses of sub-section 4 of present section.

2 / As a system of separate or denominational schools existed in the Territories, at the time of the formation of the Province of ———— the suppression of such a system shall be beyond the powers of the local Legislature of said Province to be established, and of any subsequent legislature, and of any provincial authority, even the Lieutenant Governor in Council.

3 / In the Ordinances which may be enacted and amended from time to time in respect to Education, it shall be provided always that the minority of the ratepayers in a school district, whether Protestants or Roman Catholics, may establish a separate school-district therein, with same or different limits, in the same manner as undenominational school districts are established.

4 / The essentials of a really separate or denominational school system shall be deemed to refer to (a) the taxation; (b) the representation in the Board of Education or Council of Public Instruction, of whatever name it may be designated; (c) the appointment of Inspectors; (d) the selection of school books; (e) certain provisions concerning courses of normal school and pedagogical training.

a / Whenever a separate school-district has been established, the ratepayers establishing such protestant or roman catholic school-district and all the ratepayers of the same denomination therein shall be liable to taxation only for the support of their respective schools and shall be subject only to assessment of such school rates as are imposed for the support of said schools.

b / The minority whether protestant or roman catholic, in the whole Province shall be entitled to a representation on the Board of Education or Council of Public Instruction of whatever name it may be designated, to the extent of at least one third of the total number of members of said Board or Council.

c / The minority whether Protestant or Roman Catholic in the whole Province, shall also be entitled to have a number of inspectors being appointed in the same proportion of at least one third of the total number of inspectors. The duties of said inspectors will be to inspect schools of their respective denomination and to preside over the courses of normal training in special cases, as hereinafter provided, (e).

d / A special series of books shall be approved for the separate schools, at least for Readers, History, Geography and the technical teaching of Religion; the selection of such books being instructed, for either class of separate schools, to the respective members of the same denomination, in the Board of Education or Council of Public Instruction, of whatever name it may be known.

e / With respect to the courses of normal school and pedagogical training it shall be provided that at least one special course for members of religious communities of men, and also one at least for religious communities of women shall be authorized; the pedagogical training being intrusted to some members of such religious communities, always under the direction and supervision of the inspectors of the same denomination.

5 / Any act or decision or regulation of the local Legislature or of any provincial authority affecting the rights or privileges of the Protestant or Roman Catholic minority of the King's subjects, in relation to Education shall be void and of no effect.

6 / An appeal shall lie to the Governor General in Council from any such

act, decision or regulation of any provincial authority, affecting any right or privilege of the Protestant or Roman Catholic minority of the King's subjects, in relation to Education and the Governor General in Council will make necessary provisions for the due execution of this section.

7 / And in case such provisions as made and ruled by the Governor General in Council, are not duly executed by the proper provincial authorities, then and in every such case, and as far only as the circumstances of each case require, the Parliament of Canada applied to by a comity [*sic*] of at least three members of the Protestant or Roman Catholic minority of the King's subjects shall make remedial law, for the faithful execution of the provisions of this section, in relation to Education.

(SOURCE: AAStB, 'Provisions respecting EDUCATION to be introduced in the ACT constituting part of the N.W. territories in a province known as the Province of ———' [29 April 1904]. For the date, see ibid., Legal to Sbaretti, 29 April 1904)

CLAUSE NO. 2
Proposed by N.C. Beck, 29 December 1904
The Legislature of the Province may exclusively make laws in relation to Education, subject and according to the following provisions:

1 / Nothing in any such law shall prejudicially affect any right or privilege which His Majesty's Roman Catholic subjects have *at the date of the passing of this Act* by virtue of the North-West Territories Act or by virtue of any Ordinance of the Territories relating to schools or Government grants thereto or taxation for the maintenance thereof or by virtue of any regulation made thereunder.

2 / An appeal shall lie to the Governor-General in Council from any valid Act of the Legislature or decision of any provincial authority affecting any right or privilege of His Majesty's Roman Catholic subjects in relation to any of the matters aforesaid. In case any act or decision, as from time to time seems to the Governor-General in Council requisite for the removal of such grounds of complaint as the Governor-General in Council shall find to be established, be not duly executed by the Legislature or other proper provincial authority in that behalf, and as far only as the circumstances of such case require, the Parliament of Canada may make remedial laws for the removal of such grounds of complaint and the due execution of such decision of the Governor-General.

(SOURCE: Ibid., Beck to Langevin, 29 December 1904)

CLAUSE NO. 3

Proposed by C. Fitzpatrick with modifications by Mgr Sbaretti in parentheses, 11 January 1905

The Legislature of the said Province shall pass all necessary laws in respect to education; but it shall therein always be provided that a majority of the ratepayers of any district or portion of said Province or of any less portion or sub-division thereof, by whatever name the same is known may establish such schools therein as they think fit and make the necessary assessment and collection of rates therefor; and that the minority of the ratepayers therein whether Protestant or Roman Catholic (and whether a public school has been established therein or not) may establish separate schools therein and in such case the ratepayers establishing such Protestant or Roman Catholic separate schools shall be liable only to assessment of such rates as they impose upon themselves in respect thereof (and shall be entitled to receive their proportionate share of the trust funds created by the sale and investment of school lands as provided by Section 23, 24, and 25 of the Dominion Lands Act.)

(SOURCE: Ibid., Sbaretti to Langevin, secret and confidential, 11 January 1905)

CLAUSE NO. 4

Proposed by Mgr Sbaretti, 16 January 1905

The Legislature of the said Province, *subject to the provisions of section 93, B.N.A. Act, shall have power to pass all* necessary laws in respect to education; but it shall therein always be provided *for the continuation of separate schools* and that the majority of the rate-payers of any district or portion of said Province or of any less portion *shall have the right* to establish *and maintain* such schools therein as they think fit, *with power* to make the necessary assessment and collection of rates therefor; and that the minority of ratepayers therein, whether Protestant or Roman Catholic *and whether a public school has been established therein or not shall have the right to* establish *and maintain such separate* schools therein *as they think fit with the power to make the necessary assessment and collection of rates therefor,* and in such case the ratepayers establishing such Protestant or Roman Catholic separate schools shall be liable only to assessment of such rates as they impose upon themselves in respect thereof. *No discrimination shall be made between separate and other schools of a public character, with reference to their support of aid by public funds, resources, or powers, –*

whether Dominion, Provincial, municipal or other, – or with respect to privileges or exemptions of any kind.
(SOURCE: Laurier Papers, Sbaretti to Laurier, 16 January 1905)

CLAUSE NO. 5
Proposed by C. Fitzpatrick with modifications in italics by Mgr Sbaretti, 7 February 1905
The Legislature of the said Province shall, subject to the provisions of Section 93 of the British North America Act, pass all necessary laws in respect to education; but it shall therein always be provided – *for the continuation (or existence) of Separate Schools* – and that a majority of the ratepayers of any district or portion of said Province or of any less portion or subdivision thereof by whatever name the same is known may establish such schools therein as they think fit, and make the necessary assessments and collection of rates therefor; and that the minority of the ratepayers therein whether Protestant or Roman Catholic, and whether a public school has been established or not, may establish separate schools therein – *and make the necessary assessments and collection of rates thereof* – and in such case the ratepayers establishing such Protestant or Roman Catholic separate schools shall be liable only to assessment of such rates as they impose upon themselves in respect thereof.

In the *appropriation of public moneys by the Legislature* in aid of education, or *in the distribution* of the moneys arising from the school fund established by the Dominion Lands Act and paid to the Government of the Province, there shall be no discrimination between the public schools, and the separate schools and an equitable share or proportion of such moneys shall be applied to the support of such schools both public and separate.
(SOURCE: Ibid., Sbaretti to Laurier, 7 February 1905)

CLAUSE NO. 6
Proposed by C. Fitzpatrick with modifications by Mgr Sbaretti in parentheses, 12 February 1905
The Legislature of the said Province shall pass all necessary laws in respect to education; but it shall therein always be provided that a majority of the ratepayers of any district or portion of said Province or any less portion or subdivision thereof, by whatever name the same is known, may establish such schools therein as they think fit, and make the necessary assessments and collection of rates therefor, and that the minority of the ratepayers therein whether Protestant or Roman Catholic (and whether a public school

has been established or not) may establish separate schools therein (and make the necessary assessments and collection of rates therefor) and in such case the ratepayers establishing such Protestant or Roman Catholic separate schools shall be liable only to assessment of such rates as they impose upon themselves in respect thereof. etc. etc.

(SOURCE: AAE, Sbaretti to Legal, private and strictly confidential, 12 February 1905)

CLAUSE NO. 7
Proposed by C. Fitzpatrick, 12–20 February 1905

1 / The Legislature of the said Province shall pass all necessary laws in respect to education; but it shall therein always be provided that a majority of the ratepayers of any district or portion of said Province or of any less portion or subdivision thereof, by whatever name the same is known, may establish such schools therein as they think fit, and make the necessary assessments and collection of rates therefor, and that the minority of the ratepayers therein, whether Protestant or Roman Catholic, may establish separate schools therein, and make the necessary assessment and collection or rates therefor, and in such case the ratepayers establishing such Protestant or Roman Catholic separate schools shall be liable only to assessment of such rates as they impose upon themselves in respect thereof.

2 / In the appropriation of public moneys by the legislature in aid of education, and in the distribution of any moneys paid to the Government of the Province arising from the school fund established by the Dominion Lands Act, there shall be no discrimination between the public schools and the separate schools and an equitable share or proportion of such moneys shall be applied to the support of such schools both public and separate.

3 / The provisions of section 93 of the British North America Act, 1867, shall apply to the said Province as if the date upon which this Act comes into force the territory comprised therein were already a province; and the expression 'the Union' in the said section being taken to mean the same date.
(SOURCE: AAStB, Sbaretti to Langevin, confidential, 20 February 1905)

CLAUSE NO. 8
Introduced by the federal government on 21 February 1905

1 / The provisions of section 93 of the British North America Act, 1867, shall apply to the said provinces as if, at the date upon which this Act comes

into force, the territory comprised therein were already a province, the expression 'the union' in the said section being taken to mean the said date.

2 / Subject to the provisions of the said section 93, and in continuance of the principles heretofore sanctioned under the Northwest Territories Act, it is enacted that the legislature of the said province shall pass all necessary laws in respect of education, and that it shall therein always be provided (*a*) that a majority of the ratepayers of any district or portion of the said province or of any less portion or subdivision thereof, by whatever name it is known may establish such schools therein as they think fit, and make the necessary assessments and collection of rates therefor, and (*b*) that the minority of the ratepayers therein whether Protestant or Roman Catholic, may establish separate schools therein, and make the necessary assessments and collection of rates therefore, and (*c*) that in such cases the ratepayers establishing such Protestant or Roman Catholic separate schools shall be liable only to assessment of such rates as they impose upon themselves with respect thereto.

3 / In the appropriation of public moneys by the legislature in aid of education, and in the distribution of any moneys paid to the government of the said province arising from the school fund established by the Dominion Lands Act, there shall be no discrimination between the public schools and the separate schools, and such moneys shall be applied to the support of public and separate schools in equitable shares or proportion.
(SOURCE: *Commons Debates*, 1905, cols. 1852–3)

CLAUSE NO. 9
Proposed by C. Sifton and Liberal Members of Parliament from the North-West Territories, 3 March 1905
In and for the Province the Legislature may exclusively make laws in relation to education, subject and according to the following provisions:

1 / Nothing in any such law shall prejudicially affect any right or privilege with respect to Separate Schools which any class of persons have at the date of the passing of this Act, under the terms of chapters 29, 30 and 31 of the ordinances of the North-west Territories passed in the year 1901.

2 / An appeal shall lie to the Governor-General in Council from any Act or decision of any Provincial authority affecting any right or privilege of the Protestant or Roman Catholic minority of the King's subjects in relation thereto.

3 / In case any such Provincial law, as from time to time seems to the Governor-General in Council requisite for the due execution of the provisions of this section is not made, or in case any decision of the Governor-General in Council on any appeal under this section is not duly executed by the proper Provincial authority in that behalf, then and in every such case, and as far only as the circumstances of each case require, the Parliament of Canada may make remedial laws for the due execution of the provisions of this section and of any decision of the Governor-General in Council under this section.
(SOURCE: *Toronto Globe*, 6 March 1905)

CLAUSE NO. 10
Proposed by C. Sifton c. 11 March 1905, after consultation with John W. Dafoe in Winnipeg
(16. Section 93 of the British North America Act, 1867, shall apply to the said province, with the substitution for paragraph (1) of the said section 93, of the following paragraph:)

1 / Nothing in any such law shall prejudicially affect any right or privilege with respect to separate schools which any class of persons have at the date of the passage of this Act, under the terms of chapters 29 and 30 of the ordinances of the Northwest Territories, passed in the year 1901.

2 / In the appropriation by the legislature or distribution by the government of the province of any moneys for the support of schools organized and carried on in accordance with said chapter 29 or any Act passed in amendment thereof, or in substitution therefor, there shall be no discrimination against schools of any class described in the said chapter 29.

3 / Where the expression 'by-law' is employed in subsection 3 of the said section 93, it shall be held to mean the law as set out in said chapters 29 and 30, and where the expression 'at the union' is employed, in said subsection 3, it shall be held to mean the date at which this Act comes into force.
(SOURCE: *Commons Debates*, 1905, col. 8269)

CLAUSE NO. 11
Passed by Parliament in 1905
17   Section 93 of *The British North America Act*, 1867, shall apply to the said province, with the substitution for paragraph (1) of the said section 93, of the following paragraph:

'1 / Nothing in any such law shall prejudicially affect any right or privilege with respect to separate schools which any class of persons have at the date of the passing of this Act, under the terms of chapters 29 and 30 of the Ordinances of the North-west Territories, passed in the year 1901, or with respect to religious instruction in any public or separate school as provided for in the said ordinances.'

2 / In the appropriation by the Legislature or distribution by the Government of the province of any moneys for the support of schools organized and carried on in accordance with the said chapter 29 or any Act passed in amendment thereof, or in substitution therefor, there shall be no discrimination against schools of any class described in the said chapter 29.

3 / Where the expression 'by law' is employed in paragraph 3 of the said section 93, it shall be held to mean the law as set out in the said chapters 29 and 30, and where the expression 'at the Union' is employed, in the said paragraph 3, it shall be held to mean the date at which this Act comes into force.

(SOURCE: *Statutes of Canada*, 4–5 Edward VII, c. 3, s. 17, (1905))

Bibliographical note

I

Of the materials consulted for this study, the most important were the un-published papers of several religious and political figures who determined the course of the school question in western Canada. The correspondence of Archbishops Alexander Taché and Adélard Langevin of the Archdiocese of St Boniface, and of Bishops Vital Grandin and Emile Legal and the letter books of Father H. Leduc of the Diocese of St Albert, were un-doubtedly the most valuable. The Archbishop's Archives in St Boniface contain a very rich collection of Taché's and Langevin's incoming letters and an equally complete collection of Langevin's outgoing mail. Either Taché kept no letter books or they have been lost. However, scattered among his incoming correspondence are copies of the most important letters he wrote. The Archbishop's Archives in Edmonton contain Grandin's and Legal's complete correspondence and Leduc's letter books. Grandin's outgoing let-ters and his journal and memoirs are also available in typewritten form as the Grandin Papers in the Provincial Archives of Alberta, Edmonton. Unfortu-nately there are no indexes to any of the religious papers (except, of course, for the letter books). At St Boniface most of the letters are filed chronolo-gically and all are filed by correspondents at Edmonton. Microfilm copies of most of the letters are also available at the Oblate Archives in Ottawa, and transcripts of those referring to the Ukrainians can be seen at the Archives of the Basilian Fathers in Mundare, Alberta.

The most important political papers were those in the Manuscript Divi-sion of the Public Archives in Ottawa. Of these the most valuable were the Sir John A. Macdonald Papers, the Sir John Thompson Papers, the Sir

Wilfrid Laurier Papers, the Sir Richard W. Scott Papers, the Sir Clifford Sifton Papers, and the Sir Charles Fitzpatrick Papers. Of secondary importance were the Sir John Abbott Papers, the Sir Mackenzie Bowell Papers, the Alexander Mackenzie Papers, the Alexander Morris Papers, the Israel Tarte Papers, the Sir Charles Tupper Papers, the Earl of Aberdeen Papers, the Earl Grey Papers, and the Earl of Minto Papers. Of particular value for the light they shed on the autonomy crisis in 1905 were the Walter Scott Papers (Archives of Saskatchewan, University of Saskatchewan, Saskatoon) and the Alexander C. Rutherford Papers (University of Alberta Archives, Edmonton). There are no papers for the three most important political figures in the North-West: Frank Oliver, F.W.G. Haultain, and N.F. Davin.

Of great value were the unpublished sessional papers of the Council and the Legislative Assembly of the North-West Territories (1877–1905), available on microfilm in the Archives of Saskatchewan, Legislative Library, Regina. Of some importance in the same archives were the 'Minutes of the Advisory Council in Matters of Finance N.W.T.' (1888–91), the 'Minutes of the Executive Committee of the North-West Territories in Canada' (1892–7), the 'Minutes of the Meetings of the Executive Council of the Territories' (1897–8), and the transcripts of the Department of the Interior files. Of much less significance were the 'Correspondence reports of the Ministers of Justice and Orders-in-Council upon the subject of Dominion and Provincial Legislation, 1867–1895' in the Saskatoon branch of the same archives.

Of the university theses consulted, the two best accounts of the evolution of the territorial school system against the background of political, economic, and social developments were M. Toombs, 'Some aspects of the growth and development of educational administrative policies in Rupert's Land and in the North-West Territories to 1905' (M ED thesis, University of Saskatchewan, 1941), and G. Langley, 'Saskatchewan's separate school system: A study of one pattern of adjustment to the problems of education in a multi-religious democratic society' (PH D thesis, Columbia University, 1951). A very interesting study of the same school system against the background of European and Canadian nationalism was N.G. McDonald, 'The school as an agent of nationalism in the North-West Territories, 1884–1905' (M ED thesis, University of Alberta, 1971). Of varying importance were the following: I. Goresky, 'The beginning and growth of the Alberta school system' (M ED thesis, University of Alberta, 1944), Sr L. Hochstein, 'Roman Catholic separate and public schools in Alberta' (M ED thesis, University of Alberta, 1954), R.S. Patterson, 'F.W.G. Haultain and education in the early west' (M ED thesis, University of Alberta, 1961), S.T. Rusak, 'Relations in education between Bishop Legal and the Alberta Liberal government, 1905–1920' (M ED thesis, University of Alberta, 1966), A. Selinger, 'The contributions of D.J. Goggin to the development of education in the North-West Territories, 1893–1902' (M ED thesis, University of Alberta, 1960), H. Sparby, 'A History of the Alberta School System to 1925' (PH D thesis, Stanford University, 1958), and W. Waddell, 'The Honorable Frank Oliver' (2 vols.; MA thesis, University of Alberta, 1950).

II

The published materials used fall into three groups: official government documents; newspapers; and books, pamphlets, and articles. The following federal publications were the most important: the *Debates* and *Journals* of the House of Commons and the Senate, and the *Sessional Papers of the Parliament of Canada*, all for the years 1875–1905. Equally indispensable were the following territorial publications: the *Ordinances of the North-West Territories* (1884–1904), the *Journals* of the Council of the North-West Territories (1877–87) and of the Legislative Assembly (1888–1904), the *North-West Territories Gazette* (1883–1904), and the *Reports* of the Board of Education (1885–92), the Council of Public Instruction (1896–1900), and the Department of Education (1901–5) in the North-West.

The territorial Hansard was the local newspaper. Fortunately papers such as the *Regina Leader* (1883–1905) and the *Regina Standard* (1891–1905) carried practically verbatim accounts of the debates at Regina, and both were relied upon heavily. Other newspapers consulted, particularly on the subject of the school question as an electoral issue, were the *Alberta Advocate* (Red Deer, 1905), *Calgary Herald* (1883–1905), *Edmonton Bulletin* (1880–1905), *Edmonton Journal* (1903–5), *Grenfell Sun* (1894–9, 1901–5), *Lethbridge News* (1885–95), *Lloydminster Times* (1905), *Macleod Gazette* (1882–1905), *Medicine Hat Times* (1885–94), *Melfort Moon* (1905), *Moose Jaw News* (1884), *Moose Jaw Times* (1890–1905), *Moosomin Courier* (1884–92), *Moosomin Spectator* (1892–9), *North Battleford News* (1905), *Ponoka Herald* (1905), *Prince Albert Times* (1892–1905), *Qu'Appelle Progress* (1885–1905), *Qu'Appelle Vidette* (1884–99), *Regina Journal* (1886–90), *Saskatchewan Herald* (Battleford, 1878–1905), *Saskatoon Phoenix* (1902–5), *Strathcona Plaindealer* (1905), *Whitewood Herald* (1905), and *Yorkton Enterprise* (1902–5).

The most useful books fall into two groups: Catholic and non-Catholic. The former, mainly religious histories, present the Catholics as a helpless, tolerant, and reasonable minority at the mercy of an all-powerful, intolerant, and unreasonable majority. The language used is frequently inflammatory, and there is no recognition of the deep political and philosophical issues raised when publicly supported schools are under the control of a church. The best brief Catholic review of both the history of the Catholic church in the Territories and the North-West school question is in L. Groulx, *L'Enseignement français au Canada* (Montreal, 1934), vol. II. Other Catholic writers generally concentrate on the Manitoba school question. A.G. Morice, *Histoire de l'Eglise catholique dans l'Ouest Canadien du Lac Supérieur au Pacifique (1659–1910)*, 3 vols. (Montreal, 1912), the most important Catholic secondary source, devotes fifty-six pages to the school question in western Canada, but only eight are on the issue in the North-West and, of these, six treat the crisis in 1905. *Vie de Mgr Langevin* (St Boniface, 1916) by the same author is too brief and too partisan to be of much value on the school question. P. Breton, *Vital Grandin* (Paris and Montreal, 1960), devotes one chapter to Bishop Grandin's difficulties with the political authorities at Regina and Ottawa from 1887 to 1893, but it is not always clear when Indian or non-Indian education is being discussed. Breton's *The Big Chief of the Prairies: The Life of Father Lacombe* [Montreal, 1955] contains only scattered references to Lacombe's political activities on behalf of the school question. These are discussed more fully in K. Hughes, *Father Lacombe: The Black-Robe Voyageur* (Toronto, 1920). E. Jonquet, *Mgr Grandin* (Montreal, 1903), provides a short general chapter on educational developments prior to the School Ordinance of 1892. D. Benoit, *Vie de Mgr Taché*, 2 vols. (Montreal, 1904), very partisan but richly documented, is the best source for the history of the Catholic church during the territorial period. It contains a four-page outline of the school legislation from 1884 to 1892, complete with an eleven-page summary of Archbishop Taché's important memorandum in 1894. Benoit relied to a great extent on the religious correspondence used in the present study, as did Breton in *Vital Grandin*. Two works which ignore the school question but are useful for the development of the Catholic church in Alberta are E.J. Legal, *Short Sketches of the History of the Catholic Churches and Missions in Central Alberta* (Winnipeg, 1914?) and *A Short History of the Catholic Church of Southern Alberta, Diocese of Calgary, 1865–1948* (Calgary, 1948?), published by the Catholic Women's League of Canada.

Undoubtedly the most important non-Catholic book on the subject of this study is C.B. Sissons, *Church and State in Canadian Education: An Historical Study* (Toronto, 1959). The North-West school question is discussed in the chapter on Saskatchewan, with some attention to the reaction of the Catholic church, especially during the autonomy crisis in 1905. Several references to the correspondence between Sir Wilfrid Laurier and Archbishop Sbaretti are included. The book is essentially an account of the constitutional basis for separate schools (which Sissons dislikes) in each Canadian province. Although friendly towards Christian education, it is very critical of school systems which do not permit Catholics or Protestants to support the school of their choice. To Sissons, a minority should not be allowed to coerce its own minority into supporting separate schools; the Canadian constitution protects the rights of individuals as individuals, not as members of minority groups. Other valuable accounts of the same subject are G.M. Weir, *The Separate School Question in Canada* (Toronto, 1934) and C.B. Sissons, *Bilingual Schools in Canada* (Toronto, 1917). Both pay little attention to Catholic views on the school and language questions, but the development of separate and/or bilingual schools in each Canadian province (Sissons excludes the Maritimes) is well portrayed. Except for the above, all references to Sissons in this book are to his more recent work.

For the political history of the territorial period, the two basic works are L.H. Thomas, *The Struggle for Responsible Government in the North-West Territories* (Toronto, 1956) and C.C. Lingard, *Territorial Government in Canada: The Autonomy Question in the Old North-West Territories* (Toronto, 1946). The first carries political developments to 1897; the second to 1905. The school question is not important in Thomas's study, but Lingard's extensive account of the school crisis in 1905 absolves Haultain of all responsibility. Another political history, L.G. Thomas, *The Liberal Party in Alberta; History of Politics in the Province of Alberta (1905–1921)* (Toronto, 1959), contains the best account of the first and only election in the Province of Alberta in which the school question was an important electoral issue. Two of the best discussions of the influence of the French-English conflict on the history of Canada are G.F.G. Stanley, *The Birth of Western Canada: A History of the Riel Rebellions* (London, 1936) and M. Wade, *The French Canadians (1760–1945)* (Toronto, 1955). The latter, in particular, clarifies the effect of ethnic and religious tensions in the west on the relations between Quebec and the federal government. Another helpful source on the same subject is J.T. Saywell's introduction to *The Canadian Journal of Lady Aberdeen 1893–1898* (Toronto, 1960). For a scholarly and objective history of Canada's religious development, consult H.H. Walsh, *The Christian Church in Canada* (Toronto, 1956).

The non-Catholic literature is generally not anti-Catholic, but there are passages and conclusions with which some Catholics would undoubtedly disagree.

The most important pamphlets were the 'Memorandum of Archbishop

Taché in answer to a report of the committee of the Honourable the Privy Council of Canada,' published in its entirety in sessional paper no. 40c, *CSP*, 1894, XXVII, no. 17, 28–67, and Father Leduc's polemic, *Hostility Unmasked: School Ordinance of 1892 of the North-West Territories and Its Disastrous Results* (Montreal, 1896). The most useful articles were A.R.M. Lower, 'Two ways of life: The primary antithesis of Canadian history,' *Report of the Canadian Historical Association* (Toronto, 1943), 5–18; L.H. Thomas, 'The reports of the Board of Education,' *Saskatchewan History*, II (autumn 1949), 15–20; R. Cook, 'Church, schools, and politics in Manitoba, 1903–1912,' *Canadian Historical Review*, XXXIX (March 1958), 1–23; G.F.G. Stanley, 'French settlement west of Lake Superior,' *Transactions of the Royal Society of Canada*, XLVIII, 3d series, 1954, sec. ii, 107–15 and by the same author, 'French and English in western Canada' in *Canadian Dualism*, edited by M. Wade (Toronto, 1960), 311–50; and D.H. Bocking, 'Saskatchewan's first provincial election,' *Saskatchewan History*, XVII (spring 1964), 41–54. Archbishop Langevin's religious periodical, *Les Cloches*, begun in 1903, was also valuable, particularly for the archbishop's movements in 1905.

Notes

1 *Statutes of Canada*, 38 Vict., c.49 (1875). For the political development of the North-West, see L.H. Thomas, *The Struggle for Responsible Government in the North-West Territories (1870–1897)* (Toronto, 1956) and C.C. Lingard, *Territorial Government in Canada: The Autonomy Question in the Old North-West Territories* (Toronto, 1946)

2 Based on calculations in M.P. Toombs, 'Some Aspects of the Growth and Development of Educational and Administrative Policies in Rupert's Land and in the North-West Territories to 1905' (M ED thesis, University of Saskatchewan, 1941), 70

3 G.F.G. Stanley, *The Birth of Western Canada: A History of the Riel Rebellions* (London, 1936), 187

4 Based on calculations in Toombs, 70; see also L.H. Thomas, 81

5 For the early history of the territorial Catholic church, see A.G. Morice, *History of the Catholic Church in Western Canada from Lake Superior to the Pacific (1659–1895)*, 2 vols. (Toronto, 1910), hereafter Morice (E); also A.G. Morice, *Histoire de l'Eglise catholique dans l'Ouest Canadien du Lac Supérieur au Pacifique (1659–1910)*, 3 vols. (Montreal, 1912), hereafter Morice (F)

6 E.J. Legal, *Short Sketches of the History of the Catholic Churches and Missions in Central Alberta* (Winnipeg, [1914]), 11

7 In 1871 the single ecclesiastical province of Quebec was divided into the provinces of Quebec, Toronto, and St Boniface, with metropolitan sees at

Quebec City, Toronto, and St Boniface respectively. Taché was raised to the rank of archbishop with three suffragans: V. Grandin (bishop of St Albert), L.J. D'Herbomez (vicar-apostolic of British Columbia), and H. Faraud (vicar-apostolic of Athabaska-Mackenzie). D. Benoit, *Vie de Mgr Taché*, 2 vols. (Montreal, 1904), I, 564-5, 571-5; II, 138–46

8 The only biography, an excellent one, is by D. Benoit: see n. 7 above

9 For the best biography, see P.E. Breton, *Vital Grandin* (Paris and Montreal, 1960); also E. Jonquet, *Mgr Grandin* (Montreal, 1903)

10 See K. Hughes, *Father Lacombe: The Black-Robe Voyageur* (Toronto, 1920); also P.E. Breton, *The Big Chief of the Prairies: The Life of Father Lacombe* ([Montreal], [1955])

11 To date there is no biography of Leduc

12 The only biography is the mediocre work by A.G. Morice, *Vie de Mgr Langevin* (St Boniface, 1916)

13 *Census of Canada*, 1890–91, I, 112, 328

14 Ibid., 1880–1, I, 202, 300

15 Ibid., 1901, I, 268, 392

16 Based on the Roman Catholic clergy listed in A.W. Thomas, ed., *The Canadian Almanac* (Toronto, 1904), 305, 309, 311–12

17 R. Maclean, 'The History of the Roman Catholic Church in Edmonton' (MA thesis, University of Alberta, 1958), 55–6

18 M. Wade, *The French Canadians 1760–1945* (Toronto, 1955), 341

19 Maclean, 36

20 Breton, *Grandin*, 224–5, 280

21 AAStB, L.F. Laflèche à Taché, 10 jan. 1880, E.A. Taschereau à Taché, 12 jan. 1880

22 G.F.G. Stanley, 'French Settlement West of Lake Superior,' Royal Society of Canada, *Transactions*, 3rd series, XLVIII (1954), 107–15

23 Hughes, *Lacombe*, 194

24 PAA, Grandin Papers, Grandin à Taché, 4 jan. 1884

25 Ibid., 21 nov. 1883

26 Ibid., 31 oct. 1883

27 Based on AAE, W.T. Urquhart, secretary, North-West Council, to Grandin, 22 Sept. 1873

28 Ibid., 26 Nov. 1873, 21 April 1874

29 PAA, Grandin au Ministre de l'Intérieur (Laird), 3 avril 1875, Grandin à Leduc, 31 dec. 1875. Contrary to statements in Morice (E), II, 125–6, and L. Groulx, *L'Enseignement français au Canada*, 2 vols. (Montreal, 1934), II, 152, it was the federal, not the territorial, government that made the first grant to Catholic schools in the North-West in 1875, not 1877; see also

H.T. Sparby, 'A History of the Alberta School System to 1925' (PH D thesis, Stanford University, 1958), 24

30 PAA, Grandin à Leduc, 31 déc. 1875, Grandin à Laird, 8 juin 1877, Grandin à Leduc, 19 juin 1877

31 *Journals of the Council of the North-West Territories*, 1877, 24, hereafter *Council Journals*

32 Laird to J.S. Dennis, deputy minister of the interior, telegram, 16 Aug. 1879, in ibid., 1879, Appendix A, 27

33 SAR, Department of Interior Transcripts, file no. 85869, Dennis to Laird, 8 Nov. 1880

34 PAC, 'Copy of the Laws and Regulations established for the Colony of St Laurent on the Saskatchewan,' 10 Dec. 1873

35 PAA, 30 jan. 1881

36 Ibid., Circulaire de Grandin, 31 août 1880

37 Ibid., 18 fév. 1881

38 The governor's powers and influence are detailed in L.H. Thomas, chap. 5, especially 107–9

39 AOE, 14 déc. 1876

40 AAE, 9 fév. 1877

41 PAA, 27 fév. 1882

42 SAS, Attorney General's Files, G series, 1876–1905, file 66L, 20 Oct. 1882 (official translation)

43 PAC, Macdonald Papers, private, 4 Nov. 1886

44 SAR, Department of Interior Transcripts, file no. 13985

45 *Council Journals*, 1878, 5

46 *Saskatchewan Herald*, 14 Feb. 1881

47 Breton, *Grandin*, 259

48 Ibid., 275

49 PAA, 8 juin 1882

50 C.B. Sissons, *Church and State in Canadian Education: An Historical Study* (Toronto, 1959), 50–6

51 Great Britain, *Statutes*, 30–1 Vict., c.3 (1867)

52 Breton, *Lacombe*, 104

53 *Statutes of Canada*, 38 Vict., c.49 (1875)

54 D.C. Thomson, *Alexander Mackenzie: Clear Grit* (Toronto, 1960), 26, 74

55 Late in 1874 Morris referred to it in two letters to Mackenzie (27 Nov., 25 Dec.), to which Mackenzie replied on 11 Dec. and 27 Jan. PAC, Morris Papers

56 Ibid., private, 15 March 1875

57 Canada, House of Commons, *Debates*, 1875, 658–9, hereafter *Commons*

Debates. The reference to 'other portions' was undoubtedly to Ontario and Quebec, but New Brunswick, with its 1874 appeal to the Privy Council in London and the 'riotous proceedings' at Caraquet, County of Gloucester (where two men lost their lives early in 1875), qualified also. For the New Brunswick school question, see Sissons, *Church and State,* 238–47.

58 Canada, Senate, *Debates,* 1875, 509, hereafter *Senate Debates*

59 *Journals of the Senate of Canada,* 1875, 289, hereafter *Senate Journals*

60 *Senate Debates,* 1875, 767, 769–72

61 Ibid., 1876, 93, 206–10, 281; 1880, 505–6

62 Grandin wrote Taché nine letters in 1875 and sixteen in 1876. There are no letters from Taché to Grandin in 1875–6. Neither Benoit nor Breton indicates that either bishop noticed the act

63 *Proposed School Ordinance for the North-West Territories* ([Moose Jaw], 1883). The Edmonton Legislative Library has a copy

64 *Edmonton Bulletin,* 5 May 1883

65 Oliver's position on the school and language questions is discussed in W. Waddell, 'The Honorable Frank Oliver,' 2 vols. (MA thesis, University of Alberta, 1950), II, 216–22; see also infra, 47–9, 54, 59, 63

66 *Edmonton Bulletin,* 12 May 1883, where the injection of sectional and religious issues was criticized.

67 Ibid., 26 May 1883

68 *Council Journals,* 1883, 6–9

69 *Saskatchewan Herald,* 9 June 1883

70 *Macleod Gazette,* 14 Sept. 1882, 14 Sept. 1883

71 *Council Journals,* 1883, 33, 58–9. There are no debates on the bill, as extensive reporting by the *Regina Leader* did not begin until 1885

72 The Manitoba Act (1870) and the first provincial School Act (1871) established a church-controlled school system with local trustees supervised by Protestant or Catholic sections of the Board of Education. The latter, although independent of the provincial government, received public grants which the sections divided, at first equally and after 1875 on a per pupil basis. W.L. Morton, *Manitoba: A History* (Toronto, 1957), 18b

73 PAA, 4 jan. 1884

74 Ibid., Grandin à Lacombe, 20 jan. 1884. The first Catholic church in Regina was consecrated in August 1884. Morice (E), II, 156

75 7 fév. 1884, Benoit, *Taché,* II, 439

76 PAA, Grandin à Taché, 7 mars 1884

77 27 mars 1884. The letter, not seen, is mentioned in AAE, Dewdney to Grandin, 28 April 1884

78 Although outside the pale of white settlement, Faraud's vicariate was part of

the Territories and was affected by legislation passed at Regina
79 AAE, 15 oct. 1883
80 L.H. Thomas, 111–12; J. Blue, *Alberta: Past and Present*, 3 vols. (Chicago, 1924), I, 106
81 PAA, Grandin à Taché, 30 mars 1884
82 AAStB, 1 juillet 1884
83 AAE, Lacombe à Grandin, 2 avril 1884

CHAPTER 2

1 *Edmonton Bulletin*, 17 Jan. 1885
2 Ibid., 2 Aug. 1884
3 AAStB, 8 juillet 1884
4 Macdonald Papers, private, 22 July 1884
5 *Council Journals*, 1884, 81
6 Macdonald Papers, private, 5 Aug. 1884
7 *Regina Leader*, 7 Aug. 1884
8 Cf. *The Consolidated Statutes of Manitoba*, 1880–1, c.62, ss.1–8 and *Ordinances of the North-West Territories*, 1884, No. 5, ss.1–8, hereafter *Ordinances*
9 *Ordinances*, 1884, No. 5, s.5(3)
10 Quebec's dual system, with its Council of Public Instruction and Catholic and Protestant committees, was created in 1869. In 1875 the committees became completely independent and all Catholic bishops in Quebec became members of the Catholic committee. C.E. Phillips, *The Development of Education in Canada* (Toronto, 1957), 220
11 Cf. *Proposed School Ordinance*, 1883, ss.118–25 and *Ordinances*, 1884, No. 5, ss.25–33
12 Although Ryerson, superintendent of education in Canada West from 1844 to 1876, advocated and defended a strong common school system (C.B. Sissons, *Egerton Ryerson: His Life and Letters*, 2 vols. [Toronto, 1947], II, 95, 259), he accepted separate schools, even though he thought the conscience clause made them unnecessary. A. Shortt and A.G. Doughty, eds., *Canada and Its Provinces*, 23 vols. (Toronto, 1914–17), XVIII, 312
13 For the first question, see infra, 27; for the fourth, see infra, 32–4, 35–6, 37–8
14 Sissons, *Church and State*, 280–90, 345–7
15 AOO, Girard à Taché, 30 avril 1877
16 *Statutes of Canada*, 40 Vict., c.7, s.11 (1877)
17 *Edmonton Bulletin*, 10, 17, 31 Jan.; 7 March 1885
18 Ibid., 21 March, 5 Sept. 1885

19 *North-West Territories Gazette, 1883–89*, 5 Oct. 1885, 108
20 *Edmonton Bulletin*, 5 Sept. 1885
21 Toombs, 90
22 *Regina Leader*, 10 Dec. 1885
23 *Report of the Board of Education for the North-West Territories* (18 Dec. 1885–1 Oct. 1886), 7, hereafter *RBE*, 1885–6
24 *Regina Leader*, 10 Dec. 1885
25 Ibid.
26 Catholic representation on council decreased from 25 per cent in 1878–9 to 20 per cent in 1881, and remained constant at 15 per cent from 1884 to 1887. For Catholic support in the assembly, see infra, 42, 45–6, 67
27 *Edmonton Bulletin*, 26 Dec. 1885
28 *Ordinances*, 1885, No. 3, s.6(3)
29 *Edmonton Bulletin*, 2 Jan. 1886
30 *Ordinances*, 1885, No. 3, s.5(3–5)
31 Ibid., s.5(2)
32 Sparby, 78; Groulx, II, 157–8
33 Forget to Taché, 1 March 1894, in 'Memorandum of Archbishop Taché in Answer to a Report of the Committee of the Honourable the Privy Council of Canada,' Canada, *Sessional Papers of the Parliament of Canada*, 1894, XXVII, no. 17, Appendix D, 64, hereafter Taché Memorandum, *CSP*, 1894
34 Ibid., 65
35 *Ordinances*, 1886, No. 10, s.12
36 Ibid., s.1
37 'Regulations of the Board of Education of the North-West Territories,' *CSP*, 1894, XXVII, No. 17, 169, hereafter 'Regulations of the Board of Education,' *CSP*, 1894
38 *Ordinances*, 1886, No. 10, s.1
39 *Qu'Appelle Vidette*, 14 Jan. 1886
40 AAE, Taché à Grandin, 9 oct. 1886
41 Benoit, *Taché*, II, 528
42 Macdonald Papers, 22 Oct. 1887
43 SAS, Sir John Thompson to His Excellency the Governor-General-in-Council, 10 Jan. 1890, in 'Correspondence reports of the Ministers of Justice and Orders-in-Council upon the subject of Dominion and Provincial Legislation,' vol. I, hereafter 'Correspondence reports ... 1867–1895.' For a further discussion of Thompson's letter, see infra, 62, 191, 263n, 265n
44 Breton, *Grandin*, 304–7; Benoit, *Taché*, II, 548, 551
45 23 Dec. 1886 to 7 Jan. 1887, and 22–6 July 1886, Benoit, *Taché*, II, 532, 553
46 *Council Journals*, 1887, 8

47 Macdonald Papers, 20 Nov. 1887
48 AAStB, 17 Oct. 1887
49 Ibid., 20 Oct. 1887
50 Macdonald Papers, 22, 25 Oct. 1887
51 AAStB, Lacombe à Taché, 17, 21 oct. 1887
52 PAA, Journal de Grandin, 21 oct. 1887
53 Ibid., 25 oct. 1887
54 AAStB, Lacombe à Taché, 25, 27 oct. 1887; PAA, Journal de Grandin, 26 oct. 1887
55 PAA, Journal de Grandin, 26 oct. 1887
56 AAStB, 27 oct. 1887
57 Ibid., Lacombe à Taché, 17 oct. 1887
58 PAA, Journal de Grandin, 28 oct. 1887
59 AAStB, Lacombe à Taché, 29 oct. 1887
60 Ibid., same to same, 27 oct. 1887
61 *Regina Leader*, 22 Nov. 1887. The names of the schools were not given
62 PAA, Grandin au Ministre de l'Intérieur, 3 avril 1875
63 Ibid., Grandin à Leduc, 6 oct. 1877
64 AAE, Quévillon à Grandin, 25 mars 1886
65 PAA, 20 jan. 1884
66 AAE, Leduc à Grandin, 18 dec. 1888
67 Ibid., 21 fév. 1889
68 Wade, 346
69 *Regina Leader*, 22 Nov. 1887
70 Ibid., 15 Nov. 1887
71 SAR, Department of Interior Transcripts, file no. 85869, Dewdney to the Minister of the Interior, 2 Dec. 1887
72 *Report of the Board of Education for the North-West Territories* (18 Oct. 1887–13 Sept. 1888), 7, hereafter *RBE*, 1887–8
73 AAE, 13 nov. 1887
74 Ibid., 14 Nov. 1887, quoted in Lacombe à Grandin, 14 nov. 1887
75 The telegram has not been seen; it is mentioned in n. 76 below
76 Macdonald Papers, 20 Nov. 1887
77 This is the first reference to Haultain in the Catholic correspondence. As chief spokesman for the advisory council (1888–92), the executive committee (1893–6), and the executive council (1897–1905), Haultain became the territorial 'premier' and frequently drew the ire of Catholic leaders after 1887
78 AAStB, *confidentielle*, 26 nov. 1887
79 Ibid., Macdonald to Taché, 21 Dec. 1887

80 Ibid., 19 oct. 1887

81 *RBE*, 1885–6, 12–13; 'Regulations of the Board of Education,' *CSP*, 1894, 175–80

82 *RBE*, 1885–6, 11

83 Ibid., 9

84 Ibid., 13–17

85 *Report of the Board of Education for the North-West Territories* (1 Oct. 1886–18 Oct. 1887), 8, hereafter *RBE*, 1886–7

86 Ibid., Appendix E, 51–3

87 'Regulations of the Board of Education,' *CSP*, 1894, 169–70, 172–4

88 *Report of the Board of Education for the North-West Territories* (13 Sept. 1888–16 Oct. 1889), 3–7, hereafter *RBE*, 1888–9

89 *Report of the Board of Education for the North-West Territories* (1 Sept. 1889–10 Sept. 1890), 9–10, hereafter *RBE*, 1889–90

90 Ibid., 1885–6, 8

91 Ibid., 1887–8, 8

92 Supra, 26

93 *Ordinances*, 1885, No. 3, s.5(5)

94 Ibid., 1886, No. 10, s.1

95 Supra, 34

96 'Regulations of the Board of Education,' *CSP*, 1894, 172–4

97 Supra, 34

98 *RBE*, 1885–6, 18

99 *Regina Leader*, 16 Nov. 1886

100 *RBE*, 1886–7, 12

101 Quoted in Haultain to the Lieutenant-Governor (NWT), 4 Jan. 1894, *CSP*, 1894, XVII, No. 17, 13

102 AAStB, 29 jan. 1888

103 AAE, Leduc à Grandin, 23 mars 1888

104 PAA, Grandin à Leduc, 29 août 1888

105 *RBE*, 1887–8, Appendix A, 12–43

CHAPTER 3

1 *Statutes of Canada*, 51 Vict., c.19, s.13 (1888)

2 L.H. Thomas, 155, 157

3 Wade, 353–4

4 Morice (E), II, 173–4

5 Taché to Laflèche, 26 May 1885, quoted in Wade, 418; PAA, Grandin à Taché, 22 juin 1885

6 PAA, Grandin à Taché, 28 juin 1887
7 Ibid., 9 nov. 1887
8 Based on account in AAE, J.P. Tardivel à Grandin, 28 nov. 1887
9 Morice (E), II, 65
10 PAA, Grandin à Taché, 18 jan. 1887; AAStB, Rouleau à Taché, 15 nov. 1887
11 PAA, Grandin à Taché, 25 juillet 1888; AAStB, Forget à Taché, 24 sept. 1888, Leduc à Taché, 6 déc. 1887
12 *Calgary Herald*, 19 Sept. 1888
13 PAA, 11 jan. 1888
14 The series ran from 13 Sept. 1888 to 26 Sept. 1889
15 *Qu'Appelle Vidette*, 8 Dec. 1887, 19 July 1888
16 PAC, Thompson Papers, private, 1 Oct. 1888
17 AAStB, Thompson to Taché, private, 5 Oct. 1888
18 Thompson Papers, 12 Oct. 1888
19 *Regina Leader*, 6 Nov. 1888
20 Ibid., 20 Nov. 1888
21 Ibid.
22 Thompson Papers, Dewdney to Thompson, 16 April 1888
23 Manitoba introduced compulsory education in 1916. Sparby, 77n
24 *Regina Leader*, 27 Nov. 1888
25 AAStB, 3 déc. 1888
26 Infra, 78–9; also 136–7
27 AAStB, Royal à Taché, 10 oct. 1888, Royal à Grandin, 16 oct. 1888
28 *Regina Leader*, 4 Dec. 1888
29 Thompson Papers, telegram, 3 Dec. 1888
30 Ibid., telegram, private, 4 Dec. 1888, vol. 13, 17
31 *Regina Leader*, 11 Dec. 1888
32 *Revised Ordinances*, c.59, s.82(1) (1888)
33 AAStB, Leduc à Taché, 18 déc. 1888
34 Ibid., 22 nov. 1888
35 AAE, *personnelle*, 3 déc. 1888
36 Thompson Papers, 24 Nov. 1888
37 For a further discussion of this point, see infra, 67
38 PAA, 12 déc. 1888
39 *Calgary Herald*, 14 Aug. 1889
40 *Lethbridge News*, 14 Aug. 1889
41 Morice (E), II, 229
42 *Regina Journal*, 27 Sept., 6 Dec. 1888, 31 Jan., 7 March, 18 April, 23 May, 13, 27 June, 8 Aug 1889
43 *Qu'Appelle Vidette*, 17 Oct. 1889

44 *Moosomin Courier*, 10 Jan. 1889
45 *Lethbridge News*, 21 Aug. 1889
46 *Qu'Appelle Progress*, 9 Aug., 6, 20 Sept. 1889
47 *Regina Leader*, 23 Oct., 20 Nov., 18 Dec. 1888, 5 March, 7 May, 18 June, 2, 16 July 1889
48 *Regina Journal*, 29 Nov., 20 Dec. 1888, 7 Feb. 1889
49 Benoit, *Taché*, II, 622
50 *Northwest Review*, 14, 28 Nov. 1888, 8, 29 May, 18 Sept., 27 Nov. 1889
51 Ibid., 14 Aug. 1889
52 Ibid., 30 Jan., 29 May, 12 June, 31 July, 4, 11 Sept. 1889
53 Ibid., 27 Nov. 1889
54 Infra, 134
55 Morton, *Manitoba*, 200–3
56 SAR, 'Minutes of the Advisory Council in Matters of Finance, NWT,' 13 Aug. 1889, hereafter Minutes of Advisory Council
57 AAStB, 14 août 1889, Leduc à Taché, 20 août 1889
58 Macdonald Papers, 18 Aug. 1889
59 Ibid., 22 Aug. 1889
60 Ibid., 18 Aug. 1889
61 Ibid., 28 Aug. 1889
62 Ibid., private, 6 Oct. 1889
63 *Regina Leader*, 22 Oct. 1889
64 *Assembly Journals*, 1889, 17–18
65 Ibid., 41
66 Ibid., 34–6
67 *Regina Leader*, 1 Nov. 1889; *Assembly Journals*, 1889, 41
68 Ibid., 64–5. The *Regina Leader*, which reported debates extensively by this time, carried no debate on the resolution
69 *Assembly Journals*, 1889, 108–9
70 *Regina Leader*, 1 Nov. 1889
71 *Qu'Appelle Vidette*, 11, 18 July 1889; *Northwest Review*, 4 Sept. 1889
72 *Assembly Journals*, 1889, 35
73 Sissons, *Church and State*, 234–5
74 *Regina Leader*, 1 Nov. 1889
75 Macdonald Papers, Dewdney to Macdonald, 18 Aug. 1889
76 L.H. Thomas, 21–2, 31, 44, 129–30, 184; Lingard, 19–20
77 *Regina Leader*, 1 Nov. 1889
78 *Assembly Journals*, 1889, 45
79 AAE, Leduc à Grandin, 4–6 nov. 1889; PAA, Grandin à Leduc, 13 nov. 1889; *Regina Leader*, 1 Nov. 1889

80 *Lethbridge News*, 30 Oct. 1889; AAE, Leduc à Grandin, 2 oct., 27 nov. 1889; *Northwest Review*, 17 Oct. 1889

81 *Regina Leader*, 12 Nov. 1889

82 PAA, Grandin à Royal, 29 oct. 1889

83 Macdonald Papers, 29 Oct. 1889

84 AAE, 30 oct. 1889; AAStB, 30 oct. 1889 (two letters each)

85 AAE, Leduc à Grandin, 4 nov. 1889

86 Ibid., 6 nov. 1889

87 PAA, Grandin à Rouleau, 13 nov. 1889

88 Ibid., Journal de Grandin, 14 nov. 1889

89 AAE, Rouleau à Grandin, 26 nov. 1889

90 Ibid., Royal à Grandin, 24 nov. 1889

91 PAA, Journal de Grandin, 16 nov. 1889

92 Quotations are from the English translation of the letter as tabled in *Commons Debates*, 1890, cols. 119–21

93 AAE, Taschereau à Grandin, 1 déc. 1889

94 Ibid., Duhamel à Taschereau, 4 déc. 1889

95 Ibid., Taschereau à Duhamel, 6 déc. 1889

96 Ibid., Laflèche à Grandin, 20 déc. 1889

97 Ibid., Royal à Grandin, 9 jan. 1890

98 Ibid., Lacombe à Grandin, 'la fête de la Purification' (2 fév. 1890)

99 Mercier suggested Grandin look to France, Belgium, and Switzerland for colonists; it was enough for Quebec to colonize the Gaspé peninsula, the Ottawa valley, and Manitoba (ibid., 19 déc. 1889)

100 Ibid., Leduc à Grandin, 29 jan. 1890

101 Ibid., 8 fév. 1890

102 PAA, 19 fév. 1890

103 At Royal's request Grandin had written Dewdney (25 July 1888), giving qualified approval to his administration in the North-West. To silence government critics Dewdney published the letter minus the qualifications and embarrassed Grandin and Taché, who had complained of their difficulties at Regina and Ottawa. PAA, Grandin à Royal, *privée*, 3 oct. 1888, Grandin à Taché, 30 oct. 1888; Thompson Papers, Grandin à Langevin, *privée*, 4 mars 1889

104 AAE, Taché à Grandin, 2 mars 1890

105 *Calgary Herald*, 23 Dec. 1889; *Macleod Gazette*, 9 Jan. 1890; *Lethbridge News*, 15 Jan. 1890; *Saskatchewan Herald*, 29 Jan. 1890

106 AAStB, 17 jan. 1890

107 *Commons Debates*, 1890, cols. 119–21

108 Ibid., cols. 969, 560

109 *Calgary Herald*, 18 Jan. 1890
110 PAA, Circulaire de Grandin, 18 jan. 1890
111 AAStB, 31 déc. 1889
112 PAA, 18 mai 1890
113 Ibid., Grandin à Laflèche, 22 août 1890

CHAPTER 4

1 *Commons Debates*, 1890, col. 38
2 *Commons Journals*, 1890, 86; *Commons Debates*, 1890, col. 882
3 AAStB, 24 fév. 1890; AAE, 26 fév. 1890
4 PAA, Grandin à LaRivière, 12 mars 1890
5 AAStB, Taché à LaRivière, 5 mai 1890
6 *Commons Debates*, 1890, cols. 677, 636, 853, 995
7 *Senate Debates*, 1890, 609
8 Thompson to the Governor-General-in-Council, 10 Jan. 1890, in 'Correspondence report ... 1867–1895'
9 See infra, 191, 263n, 265n
10 PAC, Laurier Papers, confidential, 24 Feb. 1890
11 *Prince Albert Times*, 13 Dec. 1889
12 *Saskatchewan Herald*, 25 Dec. 1889
13 *Edmonton Bulletin*, 7 June 1890
14 Ibid., 14 June 1890
15 Ibid., 1 Nov. 1890
16 Ibid., 22 Nov. 1890
17 *Regina Leader*, 18 Nov. 1890
18 Advisory Council to the Lieutenant-Governor, 29 Oct. 1889, quoted in L.H. Thomas, 171
19 *Assembly Journals*, 1890, 56
20 *Regina Leader*, 25 Nov. 1890
21 There is no evidence of difficulties with constituents
22 *Assembly Journals*, 1890, 56
23 Ibid., 129
24 Ibid., 130, 134–5
25 *Saskatchewan Herald*, 13, 20, 27 Feb. 1891
26 Ibid., 13 March 1891
27 *Commons Debates*, 1891, cols. 174–5
28 Thompson Papers, Brett and Betts to the Secretary of State, 23 June 1891
29 *Commons Debates*, 1891, cols. 1760–1
30 Ibid., col. 3909

31 Ibid., col. 3913
32 Infra, 177
33 *Commons Debates*, 1891, cols. 3910–12, 3921-2
34 Ibid., col. 3941
35 *Senate Debates*, 1891, 554; *Moosomin Courier*, 18 June 1891, *Qu'Appelle Vidette*, 18 June 1891
36 AAE, 17 Dec. 1889
37 Ibid., Leduc's Letter Book, 1889–1, 14 Sept. 1891, 959
38 *Commons Debates*, 1890, col. 882; *Senate Debates*, 1890, 622, 629; *Statutes of Canada*, 54–5 Vict., c.22, s.20 (1891)
39 PAA, Grandin à Royal, 23 déc. 1890
40 *Saskatchewan Herald*, 13 March 1891
41 AAE, Royal à Grandin, mars 28 1891
42 PAA, Grandin à Taché, 8 avril 1891; AAE, Taché à Grandin, 20 avril 1891
43 PAA, Journal de Grandin, 6 nov. 1891
44 Ibid., 1, 6 nov. 1891
45 *Edmonton Bulletin*, 14 Nov. 1891; PAA, Journal de Grandin, 7 nov. 1891
46 *Edmonton Bulletin*, 17 Oct. 1891
47 *Macleod Gazette*, 12, 21 Feb. 1891
48 *Prince Albert Times*, 25 Nov. 1891
49 *Saskatchewan Herald*, 2, 30 Oct. 1891
50 Ibid., 13 Nov. 1891
51 E.g., *Qu'Appelle Vidette*, 13 March 1890, 21 May 1891
52 Ibid., 5, 12 Nov. 1891; *Regina Leader*, 10 Nov. 1891
53 *Qu'Appelle Vidette*, 12 Nov. 1891
54 Ibid., 5 Nov. 1891
55 Ibid., 26 Nov. 1891
56 L.H. Thomas, 200
57 *Statutes of Canada*, 54–5 Vict., c.22, s.6 (1891)
58 *Regina Standard*, 18 Dec. 1891
59 Ibid., 29 Jan. 1892
60 AAStB, Rev. J. Caron à Taché, 26 déc. 1891
61 3 déc. 1891, Benoit, *Taché*, II, 726
62 AAE, Leduc à Grandin, 27 déc. 1891
63 AAStB, Forget à Taché, 31 déc. 1891; PAA, Grandin à Forget, 16 jan. 1892, Grandin à Prince, 16 jan. 1892
64 PAC, Abbott Papers, 15 Jan. 1892
65 *Assembly Journals*, 1891–2, 110
66 *Regina Standard*, 29 Jan. 1892
67 *Assembly Journals*, 1891-2, 110

68 *Regina Standard*, 29 Jan. 1892

69 *Assembly Journals*, 1891–2, 110

70 *Regina Standard*, 5 Feb. 1892

71 *Assembly Journals*, 1891–2, 133

72 *Regina Standard*, 5 Feb. 1892

73 *Ordinances*, 1891–2, No. 28, ss.1–2, 5–7

74 *Assembly Journals*, 1891–2, 134

75 *Regina Standard*, 5 Feb. 1892

76 Thompson Papers, Leduc to James Brown, 3 July 1891

77 *Report of the Board of Education for the North-West Territories* (10 Sept. 1890 – 2 Sept. 1891), 12–19, hereafter *RBE*, 1890–1

78 *Regina Standard*, 26 Aug. 1892

79 AAE, Leduc à Grandin, 30 jan. 1889

80 PAA, Grandin à Prince, 16 jan. 1892

81 AAE, 30 jan. 1892

82 AAStB, 3 mars 1892

83 Minutes of the Executive Committee of the North-West Territories in Canada, 23 March, 13 July 1892, hereafter Minutes of the Executive Committee

84 AAStB, Gillies to Taché, 26 Dec. 1893

85 Minutes of the Executive Committee, 13 April 1894. For a further discussion of Gillies's resignation, see infra, 116

86 Quoted in *Commons Debates*, 1896, col. 2408

87 AAE, Thompson à Grandin, 15 mars, 1892

88 PAA, 7 avril 1892

89 *Commons Debates*, 1892, cols. 2462–3

90 Ibid., cols. 3062, 3069, 3077–88

91 *Assembly Journals*, 1892 (first session), 13; *Regina Standard*, 19 Aug. 1892

92 *Assembly Journals*, 1892 (first session), 30

93 *Saskatchewan Herald*, 1 April 1892

94 *Regina Standard*, 19 Aug. 1892

95 *Ordinances*, 1892, No. 22, s.83(1)

96 *Regina Standard*, 26 Aug. 1892

97 Quoted in ibid., 2 Sept. 1892

98 *Saskatchewan Herald*, 12 Feb. 1892

99 L.H. Thomas, 214

100 *Regina Standard*, 2 Sept. 1892

101 L.H. Thomas, 219

102 *Regina Standard*, 19 Aug. 1892

103 Thompson Papers, Royal to Thompson, 1 Sept. 1892

104 *Macleod Gazette*, 15 Sept. 1892

105 L.H. Thomas, 221

106 Resort to the courts proved fruitless; on 30 July 1892, the judicial committee of the Privy Council declared the 1890 legislation *intra vires*. Benoit, Taché, II, 690–1

107 Quoted in L.H. Thomas, 225

108 *Regina Standard*, 7 Oct. 1892

109 Ibid., 18 Nov. 1892; *Regina Leader*, 24 Oct. 1892

110 *Regina Standard*, 16 Dec. 1892. Several members 'simultaneously' gave him 'the only possible answer': the 1875 Act gave 'special rights' only to Protestants and Roman Catholics in 'general terms'

111 Thompson Papers, Thompson to Royal, 20 Sept 1892, vol. 33, 235

112 *Assembly Journals*, 1892 (second session), 44

113 [Haultain] to Royal, 20 Dec. 1892, quoted in L.H. Thomas, 227

114 Daly to Thompson, 22 Dec. 1892, quoted in ibid.

115 *Ordinances*, 1892, No. 1, 'An Ordinance Respecting Expenditure'; also *Regina Standard*, 30 Dec. 1892, 6 Jan. 1893

116 Thompson Papers, n.d. (either 20 or 21 Dec. 1892), vol. 34, 268

117 *Regina Standard*, 2 Sept. 1892

118 *Revised Ordinances*, c.59, s.41 (1888)

119 *Regina Standard*, 23 Dec. 1892

120 *Ordinances*, 1892, No. 22, s.32

121 *Regina Standard*, 6 Jan. 1893

122 Thompson Papers, telegram, private, 27 Dec. 1892, vol. 34A, 288

123 Formerly, inspectors, at the trustees' request, examined candidates who lacked certificates (*Revised Ordinances*, c.59, s.89(2) (1888)), assisted at the examination of teachers at the Board of Education's request (ibid., s.89(6)), and granted provisional certificates to 'competent' applicants recommended by trustees (ibid., s.89(10)).

CHAPTER 5

1 *Commons Debates*, 1893, col. 606

2 *Commons Journals*, 1893, Index, xxxv

3 Taché Memorandum, *CSP*, 1894, 41. For evidence that the letter was to Angers, see AAE, Leduc à Grandin, 21 sept. 1893

4 AAStB, 10 juillet 1893

5 Quoted (in English) in ibid., Leduc à Taché, 19 août 1892

6 AAE, 23 July 1892

7 L.H. Thomas, 207

8 Minutes of the Executive Committee, 4 Jan., 4 April, 27 Dec. 1893
9 *Parliamentary Debates on the Subject of Confederation of the British North American Provinces* (Quebec, 1865), 640–4
10 R.S. Patterson, 'F.W.G. Haultain and Education in the Early West' (M ED thesis, University of Alberta, 1961), 58, n.38
11 Quoted in ibid., 9
12 'Haultain, known locally as "that little Englishman" because he spoke with an "English accent" and "the tweeds and serges which he affects are all English," was English-born but came to Canada at an early age.' N.G. McDonald, 'The School as an Agent of Nationalism in the North-West Territories, 1884–1905' (M ED thesis, University of Alberta, 1971), 104
13 Sissons, *Church and State*, 284
14 Selinger's mediocre study pays little attention to either: A.D. Selinger, 'The Contributions of D.J. Goggin in the Development of Education in the North-West Territories 1893–1902' (M ED thesis, University of Alberta, 1960)
15 *Regina Leader*, 7 Sept. 1893
16 Thompson Papers, 6 Dec. 1893
17 Based on discussions with R.S. Patterson
18 McDonald, 131–4
19 H.A. Rommen, *The State in Catholic Thought: A Treatise in Political Philosophy* (St Louis and London, 1947), 596n.
20 Thompson Papers, Taché to Thompson, 6 Dec. 1893
21 H. Leduc, *Hostility Unmasked: School Ordinance of 1892 of the North-West Territories and Its Disastrous Results* (Montreal, 1896), 35–6, hereafter Leduc, *Hostility Unmasked*
22 Ibid., 36
23 Minutes of the Executive Committee, 8 June 1893
24 Leduc, *Hostility Unmasked*, 36
25 Sessional Paper no. 11, in unpublished sessional papers of the Council and the Legislative Assembly in the North-West Territories, 1894, microfilm no. 2.95, p. 11, hereafter TSP
26 Haultain to the Lieutenant-Governor (NWT), 4 Jan. 1894, *CSP*, 1894, XXVII, no. 17, 14. For Haultain's substitution of 'determined upon' for 'prescribed,' see infra, 95
27 Caron to Taché, 24 Feb. 1894, quoted in Taché Memorandum, *CSP*, 1894, Appendix B, 59
28 *RBE*, 1885–6, 12–13
29 Haultain to the Lieutenant-Governor (NWT), 12 Jan. 1894, *CSP*, 1894, XXVII, no. 17, 17

30 *RBE*, 1889–90, 12–14
31 Ibid., 1890–1, 12–14
32 TSP, no. 12, 1894, microfilm no. 2.95, p. 11
33 Neff's income to 14 Aug. 1894 was the same as Haultain's, indicating that Neff spent as much time in Regina as Haultain and constituted the two-man quorum of the Council. Ibid
34 'Circular to Teachers of Roman Catholic Schools in the Territories,' 30 Sept. 1893, *CSP*, 1894, xxvii, no. 17, 197
35 Haultain to the Lieutenant-Governor (NWT), 12 Jan. 1894, ibid., 17
36 Same to same, 4 Jan. 1894, ibid., 14
37 Taché Memorandum, ibid., 36
38 'Regulations of the Council of Public Instruction Governing Teachers' Certificates, 1894,' ibid., 193–6. For the date, see TSP, no. 9, 1894, microfilm no. 2.95, p. 10
39 *Revised Ordinances*, c.59, s.179 (1888). 'In practice, any school having a High School Branch was termed a Union School': Toombs, 109
40 *RBE*, 1888–9, 8–10
41 *Report of the Council of Public Instruction of the North-West Territories*, 1896, 16, hereafter *RCPI*
42 *RBE*, 1889–90, 7
43 'Regulations of the Board of Education of the North-West Territories,' 15 March 1888, *CSP*, 1894, xxvii, no. 17, 169
44 *RBE*, 1889–90, 6–10
45 *RCPI*, 1896, 16
46 *RBE*, 1890–1, 21
47 Supra, 38
  RCPI, 1896, 16–17
  Thompson Papers, no. 24013, notice entitled 'Normal Schools, N.W.T.,' egina, 1 Sept. 1893
  duc, *Hostility Unmasked*, 10
  luc to Taché, 17 Feb. 1894, in Taché Memorandum, *CSP*, 1894, endix A, 55
  1889–90, 8
  to Taché, 17 Feb. 1894, in Taché Memorandum, *CSP*, 1894, lix A, 55
  Ordinances, c.59, s.89(1) (1888)
  losed in Leduc à Taché, 26 fév. 1894
  , 1892, No. 22, s.91(10)
  c à Taché, 17 sept. 1893
  Grandin, 4 sept. 1893
  same, 6 sept. 1893. For Leduc's movements, see ibid., same to

same, 20 sept. 1893 and AAStB, Leduc à Taché, 17 sept. 1893. The text, unless otherwise indicated, is based on the more comprehensive letter to Grandin

60 Leduc, *Hostility Unmasked*, 9
61 AAStB, 17 sept. 1893
62 Ibid., Leduc à Taché, 6, 31 oct. 1893
63 Taché Memorandum, *CSP*, 1894, Appendix B, 59, Appendix D, 66
64 AAStB, Leduc à Taché, 17 sept. 1893
65 Based on account in AAE, Leduc à Grandin, 21 sept. 1893
66 Thompson Papers, 24 Oct. 1893, vol. 39, 471
67 AAE, Leduc à Grandin, 16 oct. 1893
68 Maclean, 100–2
69 AAE, Leduc à Grandin, 31 oct. 1893
70 The petitions are listed in *CSP*, 1894, XXVII, no. 17, 18
71 AAStB, Lacombe à Taché, 12 nov. 1893
72 Ibid., 27 Nov. 1893
73 Petition of the Board of Trustees of St Joachim Roman Catholic Separate School District No. 7, Edmonton, 2 Nov. 1893, *CSP*, 1894, XXVII, no. 17, 1–4
74 Thompson Papers, 17 Nov. 1893, vol. 40, 315
75 Ibid., no. 24013, 'Regulations With Respect to Teachers' Examinations and Entrance Examinations to Union Schools,' 3 Sept. 1891
76 Ibid., unofficial, 28 Nov. 1893
77 Ibid., 6 Dec. 1893
78 Taché Memorandum, *CSP*, 1894, 38
79 Thompson Papers, private and confidential, 4 Jan. 1894
80 Haultain to the Lieutenant-Governor (NWT), 4 Jan. 1894, *CSP*, 1894, XXVII, no. 17, 12–15
81 AAStB, 11 Jan. 1894
82 *Moose Jaw Times*, 28 Aug. 1891; *Moosomin Spectator*, 9 Nov. 1893
83 *Regina Leader*, 22 Aug. 1892
84 Ibid., 1 June 1893
85 *Regina Standard*, 29 April 1892; also ibid., 1 April 1892
86 *Edmonton Bulletin*, 16 April 1892
87 *Regina Standard*, 18 Jan. 1894
88 *Saskatchewan Times*, 8 Sept. 1893; *Moosomin Spectator*, 28 Dec. 1893
89 Ibid., 5 Oct. 1893
90 *Regina Standard*, 2 Nov. 1893
91 Ibid., 7 Sept. 1893
92 *Lethbridge News*, 8 Feb. 1893
93 *Medicine Hat Times*, 23 March 1893
94 *Calgary Herald*, 6 Feb. 1894

95 TSP, no. 4, 1894, microfilm no. 2.95, p. 10, Daly to R.B. Gordon, telegram, 12 Jan. 1894
96 Haultain to the Lieutenant-Governor (NWT), 12 Jan. 1894, *CSP*, 1894, XXVII, no. 17, 16–17
97 TSP, no. 4, 1894, microfilm no. 2.95, p. 10, telegram, 18 Jan. 1894
98 Ibid., telegram, 18 Jan. 1894
99 Thompson Papers, private, 23 Jan. 1894
100 The Provincial Protestant Association (PPA) succeeded the militant Equal Rights Association of Ontario, established in 1889 to have the Jesuit Estates Act repealed. The Patrons of Industry, a rural movement of political protest, entered Ontario from Michigan in 1887 and spread to the Territories via Manitoba
101 Ibid., private, 7 Feb. 1894
102 Ibid., Thompson to Mackintosh, 30 Jan. 1894, vol. 42, 263
103 L.H. Thomas, 208, n.24
104 *Regina Standard*, 19 Aug. 1892
105 L.H. Thomas, 245

CHAPTER 6

1 'Extract of the report of the committee of the honourable the privy council,' *CSP*, 1894, XXVII, no. 17, 18–27, hereafter Privy Council Report
2 Taché Memorandum, *CSP*, 1894, 28–67
3 Ibid., 33–4, 36
4 Ibid., 36–7
5 Ibid., Appendix D, 66; supra, 74
6 Ibid., Appendix C, 60
7 Ibid., Appendix A, 56
8 Ibid., Appendix C, 60
9 Ibid., 34
10 Ibid., Appendix A, 54
11 AAStB, 12 sept. 1890
12 Taché Memorandum, *CSP*, 1894, 29–33
13 Ibid., Appendix A, 57
14 Ibid., Appendix D, 66
15 Ibid., 37
16 Ibid., 37–8
17 Ibid., 40–1
18 Ibid., 43
19 The letter was addressed to the governor-general-in-council. Ibid., 5, 39–40

20 Ibid., 40
21 Taché's reference was to the decision of Canada's Supreme Court in answer to six questions on the Manitoba issue, submitted by the federal government on 31 July 1893. The five judges returned five separate opinions in February 1894, three against the minority's appeal for federal action to set aside the Manitoba School Act of 1890. Sissons, *Church and State*, 185
22 Taché Memorandum, *CSP*, 1894, 48
23 *Regina Leader*, 30 Oct. 1888
24 Taché Memorandum, *CSP*, 1894, 49
25 Supra, 32; also Wade, 289
26 *Regina Leader*, 3 Nov. 1891; *Regina Standard*, 18 Dec. 1891
27 Sissons, *Church and State*, 146
28 Thompson Papers, 6 Dec. 1893
29 PAC, R.W. Scott Papers, 8 March 1894; Laurier Papers, Tarte à Laurier, 9 fév. 1894
30 AAStB, 6 mars 1894
31 PAA, Grandin à Leduc, 18 mars 1894
32 AAStB, 1 avril 1894
33 Benoit, *Taché*, II, 788–9
34 AAE, 20 avril 1894
35 *Commons Debates*, 1894, cols. 138–9
36 Ibid., cols. 159–73 (Tarte); cols. 173–9 (Davin)
37 *Senate Debates*, 1894, 144–54, 161
38 Thompson Papers, Taché to Davin, 31 May 1894
39 *Commons Debates*, 1894, cols. 1601–34
40 Ibid., cols. 2058–9, 2065
41 Ibid., col. 2059
42 Ibid., cols. 2065–8
43 As quoted in *Regina Leader*, 19 April 1894
44 *Commons Debates*, 1894, col. 1607
45 There was no such series. The reference was undoubtedly to Browning's *Educational Theories*: infra, 110–11
46 Sr Greene to Leduc, 2 May 1894, quoted in *Regina Leader*, 24 May 1894
47 AAE, Leduc's Letter Book, 1891–4, 16 mai 1894, 431
48 *Commons Journals*, 1894, 134
49 AAStB, Lacombe à Taché, 9 mai 1894
50 Ibid., 'Petition of the Cardinal, Archbishops, and Bishops of the Roman Catholic Church in Canada, May 1894'
51 Quoted in Taché Memorandum, *CSP*, 1894, 44
52 *Commons Debates*, 1894, col. 6125

53 AAStB, 11 mai 1894
54 Ibid., 31 May 1894
55 Thompson Papers, 30 May 1894
56 Ibid., private, 'Memorandum for a reply to an "open letter" addressed to N.F. Davin by the late Archbishop Taché as a refutatory criticism of a Speech delivered in the House of Commons,' n.d., hereafter Davin Memorandum
57 Order-in-Council, 5 Feb. 1894, approving the Privy Council Report
58 For a further discussion of the case, see Leduc, *Hostility Unmasked*, 10
59 *RBE*, 1885–6, 13; ibid., 1890–1, 19
60 *Commons Debates*, 1894, col. 1611
61 Davin Memorandum, 14–15
62 *Commons Debates*, 1894, cols. 6079–154
63 J.T. Saywell, ed., *The Canadian Journal of Lady Aberdeen (1893–1898)* (Toronto, 1960), 242
64 SAR, Department of Interior Transcripts, file no. 226484
65 TSP, no. 7, 1894, microfilm no. 2.94, p. 10, 'Extract from a Report of the Committee of the Honorable the Privy Council, approved by His Excellency on the 26th July, 1894'
66 AAE, 25 juin 1894
67 AAStB, 'L'oraison funèbre de Mgr L.F. Laflèche, l'Evêque de Trois Rivières, juin 1894'
68 Thompson Papers, Mackintosh to Thompson, 21 April 1894
69 *Calgary Herald*, 6 March 1894; *Medicine Hat Times*, 8 March 1894
70 Thompson Papers, private and confidential, 14 April 1894, Thompson to Mackintosh, 24 April 1894, vol. 43, 401
71 TSP, no. 7, 1894, microfilm no. 2.94, p. 10 (official translation), 6 July 1894
72 AAE, Leduc's Letter Book, 1891–4, 1 Aug. 1894, 622
73 Ibid., 4 Aug. 1894
74 *Assembly Journals*, 1894, 10
75 TSP, no. 9, 1894, microfilm no. 2.95, p. 10
76 *Regina Standard*, 30 Aug. 1894
77 Ibid.
78 *Assembly Journals*, 1894, 85–6
79 Ibid., 123–4
80 Ibid., 80
81 AAE, Leduc à Grandin, 1 sept. 1894
82 In a letter to Brown (9 Aug. 1894) the trustees raised four objections to the inspections: neither clergy, trustees, parents, nor the interested public were present at the inspection, as had 'always' been the case; the questions asked were too difficult (Trustee H.W. McKenney's 'tiny little' girl, for

example, was asked 'how many legs a spider has' – a question her father could not answer); French-speaking children were questioned only in English; and the inspectors did not discuss their report with the trustees. For details, see Leduc, *Hostility Unmasked*, 19–24, 67–75

83 *Regina Standard*, 6 Sept. 1894
84 Leduc, *Hostility Unmasked*, 42–8
85 Ibid., 49
86 *Ordinances*, 1892, No. 22, s.13(1)
87 *Assembly Journals*, 1894, 120–3
88 Ibid., 126–30
89 Ibid., 136
90 *Regina Standard*, 4 Oct. 1894
91 Ibid., 11 Oct. 1894
92 *Regina Leader*, 11 Oct. 1894
93 *Regina Standard*, 1 Nov. 1894
94 *Prince Albert Advocate*, 24 Oct. 1894
95 *Saskatchewan Herald*, 12 Oct. 1894
96 Ibid., 26 Oct. 1894
97 *Edmonton Bulletin*, 5 Nov. 1894
98 *Regina Standard*, 15 Nov. 1894
99 AAE, 1 sept. 1894
100 *Galt Reformer* (Ontario), as quoted in *Edmonton Bulletin*, 5 Nov. 1894
101 AAE, 11 sept. 1894
102 Ibid., 12 sept. 1894
103 Leduc, *Hostility Unmasked*, 3
104 PAA, Grandin à Langevin, 12 oct. 1894

CHAPTER 7

1 PAA, 6 mars 1895
2 Hughes read the letter into Hansard on 26 June 1895: *Commons Debates*, 1895, cols. 3361–2
3 PAA, 12 avril 1895
4 *Edmonton Bulletin*, 5 Sept. 1895
5 PAA, Journal de Grandin, 28 fév. 1895
6 AAE, 11 March 1895
7 PAA, 15 avril 1895
8 Ibid., Grandin à Langevin, 18, 25 avril, 7, 22 juin 1895; AAE, Langevin à Grandin, 25 avril, 21 mai, 15 juin 1895
9 *Regina Standard*, 22 Oct. 1896

10 It is not known when Sinnett was appointed; for his resignation from council, see Minutes of the Executive Committee, 7 Dec. 1895

11 *Regina Leader*, 18 April 1895; *RCPI*, 1896, Appendix B, 23; Leduc, *Hostility Unmasked*, 26

12 Leduc, *Hostility Unmasked*, 62–3; AAE, Leduc à Grandin, 19 sept. 1895

13 AAE, Leduc à Grandin, 21 sept. 1895

14 Leduc, *Hostility Unmasked*, 63

15 Quoted in ibid., 64–5

16 Ibid., 10, 16–17

17 Ibid., 15

18 *CSP*, 1894, XXVII, no. 17, 193

19 Quoted in Leduc, *Hostility Unmasked*, 65–6

20 AAE, Leduc à Grandin, 21 sept. 1895

21 Grouard succeeded Faraud as vicar-apostolic in 1890. Morice (E), II, 243–4

22 Leduc, *Hostility Unmasked*, iii–iv, vii–viii

23 *Commons Debates*, 1895, col. 4671

24 PAA, Grandin à Langevin, 13 oct. 1895; AAE, Langevin à Grandin, 7 nov. 1895

25 PAA, Mémoires de Grandin, tome 5, 55

26 AAE, Cleary to Grandin, private, 28 July 1896, Duhamel à Grandin, 26 juillet 1896, Fabre à Grandin, 23 juillet 1896, Bégin à Grandin, *privée*, 7 sept. 1896, O'Brien to Grandin, 26 July 1896

27 *Edmonton Bulletin*, 19 Dec. 1895

28 Headline in *Calgary Herald*, 18 Dec. 1895

29 Ibid., 16 Dec. 1895

30 Langevin told Grandin that Fouquet was the intermediary: AAE, 20 déc. 1895

31 *Calgary Herald*, 19, 24, 28 Dec. 1895, 2, 7 Jan. 1896

32 Ibid., 4 Jan. 1896; *Edmonton Bulletin*, 30 Dec. 1895

33 *Calgary Herald*, 11 Jan. 1896

34 AAE, 10 jan. 1896; PAA, 30 jan. 1896

35 *Calgary Herald*, 13 Jan. 1896

36 Breton, *Lacombe*, 110

37 AAE, Lacombe à Langevin et Grandin, 24 jan. 1896, Lacombe à Grandin, 9, 16 fév. 1896

38 Ibid., Lacombe à Grandin, 9 fév. 1896. Bishop John Cameron had called the Liberals ' "hell-inspired hypocrites." ' Ibid.

39 PAC, Tarte Papers, 18 fév. 1896

40 O.D. Skelton, *Life and Letters of Sir Wilfrid Laurier*, 2 vols. (New York, 1922), I, 470, suggests the former, J. Schull, *Laurier: The First Canadian* (Toronto, 1965), 313, the latter

41 *Calgary Herald*, 28 March 1896. Several territorial papers carried the letter

(*Regina Leader,* 27 Feb. 1896, *Edmonton Bulletin,* 2 March 1896), but only the *Calgary Herald* criticized it severely (28 Feb. 1896)

42 PAA, 26 déc. 1895

43 Ibid., Grandin à Langevin, 16 jan. 1896

44 AAE, Grandin's Letter Book, 1894–7, 22 Jan. 1896, 661; ibid., 29 Jan. 1896

45 PAA, 5 fév. 1896

46 AAE, 13 fév. 1896

47 PAA, Grandin à Langevin, 27 fév. 1896

48 *Commons Debates,* 1896, cols. 5923, 3860, 2765, 4167–8

49 PAA, Grandin à Langevin, 18 mars 1896

50 AAE, 11 avril 1896

51 PAC, Tupper Papers, 13 April 1896

52 *Edmonton Bulletin,* 23 April 1896

53 *Macleod Gazette,* 19 June 1896

54 Ibid., 4 June 1896

55 Ibid., 3 June 1896

56 *Edmonton Bulletin,* 1 June 1896

57 *Calgary Herald,* 23 May 1896

58 Ibid., 22 May 1896

59 Ibid., 22 June 1896

60 Ibid.

61 For the Quirk incident, see ibid., 10, 12, 16 June 1896

62 PAA, Journal de Grandin, 22 mai 1896

63 Quoted in ibid., Circulaire de Grandin, 24 mai 1896

64 *Edmonton Bulletin,* 11 June 1896

65 *Calgary Herald,* 10 June 1896

66 AAStB, Leduc à Langevin, 10 juin 1896

67 PAA, Journal de Grandin, 18, 21, 23 juin 1896

68 Calculations based on results in *Calgary Herald,* 6 July 1896. Red Deer results are included in the northern Alberta vote. 1891 calculations based on results in *Macleod Gazette,* 26 March 1891

69 L.H. Thomas, 252

70 *Regina Standard,* 3 Oct. 1895 (McInnis); *Qu'Appelle Vidette,* 21 May 1896 (Douglas)

71 *Moosomin Spectator,* 23 April 1896

72 *Regina Leader,* 23, 30 April 1896; *Regina Standard,* 4 June 1896

73 *Moosomin Spectator,* 7 May 1896; *Qu'Appelle Vidette,* 7 May 1896

74 *Qu'Appelle Vidette,* 18 June 1896

75 Ibid., 9 July 1896

76 *Regina Leader,* 14 May, 25 June 1896

77 Ibid., 23 April, 7, 21 May, 4 June 1896; *Moose Jaw Times*, 8, 15 May 1896

78 Laurier Papers, 29 June 1896

79 Blue, I, Appendix 5, 436

80 *Saskatchewan Times*, 9 June 1896

81 *Qu'Appelle Vidette*, 25 June 1896; *Regina Standard*, 2 July 1896; *Regina Leader*, 2 July 1896

82 PAA, 24 juin 1896

83 AAE, Langevin à Grandin, 25 juin 1896

84 Tupper Papers, confidential, 24 June 1896, 4 July 1896, vol. 20, 240

85 PAA, 11 juillet 1896; AAE, 3 août 1896

86 Laurier Papers, *personelle et confidentielle*, 13 août 1896

87 Ibid., 2 oct. 1896

88 Ibid., n.d., no. 6150

89 Ibid., 10 août 1896; AAE, 11 août 1896

90 AAE, Leduc à Grandin, 18 août 1896

91 Laurier Papers, 14 Aug. 1896

92 *Calgary Herald*, 5 March 1896

93 *Commons Debates*, 1896, col. 61

94 Ibid., col. 2407

95 AAE, 6 mars 1896

96 *Edmonton Bulletin*, 15 June 1896

97 PAA, Journal de Grandin, 13, 15 juin 1896

98 AAstB, n.d. (between 25 June and 5 July 1896)

99 *Edmonton Bulletin*, 8 Oct. 1896

100 *Assembly Journals*, 1896, 21

101 *Regina Standard*, 8 Oct. 1896

102 *Assembly Journals*, 1896, 21

103 *Regina Standard*, 8 Oct. 1896

104 AAstB Leduc à Langevin, 6 oct. 1896

105 *Regina Standard*, 8 Oct. 1896

106 *Assembly Journals*, 1896, 44

107 *Regina Standard*, 29 Oct. 1896

108 Ibid.; *Assembly Journals*, 1896, 60

109 *Regina Standard*, 15 Oct. 1896

110 *Brophy* v. *Attorney-General of Manitoba*, 1895 A.C. 202, at 228–9

111 AAstB, Leduc à Langevin, 16 oct. 1896

112 *Regina Standard*, 29 Oct. 1896

113 Ibid., 5 Nov. 1896

114 AAE, Circulaire de Langevin, 4 nov. 1896

115 AAstB, 'Droits et Devoirs en matière d'Education – Principes et Conclusions,'

n.d. (file 'Question des Ecoles,' no. 3); 'Concile Provinciel tenu à Saint-Albert, les 7, 8, 9 avril 1902.'

116 Skelton, II, 13–19
117 PAA, Grandin à Langevin, 12 nov. 1896
118 Ibid., Journal de Grandin, 27, 27 nov. 1896, Grandin à Langevin, 25 nov. 1896; AAStB, Leduc à Langevin, 26 nov. 1896
119 *Edmonton Bulletin*, 26 Nov. 1896
120 AAE, Langevin à Grandin, 18 nov. 1896; AAStB, 3 déc. 1896
121 PAA, 30 nov. 1896; AAE, 7 déc. 1896
122 PAA, Grandin à Langevin, 19 déc. 1896; AAE, Langevin à Grandin, 4, 30 déc. 1896

CHAPTER 8

1 Based on A.R.M. Lower, 'Two Ways of Life,' *Report of the Canadian Historical Association, 1943* (Toronto, 1943), 5–18 and Lower, *Colony to Nation: A History of Canada* (Toronto, 1946), 68–9
2 *RCPI*, 1896, 11–12, 17, 22–3, 28–9, Appendix A, 12
3 Leduc, *Hostility Unmasked*, 56–7
4 AAE, Leduc à Grandin, 23 mars 1897
5 *Macleod Gazette*, 22 Oct. 1897
6 *Regina Standard*, 16 Dec. 1897
7 AAE, *absolument personnelle et confidentielle*, 30 mars 1897
8 AAStB, *notes intimes et privées*, 24 avril 1897
9 Ibid., Merry del Val à Langevin, 4 mai 1897; AAE, Langevin à Grandin, 26 mai 1897
10 AAStB, 28 juin 1897
11 AAE, 26 mai 1897
12 Ibid., 5 juillet 1897; AAStB, 3 juillet 1897
13 AAE, 4 juillet 1897; AAStB, 15 juillet 1897
14 PAA, n.d. (*c*.30 juillet 1897)
15 Ibid., 27 août 1897
16 Ibid., 16 sept. 1897; AAE, 21 oct. 1897
17 AAStB, 30 mai 1897
18 Skelton, II, 41
19 Quoted in ibid., I, 464
20 AAStB, Encyclical Letter of Pope Leo XIII (Authorized English Translation), 8 Dec. 1897
21 PAA, Grandin à Langevin, 17 jan. 1898; AAStB, 22 jan. 1898; AAE, 23 jan. 1898

22 PAA, Circulaire de Grandin, 22 jan. 1898, Lettre Pastorale de Grandin, 7 fév. 1898
23 AAE, 'Résumé des délibérations : Réunions du 15 et 16 décembre 1897'
24 AAStB, 19 déc. 1897
25 Ibid., 8 Jan. 1898
26 Ibid., Langevin to Haultain, *c.* 8 Jan. 1898
27 Ibid., 22 March 1898
28 For a detailed account of this issue, see M.R. Lupul, 'The Campaign for a French Catholic School Inspector in the North-West Territories 1898–1903,' *Canadian Historical Review*, XLVIII (Dec. 1967), 332–52, reprinted in *Minorities, Schools, and Politics*, edited by R. Cook, C. Brown, and C. Berger (Toronto, 1969), 42–62
29 AAE, Langevin à Grandin, 6 sept. 1898; AAStB, Langevin to Haultain, Letter Book, 1895–1900, 7 Sept. 1898, 232, Haultain to Langevin, 24 Sept. 1898
30 Laurier Papers, Forget à Laurier, *privée*, 26 jan. 1898
31 Ibid., telegram, 27 sept. 1898
32 AAStB, Letter Book, 1895–1900, *personnelle*, 28 sept. 1898, 288
33 AAE, Langevin à Grandin, 11 mars 1899
34 Ibid., same to same, 2 avril 1899
35 TSP, Bélanger to Haultain, 26 March 1899, sessional paper no. 8, 1899, microfilm no. 2.96
36 *RCPI*, 1896, 13
37 AAStB, Forget à Langevin, 11 avril 1899
38 TSP, Desaulniers to Haultain, 8 April 1899, sessional paper no. 8, 1899, microfilm no. 2.96; AAStB, Lacombe à Langevin, 19 avril 1899; PAA, Grandin à Langevin, 11 mai 1899
39 AAStB, Beaulieu à Langevin, 6 avril 1899; TSP, Beaulieu to Haultain, 11 April 1899, sessional paper no. 8, 1899, microfilm no. 2.96; AAStB, Haultain to Langevin, 18 Jan. 1901
40 AAStB, Legal to Haultain, 5 April 1900, copy enclosed in Legal à Langevin, 5 avril 1900, Langevin to Haultain, Letter Book, 1895–1900, 27 March 1900, 912, Haultain to Langevin, 10 April 1900
41 Laurier Papers, Legal à Laurier, 29 nov. 1899
42 AAStB, 5 April 1900, copy enclosed in Legal à Langevin, 5 avril 1900
43 *North-West Territories Gazette*, 14 July 1900, 1
44 AAStB, 18 Dec. 1900, 18 Jan. 1901
45 Ibid., Memorandum of Archbishop Langevin, 'How was kept the promise of the Hon. M. Haultain for the appointment of a catholic inspector in the North-West Territories,' 9 Nov. 1901

46 Laurier Papers, Langevin à Laurier, 18 déc. 1901; AAStB, Payment à Langevin, 23 déc. 1901, 3 jan. 1902, and n.d., 1902
47 AAE, 29 jan. 1902
48 AAStB, Payment à Langevin, 8 jan., 21 mars 1902
49 Ibid., Langevin à Legal, Letter Book, 1899–1902, 15 avril 1902, 795
50 Ibid., 18 June 1902
51 Ibid., Kramer to Langevin, 23 Nov., 3, 10 Dec. 1903, Langevin to Kramer, Letter Book, 1903–4, 28 Nov., 9 Dec. 1903, 529, 607
52 J.P. Weber o.s.b., 'Report on Separate Schools,' n.p., n.d., mimeo., 11 (St Thomas More College Library, Saskatoon, Saskatchewan)
53 Supra, 145
54 AAStB, Legal to Haultain, 8 Jan. 1898
55 AOO, 23 déc. 1898; AAStB, Letter Book, 1895–1900, 26 déc. 1898, 372
56 Laurier Papers, *personnelle*, 5 jan. 1899
57 Ibid., Forget à Laurier, *privée*, 26 jan. 1899
58 AAE, 11 mars 1899; AAStB, 24 mars 1899
59 PAA, 24 mars, 14 mai 1899; AAE, 22 avril 1899
60 AAStB, Letter Book, 1895–1900, 29 mai 1899, 640; AAE, 26 juin 1899
61 Ibid., Legal à Langevin, 3 mai 1899
62 Laurier Papers, 17 Oct. 1899
63 AAStB, Sr Greene à Langevin, 28 déc. 1899
64 For the non-professional (high school) and professional study programmes, see *RCPI*, 1896, Appendix B, 13–20. For the relationship between non-professional certificates and high school standards, see *RDE*, 1901, 23
65 *RDE*, 1901, 1902, 1903, 1904; also ibid. (Alberta), 1907
66 *Ordinances*, c.29, ss.8–11 (1901)
67 AAStB, Letter Book, 1901–2, 18 April 1902, 526, 528
68 *North-West Territories Gazette*, 30 Aug. 1902, 1
69 *RDE*, 1902, 9
70 AAStB, Legal à Langevin, 6 sept. 1902. Goggin's resignation 'for personal reasons' in October 1902 was 'reluctantly accepted' (J.A. Calder in *RDE*, 1902, 16). James Brown succeeded him in January 1903. Toombs, 114
71 AAStB, Legal à Langevin, 6 sept. 1902
72 Laurier Papers, 17 Oct. 1899
73 AAStB, Langevin à Legal, Letter Book, 1899–1902, 15 avril 1902, 795, 18 April 1902, 526, 528
74 Ibid., 19 April 1902; Haultain's reply was similar: ibid., 23 April 1902
75 *RDE*, 1903, 11
76 AAStB, 27 June 1903

77 AAE, Langevin à Grandin, 5 mars 1900
78 Supra, 123
79 AAStB, Legal à Langevin, 13 avril 1900
80 Ibid., Langevin à Sr Greene, Letter Book, 1900, 14 nov. 1900, 433. For details, see AAE, Lacombe à Grandin, 29 août 1900
81 'The Greek Catholic Church, which came into existence in 1596, was a hybrid which emerged out of the combination of the Roman Catholic Church and the Greek Orthodox Church. The name itself conveys this concept. Essentially it was that section of the Ukrainian Greek Orthodox Church which united with Rome. By this act of union, whence came the name "Uniate," the new church recognized the supremacy of the Pope as well as Roman Catholic dogma, but retained the Eastern, or the Greek Rite with all its outward forms and customs ...' (P. Yuzyk, 'The History of the Ukrainian Catholic (Uniate) Church in Canada,' MA thesis, University of Saskatchewan, 1948), 1
82 *Edmonton Bulletin*, 14 March 1902; AOO, Legal à Sbaretti, 12 mars 1905
83 PAA, Grandin à Langevin, 14, 21 mai 1900; AAStB, Langevin à Grandin, Letter Book, 1900, 7 juin 1900, 109
84 The Presbyterians and Methodists were most active. Shortt and Doughty, XI, 291–3
85 C. H. Young, *The Ukrainian Canadians* (Toronto, 1931), 139. Many years later the Greek Catholic bishop, Neil Savaryn, described the competition in the following terms: 'The Ukrainian immigrant came as a Greek Catholic, was married by a Protestant minister, had his children baptized by an Orthodox priest, and usually died completely faithless' (*Rolya Otsiv Vasyliyan v Kanadi* [The Role of the Basilian Fathers in Canada], Mundare, 1938), 11
86 Yuzyk, 59
87 ABM, Journal de Legal, 2 oct. 1897 (transcript)
88 PAA, Letter Pastorale de Grandin, 4 jan. 1900
89 Appeals are discussed in ABM, Pascal à Ledochowski, 19 déc. 1898 (transcript), Journal de Legal, 30 oct. 1898 (transcript); also Breton, *Lacombe*, 121–5
90 PAA, Grandin à C. Augier, 8 mars 1899
91 Based on Lingard, Appendix, 256
92 Quoted in ibid., 9
93 *Regina Standard*, 2 May 1900. The chairman of the Council of Public Instruction could appoint a commissioner 'to conduct the affairs of any school district.' *Consolidated Ordinances*, c.75, s.10(3) (1898)

94 *Regina Standard*, 23 May 1900

95 PAC, Sifton Papers, Ross to C. Sifton, 25 Feb. 1901

96 *Regina Standard*, 31 July 1901

97 *Assembly Journals*, 1901, 13, 20, 36

98 *Regina Standard*, 14 Aug. 1901

99 Where parents or guardians desired instruction in a language other than English, the trustees could employ one or more 'competent' persons and impose 'a special rate' on the interested parents. *Ordinances*, c.29, s.136(2–3) (1901)

100 AAStB, Langevin à V. Zholdak, Letter Book, 1901–2, 2 jan. 1902, 113, Langevin à Tardivel, 4 fév. 1902, 281

101 Ibid., Langevin à W. Blumhart, 30 jan. 1902, 249

102 AAE, 4 jan. 1902

103 *Les Cloches*, 15 jan. 1902, 8–13. *Les Cloches* was a church periodical published by Langevin at St Boniface, beginning 15 Jan. 1902

104 Yuzyk, 56–7

105 AAStB, Langevin à Zholdak, Letter Book, 1901–2, 2 jan. 1902, 113

106 *Edmonton Bulletin*, 2 Aug. 1890

107 Ibid., 17 Jan. 1902

108 For details, see J.G. MacGregor, *Vilni Zemli. Free Lands: The Ukrainian Settlement of Alberta* (Toronto and Montreal, 1969), 175–82, 198–203

109 AAStB, Falconio à Langevin, 18 jan. 1902

110 Ibid., Girod à Langevin, 3 fév. 1902

111 The campaign began on 12 April 1902, with a letter to a Dr F. Wimmers, secretary-general in Vienna 'd'un société pour aider les missions' (ibid., Letter Book, 1901–2, 545), and ended on 16 May with a letter to Fr A. Lemieux, provincial of the Redemptorist order in Quebec (ibid., 696). On each letter appeared the words 'Dieu le veut.' See also ibid., 20 fév., 22 avril, 9 mai, 20 juin, 305, 592, 662, 841

112 Ibid., Girod à Langevin, 10 mai 1902

113 Ibid., Langevin à Legal, Letter Book, 1899–1902, 14 juillet, 23 sept. 1902, 924, 971

114 Ibid., Haultain to Langevin, 7 Feb. 1903, Langevin to Haultain, n.d., 1903, in reply to Haultain's letter, dated 'the 7th instant'

115 Ibid., Langevin à Pascal, Letter Book, 1902–7, 13 mars, 19 juillet 1903, 84, 161

116 Ibid., Langevin à Legal, 19 juillet 1903, Legal à Langevin, 7 août 1903

117 Ibid., 'Réunion épiscopale tenue à Archevêché de Saint-Boniface,' 9–13 sept. 1903

CHAPTER 9

1 The discussion of autonomy, insofar as it does not relate to the school question, is based on L.H. Thomas, 197, 256–7, and Lingard, 24, 31, 33, 34

2 Sifton to Haultain, 21 March 1901, in E.H. Oliver, ed., *The Canadian North-West: Its Early Development and Legislative Records*, 2 vols. (Ottawa, 1914–15), II, 1160

3 Reports of debates in *Regina Standard*, 29 May, 19, 26 June, 17 July 1901

4 Lingard, 38

5 The draft bill is found in Oliver, II, 1174

6 *Great Britain, Statutes*, 30–1 Vict., c.3, s.93(1) (1867)

7 Laurier Papers, 11 March 1905

8 Lingard, 175

9 Quoted in *Calgary Herald*, 2 March 1905

10 Oliver, II, 1174

11 Laurier Papers, Haultain to Laurier, 11 March 1905

12 27 March 1902, quoted in Oliver, II, 1202

13 Lingard, 55–6

14 *Senate Debates*, 1902, 101–2

15 *Commons Debates*, 1902, cols. 3085, 3090, 3101–2, 3113, 3115

16 *Macleod Gazette*, 23 May 1902

17 Lingard, 79

18 Laurier Papers, 13 Jan. 1903

19 *Commons Debates*, 1903, cols. 13894, 13904–5, 13928–9

20 Quoted in *Edmonton Bulletin*, 2 Dec. 1901

21 *Canadian Annual Review, 1902* (Toronto, 1903), 38

22 Quoted in Lingard, 104

23 Laurier Papers, 30 sept., 1 oct. 1903

24 PAC, Fitzpatrick Papers, 1 fév. 1905

25 Laurier Papers, 3 fév. 1905

26 Ibid., 7 fév. 1905, *confidentielle*, 14 fév. 1905

27 PAA, 12 nov. 1896

28 AAE, 'Concile provincial tenu à Saint-Albert,' 7–9 avril 1902; AASTB, 'Réunion épiscopale tenue à l'Archevêché de Saint-Boniface,' 13 sept. 1903

29 Ibid., Letter Book, 1903–4, 11 sept. 1903, 316

30 AAE, 27 sept. 1903

31 Most companies were in the 'anonymous' category. The law required that a company apportion funds between Catholic and non-Catholic schools on its own initiative and with the 'consent' of the Board of Directors, 'a thing which is ordinarily almost impossible,' because companies preferred

anonymity to probing the religious affiliation of their shareholders. Companies in Catholic school districts, Legal declared, should therefore pay taxes to Catholic schools 'proportionally to the school population of these Catholic schools,' not on the basis of Catholic shareholders in the companies (R.W. Scott Papers, Legal to Sbaretti, 4 Oct. 1903 [official translation])

32 *Ponoka Herald*, 22 Jan. 1904
33 Laurier Papers, Fr A. Gasté to Laurier, telegram, 13 Feb. 1904
34 *Der Wanderer* (St Paul, Minnesota), quoted in Sifton Papers, J.G. Turriff to Sifton, personal, 16 Feb. 1904
35 Laurier Papers, 1 March 1904
36 Ibid., 7 March 1904
37 Supra, 114
38 Laurier Papers, 9 March 1904
39 Fitzpatrick Papers, 5 March 1904
40 Laurier Papers, 12 March 1904
41 Ibid., Sbaretti to Laurier, 15 March 1904
42 AAE, 15 mars 1904
43 AOO, 15 avril 1904
44 AAStB, 29 avril 1904. For Legal's clause, see Appendix, clause no. 1
45 Ibid., 'Provisions respecting EDUCATION to be introduced in the ACT constituting part of the N.W. territories in a province known as the Province of ————,' n.d.
46 AAE, Sbaretti à Legal, 6 mai 1904
47 *Statutes of Canada*, 3 Edward VII, c.60, s.2 (1903); 19 May 1904, in Oliver, 1236–7
48 *Edmonton Journal*, 26 May 1904
49 1 June 1904, in Oliver, II, 1235–6
50 Laurier Papers, Merry del Val à Laurier, *confidentielle*, 1 avril 1904, Laurier à Merry del Val, *confidentielle*, 26 mai 1904
51 30 Sept., 5 Oct. 1904, in Oliver, II, 1242–3
52 R.W. Scott Papers, 11 Oct. 1904
53 Ibid., confidential, 12 Oct. 1904
54 Laurier Papers, H. Chevrier (Manitoba MLA) to Laurier, 8 Oct. 1904; AAStB, 'Réunion Annuelle des Archevêques de la Puissance du Canada,' 12 oct. 1904
55 *Regina Leader*, 19 Oct. 1904
56 AAE, Sbaretti à Legal, 12 nov. 1904
57 R.W. Scott Papers, Sbaretti to Scott, 24 Nov. 1904; Laurier Papers, Sbaretti to Laurier, 23, 30 Dec. 1904
58 AAStB, Letter Book, 1904–5, 26 nov. 1904, 226

59 Ibid., 14 Dec. 1904, 320 (italics in original)
60 Ibid., 16 déc. 1904
61 Ibid., 26, 28 déc. 1904
62 Ibid., 28 déc. 1904, 358
63 Supra, 133
64 Laurier Papers, 22 déc. 1904
65 AAStB, 29 Dec. 1904. For Beck's clause, see Appendix, clause no. 2
66 For evidence that Bulyea, a strong party man, had found territorial non-partisan politics trying, see Laurier Papers, Bulyea to Laurier, 5 Aug. 1905
67 Lingard, 131
68 SAS, Walter Scott Papers, 25 Jan. 1905
69 Quoted in *Calgary Herald*, 11 Jan. 1905
70 Laurier Papers, 11 March 1905
71 *Commons Debates*, 1905, cols. 2506, 2575
72 Laurier Papers, Sbaretti to Laurier, 21 Jan. 1905
73 AAStB, secret and confidential, 11 Jan. 1905. For Fitzpatrick's clause with Sbaretti's bracketed amendments, see Appendix, clause no. 3. In 1872 the Dominion Lands Act had set aside sections 11 and 29 in every township as an endowment for educational purposes, and in 1879 another Lands Act directed that revenues from land sales be invested in Dominion securities and the interest arising therefrom 'paid annually to the Government of the Province or Territory within which such lands are situated towards the support of public schools therein.' The delegate was obviously concerned that only public schools could benefit from the school-lands fund
74 Ibid., Langevin à Sbaretti, Letter Book, 1904–5, 19 jan. 1905, 465
75 AOO, 'Suggestion for a Provision on the Provincial Act as to Education,' 17 Jan. 1905, enclosed in Leduc à Sbaretti, 18 jan. 1905
76 Laurier Papers, 16 Jan. 1905. For Sbaretti's clause, see Appendix, clause no. 4
77 Ibid., 19 Jan. 1905
78 Ibid., 21 Jan. 1905 (two letters)
79 Ibid., 23 Jan. 1905
80 Ibid., 3 Feb. 1905
81 Ibid., 7 Feb. 1905. For Fitzpatrick's clause and Sbaretti's modifications, see Appendix, clause no. 5
82 Ibid., Sbaretti to Laurier, 11 Feb. 1905. For the clause, see Appendix, clause no. 6
83 Ibid., 11 Feb. 1905
84 Ibid., 11 Feb. 1905
85 AAE, private and strictly confidential, 12 Feb. 1905
86 Based on letter below, n.88. Legal's letter could not be located

87 The Roman Catholic population in St Albert, barely 50 per cent in 1961, fell to 39 per cent by 1971. *Census of Canada*, 1961, Bulletin 1.2–6, Table 46–1; ibid., 1971, 92–724, pp. 13–16

88 Laurier Papers, 11 Feb. 1905

89 Ibid., 16 Feb. 1905

90 AAStB, 16 Feb. 1905

91 Ibid., Langevin à Sbaretti, Letter Book, 1904–5, 19 fév. 1905, 645

92 Ibid., Sbaretti to Langevin, 20 Feb. 1905. For the clause, see Appendix, clause no. 7

93 Ibid., Langevin à Gasté, Letter Book, 1902–7, 6 fév. 1905, 507

94 AOO, Leduc à Langevin, 18 mai 1905. For the date, see Legal's list of important dates on the autonomy issue in AAE, file no. 8

95 AAStB, Sbaretti to Langevin, 16 Feb. 1905

96 Quoted in A.D. MacRae, *History of the Province of Alberta*, 2 vols. (Calgary 1912), I, 453

97 AAE, 15 Feb. 1905

98 Quoted in *Edmonton Bulletin*, 15 Feb. 1905

99 Lingard, 139

100 Quoted in *Commons Debates*, 1905, col. 5352

101 Laurier Papers, 22 Jan. 1905

102 26 Jan. 1905, quoted in Sissons, 263

103 *Calgary Herald*, 17 Feb. 1905; *Edmonton Journal*, 17 Feb. 1905

104 *Commons Debates*, 1905, col. 1852; Sifton Papers, Sifton to Dafoe, personal, 25 Feb. 1905, vol. 263, 209

105 *Senate Debates*, 1905, 9

106 *Commons Debates*, 1905, cols. 1421–63

107 For the clause, see Appendix, clause no. 8

108 *Commons Debates*, 1905, col. 5339

109 For Fitzpatrick, see ibid., cols. 2576, 5334; for Laurier, ibid., col. 2925

110 Ibid., col. 3104

111 Skelton, II, 275

112 Quoted in ibid., 234n.; J. W. Dafoe, *Clifford Sifton in Relation to His Times* (Toronto, 1931), 278

113 *Commons Debates*, 1905, col. 1458

114 Ibid., col. 1466

CHAPTER 10

1 AUA, Rutherford Papers, P. Talbot to A.C. Rutherford, 21 Feb. 1905; *Calgary Herald*, 22 Feb. 1905; *Regina Leader*, 22 Feb. 1905; *Saskatoon Phoenix*, 24 Feb. 1905

2 Laurier Papers, Laurier to N.W. Rowell, 22 Feb. 1905, Laurier to P.L. Potter, 25 Feb. 1905
3 Rutherford Papers, 24 Feb. 1905
4 Both Skelton and Dafoe attest to personal antagonism between Sifton and Fitzpatrick: Skelton, II, 236; Dafoe, 279–80
5 Sifton Papers, personal, 25 Feb. 1905, vol. 263, 209
6 Ibid., personal, 26 Feb. 1905, 213
7 Ibid., Sifton to Dafoe, 27 Feb. 1905, 228
8 Sifton to Laurier, 27 Feb. 1905, Laurier to Sifton, 28 Feb. 1905, reproduced in *Commons Debates*, 1905, cols. 1851, 1853
9 Ibid., col. 1857
10 Sifton Papers, Sifton to Fielding, 1 March 1905, vol. 263, 277
11 Ibid., Fielding to Sifton, 2 March 1905
12 Quoted in *Edmonton Journal*, 21 March 1905
13 Laurier Papers, McGuire to Laurier, 23 Feb. 1905
14 Ibid., personal, 13 March 1905
15 Ibid., 9, 14 (telegram), 15, 18 Feb. 1905
16 *Calgary Herald*, 25 Feb. 1905
17 *Edmonton Bulletin*, 28 Feb. 1905
18 Quoted in *Calgary Herald*, 2 March 1905
19 *Edmonton Bulletin*, 15 March 1905
20 Laurier Papers, 1 March 1905. Ewan, a Laurier admirer, hoped to effect 'some good' by 'discouraging agitation' (ibid., Ewan to Laurier, 24 Feb. 1905)
21 *Commons Journals*, 1905, *passim*
22 Laurier Papers, vol. 738, *passim*
23 AAStB, 23 fév. 1905
24 Laurier Papers, 24 fév. 1905
25 Quoted in *Edmonton Bulletin*, 28 Feb. 1905
26 Based on Fr E.J. Auclair in *A Standard Dictionary of Canadian Biography*, edited by C.G.D. Roberts and A.L. Tunnell, 2 vols. (Toronto, 1938), II, 234–5
27 G.R. Cook, 'Church, Schools, and Politics in Manitoba, 1903–12,' *Canadian Historical Review*, XXXIX (March 1958), 17
28 Sifton Papers, Sifton to Laurier, 3 March 1905, vol. 263, 400; *Edmonton Journal*, 6 March 1905. For the clause, see Appendix, clause no. 9
29 Laurier Papers, Sbaretti to Laurier, 7, 11 March 1905
30 Sifton Papers, Sifton to the Rev. C.W. Gordon, 7 March 1905, vol. 263, 577
31 Laurier Papers, 9 March 1905
32 Ibid., 11 March 1905

33 Sifton Papers, telegram, 10 March 1905

34 Quoted in *Commons Debates*, 1905, col. 8269. For the clause, see Appendix, clause no. 10

35 The following made public statements supporting the clause: the Revs. G. Bryce (*Edmonton Bulletin*, 2 June 1905), A.B. Baird (ibid., 31 May 1905), and J.A. Carmichael (ibid., 7 June 1905). There is no evidence that Methodist and Baptist clergy in Winnipeg joined them

36 Sifton Papers, personal, 11 March 1905, vol. 263, 660

37 Rutherford Papers, 21 March 1905

38 Laurier Papers, Sbaretti to Laurier, 13 March 1905

39 AAE, 15 mars 1905. Beck's telegram, not seen, was mentioned in Legal's reply, AOO, 17 March 1905

40 AAE, 19 mars 1905

41 AAStB, *personnelle*, Letter Book, 1904–5, 20 mars 1905, 763

42 Ibid., *confidentielle*, 25 mars 1905

43 AAE, 'Confidential Memorandum' of N.D. Beck, 10 July 1905

44 AAStB, 25 mai 1905

45 Laurier Papers, 11 March 1905

46 Ibid., n.d., no. 93226

47 *Commons Debates*, 1905, cols. 2913–5424; cols. 2519–24 (McCarthy, Lake), 2557 (Herron), 3168 (Oliver), 3829 (Turriff), 3161–2 (Oliver), 4346 (Lamont), 4183 (Talbot), 4840–1 (Cash), 3164 (Oliver), 3623–4, 3614 (Scott), 3344–55 (McCarthy), 4878 (Herron), 3350 (Lake)

48 Several Sheho constituents, led by the Rev. A. Mactavish (Methodist), were unhappy with Cash's position. *Yorkton Enterprise*, 12, 19 April 1905

49 Laurier Papers, personal, 4 April 1905 (Bulyea), personal, 14 April 1905 (Davis)

50 W. Scott Papers, 3 April 1905

51 Sifton had added that 'legal authorities, like my friend Mr. Haultain, a quotation from whom I could read if I saw fit ... thought that when those privileges were curtailed and taken away, they were taken away in defiance of the clause of the Act of 1875' (*Commons Debates*, 1905, col. 3105). Haultain denied 'absolutely' he had ever admitted the 1892 law was unconstitutional. The ordinance was 'a consolidation.' The principal legislation that ' "swept away" ' (Sifton's expression, ibid., col. 3100) the dual system 'had been passed in 1891 and earlier.' *Calgary Herald*, 26 April 1905

52 Laurier and Fielding knew Thompson's opinion. Laurier Papers, Laurier to Fielding, n.d., no. 93105. Fitzpatrick was impressed by it: *Commons Debates*, 1905, cols. 7125–30

53 Based largely on ibid., cols., 1428–31, 3834–4186

54 G.R. Cook, 'Church, Schools, and Politics in Manitoba, 1903–12,' 3–4

55 *Commons Debates*, 1905, col. 3944

56 Rutherford Papers, Talbot to Rutherford, 7 April 1905. Talbot's statement, 'I fear Fitzpatrick was in consultation with him,' indicates the territorial members were unaware of the government's negotiations with Sbaretti

57 J.S. Ewart was a 'libéral protestant' lawyer (Morice(F), III, 8) who defended the minority after 1890 and was 'frequently' consulted by Sbaretti in 1905. AAE, Sbaretti to Legal, 24 March 1905

58 To the *Calgary Herald* (7 April 1905) the delegate was practically out of the country: 'MGR. SBARETTI IS RECALLED/ EASTERN CANADA IS FURIOUS/ Not In Many Years Has Ontario Witnessed Such a Situation as Now Confronts The Country.'

59 R.W. Scott Papers, 15 April 1905

60 *Commons Debates*, 1905, col. 2979

61 Ibid., cols. 5400–1, 5423

62 AAStB, Letter Book, 1904–5, 27 mars 1905, 802, Langevin à Louis Hacault, 26 mars 1905, 786

63 Armand Levergne in *Commons Debates*, 1905, col. 6187. *Le Canada* quoted Legal as follows: 'Nous sommes satisfaits du système d'écoles que nous avons, et nous espérons qu'on nous le laissera.' Quoted in A. Lavergne, *La vérité sur la question scolaire du Nord-Ouest* [Montreal, 1907], 59

64 AAStB, the Rev. J.H. Bouffard à Langevin, 23 mars 1905, the Rev. G. Dugas à Langevin, 25 mars 1905, Langevin à Bouffard, Letter Book, 1904–5, 29 mars 1905, 809

65 Ibid., Letter Book, 1902–7, 29 mars 1905, 559

66 Ibid., Letter Book, 1904–5, 30 mars 1905, 803

67 Ibid., 27 mars 1905, 792, 28 mars 1905

68 Ibid., Langevin à G. Dugas, Letter Book, 1904–5, 29 mars 1905, 812

69 Ibid., 4 April 1905

70 AOO, 31 mars 1905

71 Laurier Papers, Leduc to Beck, 31 March 1905

72 AOO, Legal à Langevin, 5 avril 1905

73 AAStB, 14 avril 1905

74 Ibid., confidential and *sub secreto*, 6 April 1905

75 Ibid., Letter Book, 1902–7, 8 avril, 576

76 Quoted from the English translation, *Edmonton Bulletin*, 26 April 1905

77 AAStB, 4 avril 1905

78 Report quoted in *Commons Debates*, 1905, col. 5293. For the date, see *Edmonton Bulletin*, 11 April 1905

79 AAStB, Letter Book, 1904–5, 9 avril 1905, 873

80 Ibid., Langevin à Dugas, 8 avril 1905

81 Ibid., Dugas à Langevin, 15 avril 1905. There may have been some truth to the rumour. Among the papers in ibid. is an unsigned document in English, dated Ottawa, 17 June 1905, and addressed to Cardinal Merry del Val, stating the writer had been asked 'to join in a movement in favour of appointing Bishops of English speaking nationalities in the new Provinces of Saskatchewan and Alberta.' The writer 'thoroughly' approved of the idea and was 'satisfied' that the same policy should be followed in Manitoba and British Columbia. Langevin criticized the document in ibid., 'Réponse aux assertions contenues dans le Mémoire adressé à Son Eminence le Cardinal Merry del Val, le 17 juin 1905,' 1908, n.d.

82 Ibid., Letter Book, 1904–5, 8 avril 1905, 874

83 Ibid., Langevin à Lemius, Letter Book, 1902–7, 21 avril 1905, 578

84 Ibid., Letter Book, 1904–5, 21 avril 1905, 920, 938

85 Ibid., Omer Héroux à Langevin, 17 avril 1905, Langevin à Héroux, Letter Book, 1904–5, 22 avril 1905, 956

86 Les Cloches, 15 mai 1905, 138

87 AAStB, Legal à Langevin, 8 mai 1905

88 Les Cloches, 15 mai 1905, 140

89 AAStB, private and confidential, 15 May 1905

90 AAE, privée et confidentielle, 16 mai 1905

91 Les Cloches, 15 mai 1905, 140

92 Infra, 202

93 Laurier Papers, Sbaretti to Laurier, 2 May 1905; Commons Debates, 1905, cols. 8333–4

94 Legal had sent Bruchesi a telegram in Latin, in reply to one in Latin asking Legal's opinion of Sifton's clause. Neither telegram has been seen, but the exchange took place about the same time (21 April: supra, 197) that Langevin gave his opinion to Bruchesi (AAStB, Langevin à Gotti, 29 déc. 1906). Langevin gave two versions of Legal's telegram: 'Omnibus perpensis lex desiderabilis et optanda' (Ibid., Langevin à Legal, 17 mai 1905) and 'Datis circumstantiis, lex acceptabilis et optanda' (ibid., Langevin à Gotti, 29 déc. 1906).

95 The available evidence does not support Langevin. Fitzpatrick made no such statement in his single speech on the school question before 17 May (Commons Debates, 1905, cols. 5317–54). Fitzpatrick, like Sifton, was impressed by Thompson's report of 10 Jan. 1890, but this fact did not come out until 8 June (ibid., cols. 7125–30).

96 AAStB, 17 mai 1905

97 AAE, Legal à Langevin, Letter Book, 1904–5, 22 mai 1905, 166
98 AAStB, Langevin à Gotti, 29 déc. 1906
99 Ibid., Letter Book, 1902–7, 31 mai 1905, 595
100 Ibid., Langevin à Hacault, *personnelle et confidentielle*, Letter Book, 1905–6, 1 juin 1905, 50; also Langevin à Bégin, 10 juin, 94, Langevin à Cloutier, 10 juin, 93, Langevin à Gotti, 17 juin, 113; and Langevin à Lemius, Letter Book, 1902–7, 10 juin 1905, 599, Langevin à Pascal, 23 juin, 611
101 Ibid., Letter Book, 1902–7, 23 juin 1905, 611
102 *Commons Debates*, 1905, cols. 6187–8
103 Ibid., cols. 8284, 8335, 8428
104 Laurier Papers: Sbaretti and Laurier exchanged letters on 2 May 1905 and Sbaretti followed with two private and confidential letters on 7 May
105 Ibid., Sbaretti to Laurier, 26 May 1905, and same to same, confidential, 5 June 1905
106 Ibid., Sbaretti to Laurier, private and confidential, 20, 25, 26, 29 June 1905; Laurier to Sbaretti, 22, 26 June; Beck to Laurier, 26 June 1905
107 *Commons Debates*, 1905, cols. 7103–75
108 Ibid., cols. 8292–4
109 Ibid., col. 8341
110 Ibid., col. 8335
111 T.E. Perrett in *RDE*, 1903, 57–9
112 *Commons Debates*, 1905, col. 8377
113 For an account of the Bourassa-Lavergne philosophy, see Wade, 524–6.
114 *Les Cloches*, 15 sept. 1905, 240
115 *Commons Debates*, 1905, cols. 8387–8
116 Ibid., col. 8525. For the clause in its final form, see Appendix, clause no. 11
117 Ibid., col. 8506
118 Ibid., cols. 8530–8634
119 Ibid., cols. 8816–17, 8831–3, 8835–56, 8833–5, 8882–3
120 R.W. Scott Papers, private and confidential, 7 July 1905
121 *Senate Debates*, 1905, 620–55, 715–22, 776, 814–15, 825, 845–6
122 The best accounts of the elections are in L.G. Thomas, *The Liberal Party in Alberta: History of Politics in the Province of Alberta (1905–1921)* (Toronto, 1959), chap. 1 and D.H. Bocking, 'Saskatchewan's first provincial election,' *Saskatchewan History*, XVII (spring 1964), 41–54
123 *Canadian Annual Review*, 1905 (Toronto, 1906), 18, 49–50, 57, 69, 86, 89, 117, 156, 241, 243, 588
124 *Edmonton Bulletin*, 7 Nov. 1905
125 *Macleod Gazette*, 17 Aug. 1905
126 *Regina Standard*, 30 Aug. 1905

127 Fitzpatrick Papers, 11 May 1905
128 *Edmonton Journal*, 19 April 1905
129 *Les Cloches*, 1 mai 1905, 121
130 AAE, Leduc's Letter Book, 1905–9, personal, 15 June 1905, 23
131 Ibid., Letter Book, 1904–5, *personnelle*, 22 juin 1905, 239
132 Rutherford Papers, Talbot to Rutherford, 4 July 1905
133 *Edmonton Journal*, 2, 3 Aug. 1905; S.T. Rusak, 'Relations in education between Bishop Legal and the Liberal government, 1905–1920' (MED Thesis, University of Alberta, 1966), 17
134 AAE, Legal à J.J. Lestanc, Letter Book, 1904–5, 3 sept. 1905, 403, Legal to S. Swoboda, Letter Bank, 1905–7, 12 Nov. 1905, 15
135 Ibid., Legal à C. Cohiet, 15 dec. 1905, 194; Laurier Papers, Beck to Fitzpatrick, telegram, 10 Nov. 1905
136 L.G. Thomas, 28–9
137 *Canadian Annual Review*, 1905, 241
138 *Edmonton Journal*, 15 Nov. 1905
139 L.G. Thomas, 26–7
140 Scott Papers, Scott to W.T. Lackhart, private, 4 Jan. 1906
141 Fitzpatrick Papers, Beck to Fitzpatrick, 7 Aug. 1905
142 AAStB, Langevin à Legal, Letter Book, 1902–7, 30 août 1905, 636
143 Ibid., Langevin à V.A. Huard, Letter Book, 1905–6, 11 oct. 1905, 443
144 Ibid., Langevin to W. de Manby, 25 Nov. 1905, 692
145 Ibid., *circulaire confidentielle*, 10 oct. 1905
146 *Regina Standard*, 29 Nov. 1905
147 AAStB, Letter Book, 1905–6, 18 Nov. 1905, 656
148 *Regina Standard*, 29 Nov. 1905
149 Ibid.
150 *Regina Leader*, 29 Nov. 1905
151 Ibid., 13 Dec. 1905
152 Scott Papers, private and confidential, 22 Dec. 1905
153 AAStB, D.G. Seymour to Langevin, 1 Dec. 1905
154 Ibid., Langevin à M. Taillon, Letter Book, 1905–6, 5 dec. 1905, 735
155 Ibid., Langevin à C. Van de Velde (parish priest, South Qu'Appelle), 22 nov. 1905, 668
156 Quoted in *Manitoba Free Press*, 2 Dec. 1905
157 *Regina Leader*, 20 Dec. 1905
158 Quoted in *Regina Standard*, 20 Dec. 1905
159 Scott Papers, Scott to H.S. Woodward, private and confidential, 20 Dec. 1905
160 Quoted in *Regina Leader*, 13 Dec. 1905

161 Scott Papers, Scott to R.F. Sutherland, 22 Jan. 1906
162 Laurier Papers, 26 Dec. 1905
163 Ibid., private, 1 Jan. 1906
164 Scott Papers, private, 30 Dec. 1905
165 AAStB, Langevin à Bruchesi, 28 sept. 1905
166 Ibid., Letter Book, 1902–7, 29 sept. 1905, 650
167 Ibid., 4 oct. 905. Leduc did write Laurier a warm letter: Laurier Papers, *personnelle et confidentielle*, 7 août 1905
168 Ibid., 29 déc. 1906, 1 mai 1907
169 Ibid., 'Monseigneur L.P.A. Langevin, O.M.I., Archevêque de Saint Boniface, Manitoba, Canada, et la question des écoles de la Province du Manitoba, de la Saskatchewan, et de l'Alberta. Notes historiques servant à l'intelligence de la question,' n.d. The unsigned document is filed with the 1909 papers, hence the approximate date.
170 Rusak, 29

Index

LC
114.2
N67
L86
17,582
CAMROSE LUTHERAN COLLEGE
LIBRARY